DATE DUE

FEB 2 0 2013	

The MERCY *Factory*

THE
Mercy
FACTORY

ⅎⅎⅎⅎⅎⅎⅎ

*Refugees and the
American Asylum System*

Christopher J. Einolf

Ivan R. Dee CHICAGO

Library of Congress Cataloging-in-Publication Data:
Einolf, Christopher J., 1969–
    The mercy factory : refugees and the American asylum system /
Christopher J. Einolf.
        p. cm.
    Includes bibliographical references and index.
    ISBN 1-56663-400-8 (alk. paper)
    1. Asylum, Right of—United States—Popular works.   2. Political
refugees—Legal status, laws, etc.—United States—Popular works.
3. Political refugees—Case studies.   I. Title.

KF4836.Z9 E37 2001
325'.21'0973—dc21   2001032561

To my parents

Contents

Foreword

THE FIVE ASYLUM SEEKERS profiled in *The Mercy Factory* were my clients. I spent many hours with them in the course of working on their cases, and I still keep in touch with them now that they have won. As they all still have family in their home countries who might be persecuted if their stories were known, it was not possible to use their real names or to print photographs of them in the book. They all gave their permission to have their stories told in the book, except for Therese, whom I have not been able to locate. Most of them have read the manuscript of this book so that they could change details, such as dates and place names, which might reveal their identity to their persecutors.

In my interviews with INS officials, immigration judges, private attorneys, nonprofit staff, and volunteers, I used a tape recorder. In the few that I could not, I checked any quotations with the interview subject before publication.

While there are many people to thank, I would like particularly to thank the asylees who have shared their stories with me. I would also like to thank the many other people interviewed in the book for taking the time to talk with me. Ivan Yacub, Marisa Cianciarulo, and Anya Sykes helped me by sharing their opinions about the asylum system. They are not directly quoted in the text, but their comments are incorporated throughout.

Special thanks go to my wife, Ashley Spell, and my mother, Louise Einolf, for reading drafts of the manuscript and suggesting edits. Thanks also go to Philip Schrag for his advice and assistance.

I have tried to avoid legal jargon wherever possible, while still conveying the information correctly. I have usually used the common English meaning of legal terms, which readers expert in immigration law may perceive as an error. The following section explains the difference between the legal definition and the common English usage of several terms and how I use them in this book.

Alien: This is the technical term in immigration law for a noncitizen, but it is not a pretty term, especially in its usual form: "illegal alien." Advocates for immigrants prefer a number of other terms for aliens, such as "immigrant," "noncitizen," or "newcomer"; instead of "illegal," they prefer "undocumented" or "unauthorized." I agree that "alien" has negative connotations, and I have generally used the terms "asylum seeker" or "applicant," except in discussions of legal procedure, where I use "alien" because it is the correct legal term.

Asylum seeker and asylum applicant: I use these terms to describe people who have arrived in the United States seeking asylum, but who have not yet been approved for asylum. In immigration court, the asylum applicant is called the "respondent," but I have not used this legal jargon in the book.

Deported, excluded, and *removed:* These three words have different technical meanings in immigration law. "Deported" and "excluded" were terms used under the pre-1996 law. Aliens were "deported" if they were expelled from the country after having been admitted under a legal status; aliens were "excluded" if they were denied the right to enter the country at the border. The 1996 law replaced both these terms with the term "removed." I have used "removed" and "deported" as synonyms. None of the cases described in this book were adjudicated under the provisions of the pre-1996 law.

Refugee: This term has a colloquial meaning and an immigration law meaning. In this book I have generally used the term "refugee" in its normal, colloquial English sense—any person fleeing his home country out of fear. Thus both an asylum seeker and an asylee are "refugees" in the colloquial sense, though not in the technical legal sense.

In U.S. immigration law, a "refugee" is a person awarded "refugee" status by the U.S. government. The government affords this status to people who have fled their home countries to a second country and who cannot return home because of a well-founded fear of persecution on account of political opinion, religion, race, nationality, or social group. The United States sends INS representatives to refugee camps and other locations throughout the world and chooses a certain number of people each year—78,000 in 1999—to be granted refugee status and resettled to the United States. Thus "refugee" status is identical to "asylee" status; the only difference is that asylees receive status after arrival in the United States, refugees receive status outside the United States and are brought here by the U.S. government.

I send you out like sheep among wolves;

be wary as serpents, innocent as doves.

Jesus' advice to his followers

(Matthew 10:16)

Preface

AS THE AIRPLANE LANDS in September 1997, Therese checks one more time the passport that the priest gave her, trying to memorize her new name. "The woman in the photo doesn't look that much like me," Therese thinks, "but the priest said that Americans won't be able to tell the difference. I hope he is right."

It is hard for her to believe that only a few weeks ago she was at home with her husband and children in Bukavu, in eastern Congo. She and her husband and her children had always lived in peace. She had worked as an elementary school teacher, and her husband was a businessman and a respected community leader.

A year ago a civil war started in Congo (the former Zaire), with soldiers from the Tutsi ethnic group, led by Laurent Kabila and supported by soldiers of the Tutsi-controlled government of Rwanda, fighting the forces of Congo's former dictator, Mobutu Sese Seko. Therese and her husband are members of the Hutu ethnic group. The Tutsis and Hutus had fought many bloody wars against each other in the neighboring countries of Rwanda and Burundi, but the violence had never before spread to Congo. When Kabila's forces won the civil war a few months ago, they began a campaign against ethnic Hutus, particularly well-educated, politically active community leaders like Therese and her husband. Therese had to run away from her home town and hide with her husband and children in her grandmother's village.

Kabila's soldiers traced her there and captured her, but could not find her husband. They began to beat Therese and tear her clothes off in the street outside her grandmother's house. Her husband heard the noise and came out of hiding to protect her. The soldiers shot him on the spot and gang-raped Therese. She passed out during the rapes, and the soldiers left her for dead.

Therese woke up in a Catholic mission. The priests told her that her children were safe but would not tell her where they were. The priests told her that she had to leave the country for safety in Europe or the United States but that she would have to go alone and bring her children later. At first Therese refused to leave without her children, but she later agreed to go when the priests convinced her that by staying there she was only putting her children in greater danger.

Now Therese finds herself arriving in the United States with a false passport, a few hundred dollars, and a single change of clothing. She speaks French but no English, and she does not know a single person in the country. She is ill from an infection contracted from the rapes, she is only half-conscious from the effects of painkillers and antibiotics, and she is depressed and confused after all that has happened to her.

The flight attendant sees that she is ill and escorts her off the plane to the passport line. The immigration official can also see that she is sick, so he asks her only her name and nationality, then waves her through the immigration line. After she gets safely through the airport she throws the passport away, as the priests told her to do.

Therese looks around at the buildings, the cars, and the people. The priests told her to find a Catholic church and ask for a place to spend the night. But then what? She has heard that the United States is the country of freedom, but she has also heard that Americans don't like illegal aliens, and that one needs many different kinds of papers and identity documents to live and work in the United States. Where will she get these papers? How will she survive until she can get a job? Who will help her?

Every year thousands of people come to the United States seeking protection as asylees—more than 48,000 people applied for asylum in fiscal year 2000 alone. Our response to asylum seekers is complex and contradictory. On the one hand, America is a country of immigrants and has a proud tradition of welcoming refugees from persecution. Most Americans would not be willing to send refugees back to torture, imprisonment, or death in their home countries, and our memories of the Holocaust remind us of what can happen when refugees are returned to countries where they fear persecution.

On the other hand, most Americans are concerned about high levels of illegal immigration, and many feel that poor immigrants are a burden to society. Some Americans see the asylum system as too vulnerable to fraud and see asylum as a "loophole" in immigration laws that undocumented aliens can use to gain legal status. When large numbers of asylum seekers arrive at the same time, as has happened several times over the last few decades, both policy-makers and the general public become concerned that the country will be overwhelmed by their numbers.

To balance our desire to protect true refugees and our need to maintain secure borders, a complex system of asylum adjudication has developed over the last twenty years. It is designed to identify and assist genuine refugees while deporting undocumented aliens who falsely claim to be refugees. Determining which applicants deserve asylum is difficult and time-consuming. Each applicant should be entitled to a full immigration court hearing, but the sheer number of applicants makes it difficult for the government to give each asylum seeker's claim the time and attention it deserves.

Despite these difficulties, Americans have risen to the challenge of asylum, and the federal government has created one of the world's most effective asylum adjudication systems. More refugees receive asylum in the United States each year than in any other Western country. Over the course of two decades a system has evolved which successfully balances the need to maintain secure borders with the need to provide safe haven to those who need it.

The system balances the need to give each asylum-seeker's claim individual attention with the need to efficiently process the claims of thousands of applicants. Thousands of people, including government officials, the staffs of nonprofit organizations, church members, and volunteers, work hard to keep this system functioning.

The title of this book, *The Mercy Factory,* is meant both as an ironic statement and a compliment to the effectiveness of the system. Every asylum-seeker is a human being and deserves individual attention. At the same time the system must operate efficiently because there are thousands of asylum-seekers in need of assistance. All of us who work within the asylum adjudication program—government officials, private attorneys, social workers, and the staffs of nonprofit agencies—feel this tension between the need to give each person individual attention and the need to complete one person's case in order to move on to the next one. Over the years a system has developed that uses mass-production methods to deliver individual attention and assistance. This "mercy factory," a contradiction in terms, should not function, but it does.

While the asylum system is currently successful, it is also at risk. An anti-immigrant sentiment has developed among the general public, and policymakers have passed laws and adopted policies that make it much more difficult for refugees to win asylum. In 1996, Congress passed the Illegal Immigration Reform and Immigrant Responsibility Act (IIRAIRA), which changed many of our immigration laws to make them more strict, including the law of asylum. The new law requires aliens to apply for asylum within one year of their arrival in the United States, limits the ability of aliens to appeal adverse decisions, and allows the "expedited removal" of asylum seekers who arrive at the border with false entry documents. In recent years immigration courts have issued precedent decisions interpreting these laws that make it more difficult for aliens to receive asylum. Within the executive branch of government, the Department of Justice and the Immigration and Naturalization Service (INS) have applied these laws and court decisions in the strictest ways possible, further restricting aliens' ability to win asylum. In making the system more restrictive, we are moving toward a system where aliens have the right, in theory, to receive asylum, but where it is almost impossible, in practice, for them to do so.

If the anti-immigrant lobby succeeds in dismantling the asylum system, the result will be a tragedy, both for asylum-seekers and the American people. The United States is known worldwide as the land of freedom, and thousands of refugees come here each year because they know that America is the best place for them to seek asylum. The United States is not an area of land, nor is it a specific ethnic or national group. It is an idea, that all people, regardless of race, religion, or national origin have the inalienable right to life, liberty, and the pursuit of happiness. Through the centuries the arrival of new refugees has helped to keep alive this idea and reminded us of the importance of freedom, tolerance, and democracy. If we were to close our doors to asylum seekers, we would be challenging the ideals that make us Americans.

The MERCY *Factory*

1

ⅉ ⅉ ⅉ

Asylum in the United States

THE LAW OF ASYLUM in the United States is based on international refugee law, specifically on two treaties: "The 1951 Convention Relating to the Status of Refugees" and "The 1967 Protocol Relating to the Status of Refugees." More than 130 countries have signed and ratified one or both of these treaties. The United States signed and ratified the Protocol on Refugee Status in 1968. Our own refugee law, contained in the Immigration and Nationality Act, is closely based on this international treaty.

The Convention and the Protocol define the characteristics of a "refugee" and set out requirements for how countries should treat refugees. By signing the treaties, countries promise not to return refugees to their country of origin and promise to grant refugees basic freedoms and a means of survival while they wait for the opportunity to return to their homelands.

Before 1980, the United States was governed only by its international obligations under the Protocol on Refugee Status. The U.S. government implemented this treaty through administrative procedures, and few aliens made use of the treaty to ask for refugee status. Since the informal administrative system did not function effectively, Congress decided to put a formal system in place. The Refugee Act of 1980 instructed the Department of Justice to set up fair and systematic regulations and procedures for the adjudication of asylum claims. This act, and laws and regulations developed in later years, set out how the INS and the immigration courts should adjudicate the claims of aliens seeking asylum or refugee status. U.S. law and regulations also describe the benefits available to refugees and asylees whose applications for status are approved.

The Definition of "Refugee" Under U.S. and International Law

U.S. law contains a definition of "refugee" taken from the U.N. Protocol Relating to the Status of Refugees. The Immigration and Nationality Act, at 8 USC 1101(a)(42), defines a refugee as

> Any person who is outside any country of such person's nationality, or in the case of a person having no nationality, is outside any country in which such person last habitually resided, and who is unable or unwilling to return to, and is unable and unwilling to avail himself or herself of the protection of, that country because of persecution or a well-founded fear of persecution on account of race, religion, nationality, membership in a particular social group, or political opinion.

This definition is used in determining the status of both "refugees" and "asylees." In colloquial English the word "refugee" is often used to refer to any person who has fled his or her home country, but in immigration law the word has a technical meaning that refers to a specific immigration status. "Refugee" status is granted to people outside the United States, whom the U.S. government then transports to the United States. "Asylum" status is granted to people who ask for protection after already having arrived in the United States. The above definition of a refugee is used by adjudicators to determine if an alien qualifies for "refugee" or "asylum" status.

The definition of a refugee is complex, and many asylum applicants' claims have been approved or denied based on the courts interpretation of terms within the definition. The Justice Department's regulations, as well as immigration court decisions and INS "guidelines," have all interpreted different terms within this definition. The Board of Immigration Appeals (BIA), an administrative court within the Department of Justice charged with interpreting immigration law, has issued many precedent decisions interpreting aspects of the refugee definition for the purpose of adjudicating asylum applications. Many aspects of asylum law have also been decided by federal appeals courts, and a few U.S. Supreme Court decisions have addressed asylum law issues. Examining each phrase of the definition of "refugee," and discussing court decisions on the meaning of different terms within the definition, will provide a better understanding of the law.

"Any person who is outside any country of such person's nationality, or in the case of a person having no nationality, is outside any country in which such person last habitually resided." This section of the definition states that one must be outside of one's home country in order to be considered a refugee. Most people are nationals or citizens of some country, but some people are "stateless," having no country to call their own. These individuals can apply for refugee status if they are outside of the country where they "last habitually resided."

"[A]nd who is unable or unwilling to return to, and is unable and unwilling to avail himself or herself of the protection of that country." To be a refugee, a person must be unable or unwilling to return home. Normally, refugees are unwilling to return home because they fear the government of their home country, but they may also fear other groups, who the government cannot or will not control. For example, a refugee from Colombia might fear persecution at the hands of anti-government guerrillas, whom the government lacks the military strength to control. Thus the refugee might not be "unwilling" to avail himself or herself of the protection of his or her country, but, because of the government's weakness, the refugee is "unable" to do so.

"[B]ecause of persecution or a well-founded fear of persecution." The term "persecution" is not defined in the Immigration and Nationality Act, but the INS and several court decisions have defined the term. The courts have usually defined persecution as

"the infliction of suffering or harm on those who differ . . . in a way that is regarded as offensive."[1] The INS's proposed regulations define persecution as "the infliction of objectively serious harm or suffering."[2] The BIA has held that in order to constitute persecution, "harm or suffering must be inflicted [upon the victim] in order to punish him for possession of a belief or characteristic [the] persecutor seeks to overcome."[3] But in its decision finding that female genital mutilation constitutes persecution, the BIA made one exception to this rule. Female genital mutilation is practiced in many countries in Africa: young girls are subjected to an operation, performed without anesthesia or sterile instruments, where part or all of the clitoris and external labia are cut off. Sometimes the genital opening is also stitched closed. The BIA ruled that, even though female genital mutilation was performed on the instigation of family members, who had no "punitive" or "malignant" intent toward the person mutilated, the practice was so offensive that it could still be considered "persecution."[4] This finding was codified in the INS's proposed regulations, which state that persecution is any harm that is "subjectively experienced as serious harm by the applicant, regardless of whether the persecutor intends to cause harm."[5]

The courts have found that only extreme forms of harm constitute persecution, the U.S. Supreme Court deciding that "threats to life and freedom" always constitute persecution.[6] These include slavery, genocide, prolonged detention without trial, torture and other cruel and inhumane punishment, and the killing of individuals, except for executions conducted after due process of law. Other forms of mistreatment can also be considered "persecu-

---

1. *Fisher v. INS,* 79 F.3d 955, 961 (9th Cir. 1996); *Kovac v. INS,* 407 F.2d 102 (9th Cir. 1969).

2. Proposed 8 CFR 208.15(a). Issued as proposed regulations on December 7, 2000, published in 65 Federal Register 76588-98.

3. *Matter of Acosta,* 19 I&N Dec. 211, 223, (BIA 1985). Board of Immigration Appeals cases are always listed using the applicant's name, preceded by either "Matter of" or "In re." There is no consistent usage, and the same case might be listed "Matter of Acosta" in one source, and "In re Acosta" in another. This book always uses the English term, "Matter of."

4. *Matter of Kasinga,* Int. Dec. 3278 (BIA 1996).

5. Proposed 8 CFR 208.15 (a).

6. *INS v. Stevic,* 467 U.S. 407, 428 (1984).

tion," but courts have been careful to distinguish between "persecution" and less severe forms of harm, which have been characterized as mere "harassment" or "discrimination."[7]

Some kinds of harm are considered "persecution" even where there is no bodily harm or a threat to life and freedom. In these cases, adjudicators should consider the "cumulative effect" of all incidents suffered by the applicant.[8] The *INS Basic Law Manual* lists the types of harm that can, "especially if cumulative or persistent," be considered in the aggregate to constitute persecution. These acts include "arbitrary interference with a person's privacy, family, home or correspondence; relegation to substandard dwellings; exclusion from institutions of higher learning; enforced social or civil inactivity; passport denial; constant surveillance; and pressure to become an informer."[9]

The refugee definition states that a person is considered a refugee if he or she either was a victim of persecution in the past or has a well-founded fear of persecution in the future. Most refugees have both experienced past persecution and fear future persecution, but some refugees qualify for protection under only one of these grounds. For example, some aliens come to the United States as students, temporary workers, or diplomats, having had no experience of past persecution in their own countries. After their arrival, political conditions change in their home countries, leaving them afraid to return. A civil war or a military coup in a person's home country can make that person a refugee in the United States, even if he or she had never experienced any persecution before.

On the other hand, a refugee may have suffered persecution in the past but may no longer fear persecution in the future because of a change in home country conditions. In these cases, if the past persecution was severe enough, the alien can still receive refugee status. For example, after the fall of the Nazi regime some Jews might have returned to Germany because their persecutors were no longer in power. But the severity of the persecution they

---

7. *Balazoski v. INS*, 932 F.2d 638, 642 (7th Cir. 1991); *Ghaly v. INS*, 58 F.3d 1425, 1431 (9th Cir. 1995).

8. *Singh v. INS*, 1998 U.S. App. LEXIS 856 (9th Cir. 1998).

9. *INS Basic Law Manual*, at 21.

had suffered would have made it inhumane to force them to return there. They would qualify for refugee status on the grounds of past persecution alone.[1]

"[O]n account of race, religion, nationality, membership in a particular social group, or political opinion." The persecution suffered or feared by the alien must have been "on account of" one of these five grounds. The exact definition of these five terms, particularly that of the term "social group," has been the subject of many court decisions over the last two decades.

"[P]olitical opinion." Political opinion includes political speech, political activities within a political party, human rights group, or labor union, participation in demonstrations, or activities as a journalist. The BIA has ruled that even when the alien does not actually possess the political opinion attributed to him or her, the alien may still be granted asylum. This decision reflects the political reality of countries where human rights violations occur. In many cases, people are arrested because the government suspects them of holding opposition views when in fact they are innocent. These victims, who are persecuted on account of their imputed political opinion, are eligible to be granted asylum.[2]

"[R]ace." There are relatively few cases within U.S. law of asylum granted on account of race. Often the concept of "race" overlaps with that of ethnicity, which is considered a matter of "membership in a particular social group" or "nationality." In my own practice I have successfully represented several Indonesians of Chinese ethnicity who were granted asylum based on the persecution they suffered in Indonesia because of their race.

"[N]ationality." "Nationality" is a concept similar to "ethnicity" and "race." The Kurdish ethnic group, who constitute a minority of the populations of Iraq, Iran, Turkey, and Syria, are persecuted in these countries in part due to their nationality. Kurds can be considered a "national" group despite the fact that they have no political state of their own. Palestinians can also be con-

---

1. *Matter of Chen*, 20 I&N Dec. 16 (BIA 1989), and 8 CFR 208.13(b)(1).
2. *Matter of S-P-*, Int. Dec. 3287 (BIA 1996), and 8 CFR 208.13(b)(2)(i).

sidered a "national" group that until recently did not have its own state.

"[R]eligion." Religious persecution exists in many countries in the world, and successful cases of religious persecution include *Matter of Chen*,[3] in which an applicant was granted asylum because of his past experience of persecution as the son of a Christian minister in Communist China. In my own practice I have also successfully represented a member of the Jehovah's Witnesses who feared persecution in her home country of Eritrea. The Jehovah's Witnesses refuse to swear oaths of allegiance or salute the flag, and this refusal had caused their church to be banned and its members to be persecuted in Eritrea.

"[M]embership in a particular social group." This category is not defined in U.S. statute, but the United Nations' *Handbook on Procedures and Criteria for Determining Refugee Status* defines a social group as "persons of similar background, habits, or social status." U.S. courts have limited this broad definition by stating that members of a social group must share a "common, immutable characteristic," which members of the group "either cannot change, or should not be required to change because it is fundamental to their individual identities or consciences." This common characteristic "might be an innate one such as sex, color, or kinship ties, or in some circumstances it might be a shared past experience such as former military leadership or land ownership."[4]

The courts have found that a number of different groups constitute valid "social groups" for the purposes of asylum and refugee law. Family is a valid "social group" in a situation where a person, innocent of political opposition activity, is persecuted as retribution for the political activities of a family member.[5] Persecution on account of membership in an ethnic group, tribe, or clan is considered persecution on account of membership in a particular social group.[6] In its decision in *Matter of Toboso-Alfonso*, the BIA

3. Int. Dec. #3104 (BIA 1989).

4. *Matter of Acosta*, Int. Dec. #2986 (BIA 1985).

5. *Sanchez-Trujillo v. INS*, 801 F. 2d 1571, 1576 (9th Cir. 1986); *Gebremichael v. INS*, 10 F.3d (1st Cir. 1993).

6. *Matter of H-*, Int. Dec. 3276 (BIA 1996).

found that homosexuality constituted "membership in a particular social group" for the purposes of asylum law.[7]

What the law of asylum says about claims based on gender is complex and sometimes contradictory. Despite the fact that the BIA in *Matter of Acosta* specifically mentioned "sex" as an innate characteristic that could be the basis for a valid social group, most courts have found that gender alone is too broad a category to qualify as a social group. In several cases, asylum status was denied to women who claimed to fear persecution in fundamentalist Iran based on their gender alone.[8] The BIA did grant asylum to a woman who feared persecution, in this case female genital mutilation, on account of her gender.[9] In a later case, *Matter of R-A-*, the BIA denied asylum to a victim of domestic violence who claimed that her husband's abuse of her constituted gender-based persecution.[1] But the Attorney General vacated the decision in *Matter of R-A-*[2] and the Justice Department issued new proposed regulations overruling the board's decision. As of this writing, the regulations have not been made final, and the law on this issue is still unclear.[3] In a more recent decision, the BIA ruled in favor of an applicant who feared domestic violence, but it distinguished this case from *Matter of R-A-* by ruling that the persecution the applicant feared was on account of her religion, not her gender.[4] This area of asylum law is complex and constantly changing; it is covered in more detail in chapter ten.

The History of the Asylum Adjudication System

The system by which asylum claims are adjudicated has changed frequently in recent decades. The current one for the adjudication

7. Int. Dec. #3222 (BIA 1990).

8. *Fatin v. INS*, 12 F.3d 1233 (3rd Circuit, 1993); *Sharif v. INS*, 87 F.3d 932 (7th Cir. 1996); *Fisher v. INS*, 79 F.3d 955 (9th Cir. 1996); *Safaie v. INS*, 25 F. 3d 636, 640 (8th Cir. 1994).

9. *Matter of Kasinga*, Int. Dec. 3278 (BIA 1996).

1. *Matter of R-A-*, Int. Dec. #3403 (BIA 1999).

2. *Interpreter Releases*, January 22, 2001, p. 256.

3. Proposed regulations amending 8 CFR 208, printed in the Federal Register on December 7, 2000, pp. 76588–76598; reprinted, with analysis, in *Interpreter Releases*, December 18, 2000, pp. 1737–1746 and 1760–1770.

4. *Matter of S-A-*, Int. Dec. 3433 (BIA 2000).

of asylum claims has been in place only since 1994, and the immigration status of "asylum" was created only two decades ago, as part of the 1980 Refugee Act. Before looking at the current system, it is worthwhile to examine the history of refugee migration to the United States and the immigration laws that preceded the current asylum system.[5]

Even before the United States became an independent nation, it was a place where refugees fleeing political and religious persecution went to find safety. In the first three hundred years of our history, there were no laws to control immigration, and any refugee who could afford to travel to the United States could immigrate here to start a new life.

In the late nineteenth century, Americans began to consider limiting the number of new immigrants who were allowed to arrive each year, particularly immigrants who were regarded as racially inferior. In 1882 the first U.S. immigration law was passed, limiting the number of new immigrants who could arrive from China. In 1902 a ban on Chinese immigration was imposed, and in 1917 this ban was extended to most Asian countries. In 1922 a comprehensive immigration law was passed, setting up a quota system for immigrants from all countries outside the Western Hemisphere. The quotas were openly racist, allowing large numbers of immigrants from Western Europe, fewer from Eastern Europe, few from Asia, and none from Africa.

In the 1930s thousands of refugees from fascist and Communist regimes in Europe tried to come to the United States to find safety but were turned away when the numbers exceeded the yearly quotas set by law. In one well-known case, in 1939 a boat called the SS *St. Louis,* carrying 900 Jewish refugees, was not allowed even to land in the United States but was turned away at each port. The boat returned to Europe, and most of its passengers later perished in the Holocaust. Thousands of other Jews and opponents of the Nazis died during the 1940s after being refused visas to the United States.

5. Much of the information in this section is taken from *Calculated Kindness: Refugees and America's Half-Open Door, 1945 to the Present* by Gil Loescher and John Scanlan (New York, 1986).

After World War II, when the American public became fully aware of the extent of the genocide against European Jews, the nation began to feel that some exception to the immigration quotas should be made for refugees. Many refugees sought admission to the United States in the late 1940s, including people displaced by the Nazis and victims of Communist persecution. As the cold war developed Americans and their government wanted to help victims of Communist oppression. They also felt that by accepting refugees from Communist countries, the United States could win a moral victory in its ideological struggle against communism.

Over the next three decades the United States allowed thousands of refugees from Communist countries to enter, above the levels specified by immigration quotas. In the 1950s the United States admitted 38,000 refugees from the Hungarian uprising against Soviet power and in the 1960s thousands more refugees from Czechoslovakia. Several hundred thousand refugees were admitted in the 1960s and 1970s from Cuba. The largest single group of refugees ever admitted were Southeast Asians from Vietnam, Cambodia, and Laos; more than 600,000 of these refugees entered the United States between 1975 and 1981.

While hundreds of thousands of refugees were admitted to the United States between 1945 and 1980, there was no organized program to regulate refugee admissions. The president or Congress authorized refugee admissions on an ad hoc basis, usually in response to political events. No law existed to address the needs of aliens already present in the United States who sought protection here. As a signatory to the U.N. Protocol on Refugees, the United States had pledged not to return refugees to their countries of origin, and the immigration courts had granted a status similar to refugee status, called "withholding of deportation," to some individuals in deportation proceedings who feared persecution in their home countries. This provision was not well defined and was rarely used, and many policymakers felt there should be a better procedure.

A new legal status, called "asylum," was written into law with the passage of the Refugee Act in 1980. The main purpose of the act was to regulate the admission of refugees from overseas, but one paragraph of the law authorized the creation of a new immigration status called "asylum." Asylum would be available for people present in the United States who met the definition of a refugee, even those people who were present without legal permission. The law authorized the Department of Justice to develop its own regulations for adjudicating asylum applications. Since most asylum-seekers want protection from politically motivated persecution, this status came to be called "political asylum" in colloquial English, but since it can be granted to people fearing other kinds of persecution as well, the correct term is simply "asylum."

The Refugee Act became law on March 17, 1980, and had been in effect for only three weeks when its provisions were tested by the arrival of thousands of Cuban boat people. In an operation that came to be called the "Mariel boatlift," the Cuban exile community helped more than 130,000 people leave Cuba and ferried them to the United States, where they applied for asylum under the new law. Over the following years, hundreds of thousands of refugees from Haiti, Nicaragua, Guatemala, and El Salvador fled to the United States and sought asylum. This single paragraph in the Refugee Act had created a huge administrative burden for the U.S. government but had also held out the possibility of freedom and safety to hundreds of thousands of victims of oppression.

Because the law had left the implementation of asylum entirely up to the regulations and procedures devised by the Department of Justice, the Reagan administration was able to use the asylum process to support its foreign policy goals.[6] The Reagan administration's INS sent each asylum application to the State Department for an "advisory opinion" and followed the recommendations of that opinion over 95 percent of the time.[7] Asylum

6. For an extensive analysis of the political factors underlying U.S. asylum policy in the 1980s, see Karen Yarnold, *Refugees Without Refuge: Formation and Failed Implementation of U.S. Political Asylum Policy in the 1980's* (Lanham, Md., 1990).

7. Sarah Ignatius, *An Assessment of the Asylum Process of the Immigration and Naturalization Service* (Harvard Law School: The National Asylum Study Project), September 1993, p. 17, citing Karin Koning, U.S. Helsinki Watch Committee, *Detained, Denied, Deported: Asylum Seekers in the United States* (1989), and two U.S. General Accounting Office surveys: *Asylum: Approval Rates for Selected Applicants* (June 1987), and *Asylum: Uniform Application of Standards Uncertain*, GAO/GGD-87-33BR (January 1987).

applicants fleeing persecution in countries the United States considered hostile, such as China, the USSR, and Iran, were granted
asylum at a rate of over 50 percent, while approval rates for countries whose governments the United States supported, such as El
Salvador, Guatemala, and Haiti, were less than 3 percent, despite
the existence of extensive, well-documented human rights abuses
in those countries.[8] INS officers gave most applicants only cursory
interviews, asking few questions about their history of persecution
and focusing instead on their manner of entry into the United
States.[9] There is little evidence that INS officers went beyond the
State Department's recommendation to consider the specifics of
each case, and a General Accounting Office report found that in
over 73 percent of denied asylum cases, INS officers failed to indicate any reason for their denial of the claim.[1]

While the political bias of the Reagan administration's INS affected asylum applicants from many countries, asylum applicants
from Central America, particularly El Salvador and Guatemala,
constituted the majority of unfairly denied cases. As it became
clear that the U.S. government would not administer the asylum
laws fairly, a grass-roots movement of U.S. church groups, refugee
advocates, civil liberties groups, and individual citizens began to
provide "sanctuary" for Salvadorans and Guatemalans. They either helped them enter the country illegally and find illegal employment, or helped them cross the United States and go to
Canada, where they could receive fair, nonpoliticized hearings on
their asylum claims. Many organizations filed class-action lawsuits on behalf of the refugees, arguing that the unfair adjudication
of asylum claims violated applicants' right to due process under
the Constitution.

Many of these lawsuits were successful, and the largest of
these, brought by the American Baptist Churches, was settled by
the Justice Department in 1990 on terms favorable to Salvadoran

8. Ignatius, p. 17, citing statistics released by the INS for the period 1983–1991.

9. Ignatius, p. 18, citing Amnesty International U.S.A., *Reasonable Fear: Human Rights and U.S. Refugee Policy* (1990).

1. Ignatius, p. 18, citing the U.S. GAO, *Asylum: Uniform Application of Standards Uncertain*, GAO/GGD-87-33BR3 (January 1987).

and Guatemalan asylum applicants.[2] Under the terms of the settlement, more than 250,000 Salvadorans and Guatemalans who had arrived in the United States before 1990 were eligible to apply for asylum under new rules. Even people who had not applied for asylum before or whose asylum applications had already been denied or who had deportation orders already entered against them could get an asylum hearing. The legal settlement set out rules that would ensure that Salvadorans and Guatemalans would get fair hearings for their asylum claims and allowed them to receive work permits and permission to stay in the United States until their claims were heard.

Around the same time that the American Baptist Churches settlement was being negotiated, President George Bush's administration reformed the INS asylum system. In 1990 the Bush administration announced the creation of special asylum offices within the INS, which would operate independently of the INS district offices. There would also be a special "Asylum Corps" of adjudication officers, newly hired and specially trained, who would only adjudicate asylum applications. By separating the asylum office and its staff from the rest of the INS, the asylum adjudication process would be more efficient, compassionate, and fair. The process was designed to be less political, and asylum officers were encouraged to rely on other sources of human rights information, not exclusively on State Department reports.[3]

These reforms were successful, and the asylum offices and asylum corps are still in place today. Only one problem remained—the huge backlog of asylum applications that remained to be adjudicated. The Asylum Corps consisted of fewer than 100 officers at its inception. Its workload, already too large, was more than tripled when the American Baptist Churches settlement added over 250,000 new cases. It was impossible for the small number of asylum officers to adjudicate this many Central Ameri-

---

2. *American Baptist Churches (ABC) v. Thornburgh,* 760 F. Supp. 796 (N.D. Cal. 1991).

3. For a detailed account of the reasons for the 1990 reforms, the nature of the reforms themselves, and an early assessment of the reforms' success, see Ignatius, *Assessment of the Asylum Process.*

can cases; they could not even keep up with the number of new applications from other countries. The backlog grew each year as more and more aliens applied for asylum.

The large backlog of cases also created a new problem, that of fraudulent applications. Regulations provided that each asylum applicant would receive employment authorization if his or her application were not adjudicated within ninety days. Since very few applications were adjudicated that quickly, almost all asylum applicants received work permits within a few months of applying. With the backlog of undecided cases in the hundreds of thousands and growing each year, it seemed that it would take years for any given applicant to actually get an interview. Individuals realized that applying for asylum was an easy way to get a work permit. Many people who did not fear returning to their country applied for asylum anyway, hoping that by the time their interview was scheduled, years later, they would have found some other way of gaining legal immigration status.

The problem grew worse as dishonest lawyers and other entrepreneurs encouraged aliens to apply for asylum. In many cases they did not even tell clients that they were applying for asylum but told the applicants they were just asking for a work permit. Since most applicants could not speak or read English, they would sign the forms, sometimes even before they were filled out. The dishonest practitioners would then fill in the alien's name and personal information, and fabricate a story of persecution. These practitioners were not concerned with what would happen years later when the aliens' applications were scheduled for an interview; the practitioners collected their fee, got the alien a work permit, and moved on.

While this system helped fraudulent applicants, it hurt legitimate applicants for asylum. They wanted more than just a work permit; they wanted legal permission to stay in the United States, and they wanted asylum status so they could bring their spouses and children to join them. Advocates for both refugees and for tougher laws on illegal immigration lobbied for another reform that would put an end to the fraud.

The last major reform of the asylum system took place in

1994. As part of the reformed system, the asylum office would adopt a "last in, first out" policy for adjudicating applications. Officers would give priority to asylum applications that had just been filed and would make sure that all asylum applicants received interviews within 60 days of applying. Congress voted additional funds for the Asylum Corps, allowing it to expand its staff to the level necessary to keep up with new applications. It would go through the backlog only as time allowed. Under the new rules, applicants would not be eligible for work permits unless 180 days had passed between the time of filing and the time they received their final adjudication from the immigration court. The immigration courts changed their procedures for hearing cases as well, ensuring that almost all new asylum cases received a final adjudication from an immigration judge within this 180-day period.

These reforms were significant and successful. The government was able to meet its goals of hearing nearly all new asylum cases within 180 days of application. Aliens who made fraudulent applications for asylum no longer received work permits but orders of deportation. The total number of applications received fell sharply as the word got out on the street that it was no longer possible to get a work permit just by applying for asylum. At the same time the approval rate for asylum applications increased, and asylum seekers with valid claims were able to have their cases heard quickly and win permanent status in the United States.[4]

The Asylum System as It Exists Today

Most applicants for asylum get two chances to win their asylum cases. Their first is an interview at the asylum office of the INS. These interviews are informal and nonadversarial and are designed to identify those applicants with strong claims and grant them asylum immediately. Those applicants who do not obviously merit asylum are referred to an immigration judge for further re-

---

4. For an extensive discussion of the 1994 asylum reforms, written by one of the main architects of the reforms, see David A. Martin, "Making Asylum Policy: The 1994 Reforms," published in the *Washington Law Review,* July 1995.

view: their second chance. The immigration court hearings are formal and adversarial and are governed by rules that ensure that the hearings are conducted fairly.

If an applicant loses in court, he or she may appeal the decision to the BIA. The applicant's deportation is automatically prevented during the appeal period, but in most cases he or she is not given employment authorization. As of present writing, the BIA is far behind in its appeals and most applicants wait two to three years for their appeal to be heard. Finally, if the BIA appeal is denied, applicants can further appeal to the Federal Circuit Courts of Appeal and from there to the U.S. Supreme Court. These courts can elect not to hear the appeal, however, and the applicants' deportation is not automatically prevented during the appeal period; they must ask the INS for a stay of deportation.

This procedure varies in some cases. If an applicant in a valid nonimmigrant status, such as someone with a student or a visitor's visa, is denied by the asylum office while still in status, his or her case is not sent to court. The applicant simply reverts to his prior immigration status, and he or she can apply for asylum again when that status expires. Other applicants, such as those people apprehended at the border with false entry documents or no documents, do not get an INS hearing but go straight to court. In 1996, changes in the immigration law made it possible for the INS to deport aliens apprehended at the border without giving them a court hearing; this new law is described in more detail in chapter nine.

At both the asylum office and at immigration court, applicants are given a chance to testify on their own behalf, and they may introduce evidence or call witnesses in support of their application. The "burden of proof" is on applicants to demonstrate that they qualify for asylum status, but adjudicators also take into account the difficulties that asylum applicants face in proving the truth of their statements. Persecuting governments do not want the world to know about their abuse of the human rights of their citizens, so adjudicators cannot expect asylum applicants to have documentary evidence of their persecution.

In some cases the asylum applicant's testimony is the only evidence the applicant can provide to support his or her claim of persecution. If this testimony is sufficiently detailed, credible, and consistent, and if there is no other evidence available, adjudicators can consider this testimony adequate to meet the applicant's burden of proof. Where possible, however, applicants are expected to provide documentary evidence to back up their claims. This evidence can include general information such as newspaper articles and human rights reports about their country of origin, personal information such as identity documents and political party membership cards, and statements of witnesses who are familiar with the applicant's story. In rare cases applicants do have documentary evidence from the persecuting government, such as an arrest record or a court conviction for a political crime. In cases where an applicant has scars or other permanent physical damage from torture, a doctor's report can also be strong evidence in support of the applicant's claim.

In the period from April 1991 to September 2000, 358,207 cases were adjudicated by the INS, of which 93,245 or 26 percent were approved for asylum. In immigration court, 201,847 cases were decided in the period spanning fiscal years 1989 to 1999, and 46,984 or 23.3 percent were approved.[5] There is some overlap in these numbers, as many asylum cases are first heard by the asylum office and then referred to court, but the government does not keep statistics on how many cases were heard in both venues.

In fiscal year 2000, 48,000 new asylum cases were filed at the INS, and 62,000 cases were adjudicated—the extra cases were taken from the "backlog." The largest number of cases were filed by nationals of China, 13 percent of the total number of filings, followed by Haiti (10 percent), Mexico (8 percent), Colombia (6 percent), El Salvador (6 percent), Somalia (5 percent), Guatemala (4 percent), Ethiopia (3 percent), India (3 percent), and Liberia (2 percent). As of October, there were still 327,000 cases in the INS "backlog." Of these, however, almost 300,000 were Salvadoran and Guatemalan cases whose adjudication had been delayed until

5. These statistics are taken from *Refugee Reports* (December 2000) and from statistics released by INS in a meeting with nonprofit organizations held on November 8, 2000.

that year because of delays in implementing the American Baptist Churches (ABC) lawsuit settlement, and because of the passage of legislation in 1997 that allowed most ABC class members to obtain legal permanent resident status without having an asylum interview.[6] Of the cases adjudicated in 2000, 51.8 percent were approved, the highest rate of approval to date. Iraqi cases had the highest approval rate, of 82 percent, and Hondurans had the lowest, only 7.7 percent.

In immigration court, 50,838 cases were received in fiscal year 2000, of which 23,349 were adjudicated. China was the country of origin of the largest single group of applicants, who make up 17 percent of the total, followed by Mexico (11 percent), Haiti (10 percent), El Salvador (6 percent), the Philippines (5 percent), Somalia (3 percent), India (3 percent), Cuba (3 percent), Colombia (3 percent), and Russia (2 percent). Only 7,336 cases, or 31.4 percent of the total adjudicated, were approved; Afghanistan had the highest approval rate, 83 percent, and Nicaragua had the lowest, only 6.8 percent. Complete statistics on countries and their approval rates are reprinted in Appendix Two.

Legal practitioners and scholars interested in learning more about the law of asylum should consult one of a number of good practice manuals and academic studies listed in the bibliography. Recent developments in asylum law, and issues of concern for the future, are discussed in this book in chapter ten.

Other aspects of asylum law and procedure are discussed in the following chapters as we follow the experiences of four asylum applicants. These applicants' stories do not represent the experience of the "average" asylum applicant—in fact, two of them had an unusually difficult experience before they finally were granted asylum. I chose these four asylees to profile because their stories

6. The Nicaraguan Adjustment and Central American Relief Act (NACARA) was enacted on November 19, 1997, as Title II of the District of Columbia Appropriations Act for fiscal year 1998, Pub. L. No. 105–100, 111 Stat. 2160, but interim regulations implementing the act were not formulated until May 21, 1999 (64 Fed. Reg. 27856–82).

were unusual; their experiences illustrate the complex nature of the asylum system. Chapter Nine describes the most dangerous new development in asylum law, the mandatory detention and "expedited removal" of asylum seekers, and recounts the story of a refugee who was affected by this law.

2

ⅫⅢⅡⅢⅡ

Persecution

EACH YEAR hundreds of thousands of people become refugees
due to civil wars, political oppression, ethnic conflict, and religious persecution. The U.S. Committee for Refugees estimates that
there were 14.1 million refugees in the world in 1999.[1] An entire
branch of the United Nations, the U.N. High Commission for
Refugees (UNHCR), exists to provide for their needs; in 1999 it
had more than 5,000 staff members and a budget of $1.17 bil-
lion.[2]

What causes people to leave their countries, their homes, their
families, and their jobs for the uncertain conditions of refugee
camps in a foreign country? Fear of death: most refugees flee their
countries because of conditions of civil war. The largest single
group of refugees in the world are Palestinians, of whom over 3.9
million live as refugees in other countries. More than 2.5 million
refugees from Afghanistan live in Pakistan and Iran, and there are
millions of refugees from civil wars in other countries, such as
Iraq, Sierra Leone, Somalia, Sudan, and the former Yugoslavia.[3]

Other refugees flee because they were the victims of political

1. *World Refugee Survey,* U.S. Committee for Refugees, 2000.
2. *Refugees and Others of Concern to UNHCR—1999 Statistical Overview,*
UNHCR, July 1999.
3. *World Refugee Survey,* U.S. Committee for Refugees, 2000.

oppression within a police state or of persecution because of their religion or ethnicity. Of the 192 countries in the world, 47 are classified as "not free" and 60 as "partly free" in the most recent survey of civil and political rights done by the nonprofit research agency Freedom House.[4] Governments in 132 countries were classified as using torture against prisoners.[5]

Adele and Philippe Fontem[6]

Adele Fontem is attractive, intelligent, and well educated. At twenty-nine she is a living symbol of the "new" Africa—fluent in French, English, and her native language, Bassa; she is modern in dress and outlook, equally comfortable in an American business office or at a Cameroonian village meeting. Where she is energetic and talkative, her husband, Philippe, is calm, quiet, and relaxed. He is thirty-seven, but he looks very young. Sometimes people ask Adele if Philippe is her younger brother. When I met them, they had one child, a baby boy named Richard, and Philippe was acting as the primary caregiver. Philippe is tall and strong, an imposing presence, but gentle, soft-spoken, and self-effacingly polite.

Adele was born in 1971 in Douala, Cameroon. Her parents are middle class—her father owns a small business, and her mother is a Western-educated computer programmer. Neither of her parents were ever involved in politics. Philippe was born in Douala in 1963. His father and mother both had careers in the civil service, rising to mid-level positions before retirement. As civil servants, they had no affiliation with any political party.

Adele went to college at the University of Yaoundé in Cameroon's second largest city. She studied law at first and then changed to accounting, but left school in 1994 without a degree in order to work full-time. Philippe also attended the University of Yaoundé, and in 1987 he received a Bachelor's degree in econom-

4. *Freedom in the World 1999–2000* (New York, N.Y., 2000).
5. *Annual Report 2000*, Amnesty International.
6. Adele's name, and the names of the other refugees in this book, have been changed to protect their privacy and to protect family members still in their home countries from government reprisal. Certain details, dates, and place names have also been changed.

ics. He began a master's program but left school when he got a good job. A close friend of his owned a pharmacy but did not want to spend time in the daily management of the business. Philippe became the pharmacy's business manager, a responsible job with a high salary. Philippe and Adele met in 1994, shortly after Adele left the university. They soon began dating and after a while, Philippe hired Adele to work as an accountant at the pharmacy.

Like many African countries, Cameroon is a one-party dictatorship. Ahmadou Ahidjo, the leader of the dominant Union Camerounaise party, ruled the country from independence in 1960 until 1982, when he resigned the presidency. He nominated his successor, Paul Biya, who has led the country ever since. With foreign economic and military aid, Biya has been able to rule the country as a dictator.

This situation changed in the 1990s with the end of the cold war and the reduction of foreign aid to Cameroon. Biya had to shore up his support among his own people. He allowed demonstrations, the formation of political parties, and a more independent media. He called for elections to be held in 1992, though he never intended to give up power. He thought he could allow enough of an appearance of democracy to maintain international support and development assistance while using the media and the secret police to keep the opposition weak and divided and his control of the electoral system to win the elections.

Philippe joined the largest opposition party, the Social Democratic Front (SDF), when it was founded in 1991. All opposition parties had the same goal: to end Biya's dictatorship and the country's poverty, but the SDF was the most committed to grassroots organizing and the participation of all Cameroonians in politics.

The SDF won the largest number of votes in the 1992 elections, but Paul Biya claimed a victory in the presidential race and declared that his party had won a majority of the parliamentary seats. People knew this was not true, but the government controlled the electoral system, and Biya could falsify the election results in any way he wished.

After the elections, the SDF and other opposition groups held strikes and demonstrations, calling for Biya to step down and allow the opposition candidates to take the seats they should have won. Philippe helped organize and participated in these political activities. He had a house, a car of his own, and the use of a van owned by the pharmacy. He permitted students to use these vehicles for transportation to and from political events, and he let them use his house as a site for their meetings.

Philippe was arrested three times in 1993. The first time, early in the year, he attended a large political rally, which proceeded without interruption from the police. As he was walking home, however, a group of policemen saw him and some other SDF members on the street and guessed that they had attended the rally. They arrested Philippe and his companions and kept them in jail overnight. They beat and interrogated Philippe and his friends, who admitted nothing. "At that time, we were still strong," Philippe said. "We thought nothing could happen to us." The police had arrested many people that night, and they had no evidence other than that Philippe was walking in the street after the rally had ended. They let Philippe and his friends go. Philippe was arrested again after another demonstration later that year. Again he was beaten and interrogated, but he admitted to nothing and was released after being held overnight. The third time he was not so lucky.

In late 1993, Philippe attended a large political rally in a public meeting hall. The police waited outside the building during the rally but did not attempt to break it up or arrest all the participants because the crowd was too large for them to control. Instead the police waited for the last persons to leave, figuring they would be the demonstration's organizers. Philippe had stayed behind to help clean up, and he was arrested.

This time the police suspected him as a leader in the student movement and treated him more harshly. When he arrived at the jail, one of the policemen looked at him closely. "It's you again," he said, "I know you." Philippe was forced to strip to his underwear, and his head was shaved with a piece of broken glass. He was beaten severely over the next three days—all over his body, but mostly on his feet and on his back. Philippe told me, "If I cried out, they would say I was making so that people could hear me on the street, and they beat me harder. If I said nothing, they said that I must not be feeling it, and they beat me harder again."

After three days, he hurt so much he could not walk or lie down. They put papers in front of him and told him to sign. When he tried to read them, they beat him again. Finally, he just signed— but he did not use his true signature. He wrote his own name but in a different handwriting, so that he could later say that the signature was forged. Later he learned that sometimes the police had people sign their names many times, to see if their signature was consistent, but they did not ask him to do this that day. The paper he signed was a confession of anti-government activities and a promise never again to participate in politics.

Despite this, Philippe continued his political work after he was released, and he managed to avoid being arrested during the next few years. The level of political activity and unrest in Cameroon had declined steadily during the year after the elections, as it became clear that no amount of pressure could bring Biya or his supporters to relinquish power. The SDF party became less publicly active and concentrated on recruiting and educating new members, improving its organization, and gaining more financial support in preparation for the next round of elections, scheduled for 1997.

Philippe and Adele had begun dating in 1994, and she had soon joined in the political work. Adele was already interested in politics from her days as a university student. She explained to me that, "as a high school student, you are not aware of politics because you are mainly interested in yourself. In university, you become more aware of the state of the country. You see other people graduating with bachelor's degrees or even advanced degrees who can't get jobs. Other educated people work at government jobs, but at a greatly reduced salary." For years the Cameroonian government paid employees only a fraction of their allotted salary because of a supposed lack of funds. At the same time, government supporters and party insiders made millions from corruption. "You work hard in school, and you might have nothing; then you see someone without an education, but because he's the son of someone, he's rich. You realize that you don't want to live your whole life and have children in a situation like that."

Adele and Philippe took on a leadership role in bringing the message of the SDF party to the population of the towns and rural areas outside of Yaoundé. This area was populated by people from the same ethnic group, the Bassa, as Adele and Philippe, and they were able to speak to the villagers in their own language. Adele spoke to rural women about conditions in their villages, particularly addressing their concerns about health and their children's education. She brought medicine with her from the pharmacy and gave it to people who needed it. She recruited village women to start SDF chapters in the rural areas. These SDF chapters had a formal membership of fifteen to twenty women, who acted as a sort of executive committee, and there were hundreds of other women who attended meetings and supported the SDF.

Philippe spoke to the men about their concerns. Most of the villagers were farmers; the Biya government, however, either ignored the agricultural sector or treated it as a source of tax revenue. Development projects, funded with foreign aid, were intended to build industry and commerce but became mere mechanisms for government officials to make money from corruption. The government also controlled prices and forced farmers to sell their produce below market value. This kept food prices low for city dwellers but left farmers in a constant state of poverty.

Adele was arrested twice and jailed for short periods of time. In 1995 the government arrested Garga Haman Al-Hadji, an assistant to the leader of the SDF party and a well-known figure. Adele participated in a large demonstration in protest of this arrest, which was broken up by the police. The police took more than one hundred demonstrators to jail, including Adele, and kept them overnight.

Adele was arrested a second time in 1996. In that year the government adopted a new constitution, designed to make it possible for President Biya to win the next elections. Instead of resorting to outright fraud in the vote-counting, he rearranged the rules on voter registration, candidate eligibility, and voting practices so that he would be assured a majority of the votes cast. The new constitution mandated that people had to vote in the same district where they were born; if they moved, they would have to live at their new address five years before they could change their voting address. This constitutional scheme would have the result of separating the country into ethnic or tribal voting blocs and would encourage feelings of animosity between different tribes. The electoral districts would also be divided in such a way as to maximize the voting power of people from the president's ethnic group. The new constitution also made it a requirement that candidates for president be under sixty years of age—a change that disqualified most of Biya's competitors.

Adele and Philippe participated in a large protest against the new constitution. Adele was detained and beaten by the police. They did not interrogate her but just seemed to want to intimidate her and the others. After three days she was forced to sign a piece of paper promising that she would no longer participate in "subversive" activities, and she was released. Philippe was held in jail in a different location for one day.

Because the government controlled the electoral commission and had changed the constitution, it was clear that the 1997 elections would be unfair. The opposition had no chance of winning and after having seen Biya's party steal the election in 1992, the SDF did not intend to give credence to an election that they knew would be unfair. Along with many other parties, they boycotted the elections and encouraged their supporters not to vote at all.

Philippe and Adele went to the Bassa towns and villages outside of Yaoundé to explain the need to boycott the elections. "It was hard to tell the people not to vote," Adele explained. "For years we had been telling them to participate, to be active, to change the government, and we had been telling them their lives would get better. Then we had to tell them not to vote. They were so disappointed. But we explained to them why, and they understood."

In late August 1997 Philippe was arrested at home, where he had been holding a political meeting with a few other SDF party members. There was a knock on the door, and he went to answer it. He saw two men with dark glasses and long coats, and he went out to talk to them, closing the door behind him so that they would not enter the house and find his friends there. He saw some other men running toward him, and the next thing he knew he was being beaten over the head and dragged into a car. The men sat on him in the back seat, and he was rushed away to prison. He learned, much later, that the people who were meeting in his house were also arrested that day.

Philippe was taken to a detention center for political prisoners called the "Brigade Mixe Mobile," an "unofficial" prison that belonged to the secret police. At one time the building had been a large private home, but it had now been converted to a jail. He was held there for three months and was often beaten and interrogated. "Sometimes they beat you to get information, but sometimes they beat you just for fun. They came in drunk and they would play with us, like we were toys. All the other guards would watch and laugh. They came in even on their day off, just to beat us."

A month later, Adele too was arrested. Soldiers came to the pharmacy that evening, just before she left work, and took her away to jail. The same night, another group of soldiers stole her car and burned down the house. The soldiers took her to a police station and locked her in a room by herself. The next morning they took her to another room to be beaten. They told her she was going for her "morning coffee." They tied her hands behind her back and laid her across two tables, then beat her on the soles of her feet. They beat her until her feet swelled up and hurt so much that she could not walk, then dragged her back to solitary confinement and left her there.

The next morning she suffered the same treatment—again announced as her "morning coffee" and the next day after that and each day of the ten days she was detained there. Sometimes they pulled the tables apart so that nothing supported her body in the middle, and she had to strain to hold herself up, which was very painful. As they beat her, they insulted her and interrogated her, demanding that she name other people involved in political activities with the SDF party.

After ten days she was taken to the "Americanos," a large prison for both political prisoners and criminals, located just outside of Yaoundé. They shaved Adele's head with a piece of glass and made her strip to her underwear, which was the only clothing they allowed any of the prisoners. She was placed in a cell with twelve other women, where there were no sanitary facilities.

She was tortured several times a week at the Americanos prison. Sometimes they tied her and forced her to sit under slowly dripping water, which caused an increasing pain and eventually made her pass out. Several times each week she was taken to another room and beaten. Sometimes they beat her on both her feet and her calves with an iron bar and a police truncheon until her feet swelled up and she could not walk. Other times they beat her with a hard rubber strap until her back bled, then they threw cold water on her back because the shock of the cold water against the raw skin was very painful.

Adele was not allowed visitors at the prison, but her family found out she was there. They bribed the guards to bring her food, to make sure she was not treated too badly, and to prevent her from being raped. Many of the women in the prison had been raped by the guards, but her family's bribes saved Adele from this form of torture. Philippe and Adele's family and their friends in the SDF party began to search for someone who would accept a bribe to let one or both escape from prison. They also began to arrange for travel documents that would allow them to leave the country if they did escape.

Therese Kabongelo

Therese Kabongelo is fifty-five years old and beautiful. She has a few wrinkles around her eyes and mouth, her hair is beginning to go gray, and she has put on some weight, but this has only given her a kind, grandmotherly appearance. Therese has lived through many hardships and has learned to find joy even in the worst situations. She often seems tired and sad, but at any reason to feel happy—a joke, a kind word, the sight of a child—her face lights up with a smile.

One of my fondest memories of Therese is an event that took place at, of all places, the Department of Motor Vehicles (DMV) office in Falls Church, Virginia. We had gone there because Therese needed a photo identification card—she had come to the

United States on someone else's passport, and she had no birth certificate or other identification. Virginia state law allows for asylum applicants to obtain a state identification from the DMV, but it is a complex process and most DMV employees have never heard of it.

At the office, the first two people we talked to refused to issue any identification without seeing a passport or a birth certificate. We argued and asked to speak to a supervisor. I finally convinced them to give her an identity card, but I needed to have the form notarized. I had to leave the DMV office and go to a bank to get a notary stamp.

By the time I returned, Therese and I had been waiting for over two hours, and we still had a wait ahead of us before they would take Therese's picture and make the identity card. The office was hot, crowded, and noisy. Therese was sick with allergies and a fever, and she had been through a terrible trauma only a few months before. I was frustrated and angry, but Therese seemed unperturbed. A few minutes later she heard a baby crying behind her. She smiled and said, "Look! A baby," and turned and played with him for a while; soon he stopped crying. A minute later she was called for her photo. Her smile in the photo is radiant.

Therese was born into a middle-class family in Uvira, a small city on the eastern border of Congo, on Lake Tanganyika near what is now Rwanda and Burundi. Her father, a businessman, was an unusually modern man for the time. When Therese was six years old, he did something that had never been done before in their town: he sent his daughter to school. "Everybody in town thought he was crazy," Therese remembers, "spending money on an education for a girl." Therese's father did not change his mind, however, and she did well in school. She graduated from high school and went on to college for two years. When she left college, she went to work as a teacher at a public middle school.

At twenty-four, Therese married, and she and her husband had twin boys. When she was thirty, her husband was killed in a car accident. A close friend of her husband's helped her work through her grief and look after her children. Eventually he proposed marriage. They were married a few years after her first husband's death and had four children together. In 1985, Therese's sister and brother-in-law were killed in another car crash, and she adopted their two infant children.

Therese lived through many political changes in Congo. After the country achieved independence from Belgium in 1960, it went through a brief democratic period and elected the socialist candidate Patrice Lumumba as prime minister. The Congolese military, still controlled by Belgian officers, mutinied against the central government, and the Belgian government sent in troops to oppose Lumumba's government and support a separatist movement in one province. Lumumba declared martial law, arrested political opponents, and asked for Soviet help in maintaining power. The United Nations sent in troops to support the central government, and these troops took an active part in the civil war. At the end of 1960, Lumumba was overthrown by a group of politicians and military leaders, including the head of the army, Joseph-Désiré Mobutu, and was later killed.

After the coup, Mobutu controlled the government for several months and then allowed civilian control. The civil war continued, however, and for a time more than half the country's land area was controlled by different rebel groups. Finally, in 1965, Mobutu overthrew the civilian government again and took power for himself. He was supported by the U.S. government, which feared that chaos in Congo would allow the Soviet Union to gain influence in the country.

With U.S. support and the backing of the Congolese armed forces, Mobutu was able to stay in power for more than thirty years. He established a one-party state, controlled the media, and imprisoned, tortured, and executed his opponents. Mobutu portrayed himself as his nation's "savior" and established a Stalin-like cult of personality. Photos and portraits of him were displayed everywhere, and schoolchildren were taught songs of praise to his name.

In 1971 he announced that the names "Joseph-Désiré" and "Congo" were products of Western colonialism. He became "Mobutu Sese Seko Nkuku wa za Banga," a traditional name which means "all-conquering warrior, who goes from triumph to triumph." He changed the name of the country to "Zaire," and ordered all of the country's citizens to change their Christian names to African ones. Therese had to change her first name on her official documents to an African name, though, like most Congolese, she continued to use her Christian name as well.

As the years passed, Mobutu became more corrupt, his rule became more erratic and ineffective, and the country slipped further and further into poverty. He stayed in power because of support from foreign countries, particularly the United States. He toned down his anti-colonial rhetoric and became a vocal opponent of communism. He succeeded in making his country the United States' main cold war ally in central Africa. The benefits of this support were massive economic and military aid.

When the Cold War ended in the late 1980s, the United States cut back on its support of Mobutu, and his position began to slip. He no longer could maintain power in remote areas of the country; by the mid 1990s he had effective control of only a small area around the capital. In other parts of the country, local authorities managed things with little interference from the central government.

Where Therese lived, at the far eastern edge of the country, this situation had advantages and disadvantages. People could speak freely about politics without fear of arrest and torture. Local people managed local affairs, and corruption was less of a problem. The economy, however, declined still further as the national government no longer maintained roads, telephones, or other infrastructure, and the national currency had become worthless. Eastern Zaire reverted to a primitive economy based on subsistence farming and the barter system.

For Therese, the worst result of the economic collapse was that the government no longer paid teachers' salaries. She had to give up her job and work as a vendor in the city marketplace while her husband tried to continue with his business. The economic collapse caused problems, but the family could survive, and they adjusted to the new situation as well as they could. "We all felt like this would pass—that things would have to change," Therese told me. "We were all waiting, with the feeling that things would get better."

After the huge reduction in U.S. support in the late 1980s, Mobutu took tentative steps toward reform of the government. Among these was his decision in 1991 to allow political parties to form. In the regions outside the central government's control, a lively political debate ensued, laying the foundations of what could have become a democratic society.

Therese's husband was heavily involved in these political discussions in Uvira. He was an amiable, well-known businessman with many friends. It was natural for him to meet with other community leaders and talk about political change. As it became more clear that Mobutu no longer had the power to punish dissenters in the area, people began to speak more freely. Eventually Therese's husband became the head of the main democratic opposition party, the Union for Democracy and Social Progress (UDPS), in their district of Uvira. Therese's twin sons, now in their twenties, helped her husband promote the party among the young people of the town. Therese hosted party meetings and worked with the women members of the party.

As Mobutu's power waned, many people hoped that the UDPS or some other party could take power through democratic elections. But a series of violent events in the neighboring country of Rwanda led to an invasion of Zaire by foreign soldiers and the replacement of Mobutu with another military dictator.

For centuries, Rwanda's government and society had been dominated by the Tutsi ethnic group, a tribe that made up only about 12 percent of the country's population. In 1961, during Rwanda's transition to independence, the Hutus, the largest ethnic group in Rwanda, took control of the government from the Tutsis. As often happens, the persecuted became the persecutors, and many Tutsis fled the country. In 1993, Tutsi rebels invaded Rwanda from Uganda and began to win back control of the country. The Rwandan government was weak, corrupt, and unpopular. In an effort to mobilize public support among the Hutus, the government appealed to feelings of ethnic hatred and began a systematic campaign of genocide against Tutsi civilians. It continued for two months while the United Nations and Western governments did little to stop it; by the time the Tutsis won control of Rwanda in July 1993, the genocide had claimed 500,000 lives, more than

75 percent of the total Tutsi population of 650,000.[7] Hutu civilians, fearing it would be their turn to be attacked, fled the country in huge numbers, more than 1.5 million of them to Zaire. The U.S. army initiated a massive airlift of supplies to these refugees, and the United States and the United Nations set up refugee camps all along the border of Zaire and Rwanda.

Along with innocent civilian refugees, many armed Hutu military groups and former government members, the same people who had committed genocide against Tutsi civilians in 1993, lived in the camps. They began to use the refugee camps as military bases from which to launch attacks into Rwanda. The U.S. military had left the region, the U.N. did not possess military power with which to contain them, and the government of Zaire had no power in the area.

In July 1996, Rwandan troops invaded eastern Zaire and attacked the camps. They broke the power of the Hutu militias, and some of the Hutu refugees voluntarily returned home. Others fled further into Zaire and were pursued by the Rwandan soldiers. These soldiers did not make a distinction between Hutu refugees and Hutu militia groups, killing any Hutu they found. Reporters were not allowed into the area, but refugees who escaped told stories of massacres in which thousands of people were killed.

As the invasion continued, the Rwandan government decided to support a Zairian military leader who could take control of the entire country of Zaire from Mobutu. The leader that Rwanda chose, Laurent Kabila, had been a minor figure in a revolutionary movement of the 1960s and had lived in exile in Rwanda for twenty years. He formed a small military force and, with the support of Rwandan, Ugandan, and Burundian troops, fought his way across eastern Zaire toward the capital. The Rwandan government expected that, after he took over Zaire, Kabila would rule the country in accordance with Rwandan interests and guarantee the security of the border.

Kabila's forces met with only sporadic resistance. The people of Zaire initially welcomed his troops, assuming that any new gov-

7. *Leave None to Tell the Story: Genocide in Rwanda* by Alison Des Forges (Human Rights Watch, 1999).

ernment could only be an improvement over the old one and hoping that Kabila would honor his promises to set up a democracy. Although his forces killed many civilians through indiscriminate artillery attacks on villages and cities, and massacred people suspected of opposing them, most Zaireans thought Kabila would rule with less violence once he had won the war.

Therese had no such hope for the future because she was from the Hutu ethnic group. Although her ancestors had migrated from Rwanda nearly a hundred years before, and she was a citizen of Zaire, Kabila's soldiers made no distinction between her and Rwandan Hutus. When the war started in June, she heard about the massacres of Zairean Hutu civilians in the areas near the refugee camps. When Kabila attacked the Uvira region in October, she and her family, along with many others, fled the city for the mountains.

After she fled, Rwandan and Zairean rebel soldiers shelled Uvira with artillery before attacking with ground troops. When the soldiers occupied the city, they went on a rampage, looting and destroying private homes. They then targeted specific people for death, people whom they thought might oppose their rule. They killed some Hutus simply because of their ethnic identity, but they especially sought out Hutus who might be able to support the Hutu cause in Rwanda: wealthy or educated people, and political or community leaders. If Therese and her husband had not fled, they would certainly have been killed.

Therese stayed in the mountains for about two months. The family separated and lived in different places, so that if one or several of them were killed, at least some members would survive. Many other people had fled to the mountains, and the people lived off whatever food they could find. They dug up the roots of wild plants, hunted for birds, and scavenged for any foods that grew wild in the area.

After two months, Therese and her children had lost weight and were suffering from the cold in the mountains. Fortunately, none of them had become sick. Illness had killed many of the other refugees in the mountains, but Therese's entire family survived. Other people had begun to return to the villages because Kabila's forces had moved east, toward the capital. Therese's husband returned first, to scout out the situation, and, when he reported it safe, she and the children came to join him.

When Kabila's forces seized Kinshasa, the capital of Zaire, in May 1997, people hoped that now, with the war over and his power secure, Kabila would take steps to democratize the country. Instead Kabila appointed people from his military organization, most of them ethnic Tutsis, to all the high government positions, and he outlawed opposition parties, including the UDPS. In an effort to renounce the policies of the former regime, he changed the name of the country from Zaire back to Congo.

In eastern Congo, the effects of Kabila's rule began to be felt as the Tutsi soldiers who brought him to power consolidated their hold on the region. A new campaign of attacks on Hutus began. At first, individual Hutus died in mysterious accidents or simply disappeared—they left for work in the morning and never returned home. Later, people would find their bodies in ditches by the side of the road. In June and July, Tutsi soldiers began to raid individual houses, killing Hutus and others who had criticized Kabila or who they suspected of opposing him. They also targeted wealthy Hutus, taking advantage of their vulnerability to evict them from their homes and steal their possessions. Some Hutu citizens armed themselves and fought back, but their attempts at resistance only brought more severe reprisals. Tutsi soldiers massacred hundreds of men, women, and children, and burned entire villages and neighborhoods. They arrested, killed, or frightened away local mayors and officials and replaced them with Tutsis loyal to the new regime.

Therese and her family were first targeted on August 3, 1997, a Sunday. Soldiers came to their house while she, her husband, and her adult sons were out. Therese was attending Mass, but her husband and two oldest sons were staying away from the house out of fear. Her husband knew the soldiers would begin looking for him soon, and for a few weeks he had slept elsewhere most nights, returning home only for short visits.

About twenty-five soldiers drove into their neighborhood in military trucks and began searching houses. They came into Therese's house and asked the younger children where Therese, her husband, and the two oldest children were. They also searched for UDPS party documents in the house, taking all the papers they could find. The soldiers told the children that they knew their father was a spy, that they knew the house contained a list of other UDPS members, and that they would continue to come back until they found this list. They said they would not stop what they were doing until they had killed all the Hutus on the planet.

Therese was fortunate that no one in the family was hurt that day. Only the young children were home, and the soldiers did not abuse them in order to get information. Other families in the neighborhood were not as lucky. Their neighbor, an older man with grown children, had refused to tell the soldiers where his adult son was hiding, so the soldiers had killed him in front of his family.

After this, Therese's husband left the house for good. On August 27 the soldiers returned, but fortunately Therese was again absent when they arrived. This time they went only to Therese's house. They asked the children where Therese, her husband, and her two oldest sons were, but the children became scared and ran away. The soldiers then stole most of the things in the house and destroyed everything else. They spared nothing.

When Therese returned and found the house destroyed, she took her children and went to a village further out from the city, where her husband's mother lived. Her two oldest sons, and her third son, who was eighteen, left town to stay elsewhere. They did not tell the family where they were hiding, so that other family members could not be tortured into revealing their location. The adult sons were afraid of being killed because of their association with their father, but they also feared being forcibly recruited into Kabila's army.

Therese's husband also hid in the village, but he stayed in a different house from the rest of the family, thinking he could spare them from danger if he was not with them. Therese, her children, and her husband's mother stayed in the house of a family friend. This house had already been looted of all its furniture, and Therese thought they would be safer there because there was nothing valuable in the house that would make it a target.

On September 5, at 5 a.m., Therese and her children were awakened by the sound of heavy trucks pulling into the village.

Soldiers entered her house and forced her and the children to come outside. They began beating the adults—Therese, her mother-in-law, and the family friend—in front of the children, and the children began to cry. They beat the children too but concentrated their efforts on the women.

Her husband heard his children crying and came to give himself up to the soldiers so that he could spare his wife, mother, and children from their attack. Instead of stopping, however, they continued. They tore off the women's clothes, and raped Therese, her husband's mother, and the family friend in front of him. He struggled free of his captors when they did this and rushed to try to save his wife. They beat him repeatedly with the butts of their rifles, then shot him—round after round into his body, and continued shooting even after he was dead. The children saw all of this happen.

Therese fainted when she saw the soldiers shoot her husband. When she regained consciousness, she found herself lying in a bed in a small room. After a while, a Belgian priest came into her room to see how she was doing. They told her that she was safe for the time being and was living in a monastery in a small town outside of Uvira. She never saw anyone but the priests during her time there, but she believed that they were hiding other people: when they brought her food, she saw other plates on the tray.

The priests told Therese that her children were safe, but they would not tell her where they were—again, for their own safety. They were being taken care of by another family and had been disguised as that family's children. They also told her that her mother-in-law had died from her injuries, but they did not know what had happened to the woman who owned the house where they had stayed.

The priests told her she could stay at the monastery until she felt better but would then have to leave the country. She was endangering the other refugees and the priests by staying there, and she would not be safe anywhere in Congo. Therese did not want to leave, especially without her children, but they convinced her that her children were safer without her, since the soldiers had no interest in them and could not even tell who they were without her there to endanger them. They had only enough money to send her out of the country at this time, but she could send for her children to join her later on.

Therese did not wish to escape and did not want even to live after all that had happened to her. She slept as much as she could, and each day she prayed that she would not wake up the next morning. She lived and agreed to try to escape and start her life over again only for the sake of her children, who still needed a parent. Reluctantly, she began to work with the priests to find a way to flee to Europe or the United States.

Aster Cheru

Even now, in the United States, Aster Cheru often looks worried. A lifetime of political persecution, beginning when she was only six years old, has taken a heavy toll on her health. Aster was married but is now divorced. From her former husband she has two sons, Joseph and John, who are now five and three years old. She also has a daughter, Beth, a child from a different relationship, who is now fifteen years old. Aster is a religious woman and attends an evangelical Protestant church. Her strong religious faith and her love for her children keep her going despite the misfortunes she has suffered.

Aster does not know her exact age, but she thinks she is about thirty-seven years old. She does not know her date of birth because the persecution of her family began when she was still only a child, and the government destroyed her family records. Her parents died when she was young, and her grandparents have since passed away, so no one in her family remembers the day of her birth.

Aster does know that she was born in Dilla, a town in the region of Sidamo, Ethiopia. Her father was a government official and a member of the traditional Ethiopian nobility. At the time of her birth, Ethiopia was still ruled by the Emperor Haile Selassie, and Aster's father, as a member of the nobility, enjoyed wealth and many privileges.

In 1974, when Aster was about ten years old, the emperor was overthrown by a group of military leaders. The new rulers became known as the Dergue, an Amharic word meaning "committee." They established a Marxist state, and soon Colonel Hailemariam Mengistu emerged as the leader of this committee. The Dergue government began to take land and wealth away from the traditional nobility and redistribute it to Ethiopia's peasants. These reforms, however, were accompanied by the repression of basic freedoms and violence against any who opposed them. Aster's family were among the victims.

Her father was killed in 1975. The Dergue government had removed him from his political position and had taken away much of his land, but he retained his standing in the community. He also kept a few guns in the house, since the right to own weapons was a privilege he held as a member of the nobility. In 1975, soldiers came to his house to confiscate his weapons, but he refused to give them up. They argued and threatened, but he refused to give in, so they left. A few hours later, the soldiers returned to the house and shot him to death in his bed.

Three years later the Dergue, seeking to consolidate its control over the country, allowed the formation of political parties as long as they were socialist in orientation and did not support the return of the emperor. Since there had always been a wide opposition to Haile Selassie's reactionary rule, many people joined these parties, particularly a Communist party called the Ethiopian People's Revolutionary Party (EPRP). The Dergue regime grew alarmed at the popularity of this new party and feared that the EPRP could challenge them for power.

In a period of severe repression known as the "Red Terror," the Dergue cracked down on the EPRP. Its members were arrested, tortured, and killed. Thousands of people died, most of them young. The terror lasted from 1977 to 1978, and, at the end of it, the Dergue's power was confirmed without any political opposition.

Aster's two oldest brothers were both active in the EPRP. When the government began arresting EPRP members, her two older brothers fled. Her oldest brother, Berhane, left the country altogether, and the family never saw him again. Years later they received letters from him from Liberia, where he had started a new life, but they lost contact with him again in 1990. Her second brother, Dawit, fled to the capital, changed his name, and went into hiding.

When the authorities came to arrest Berhane and Dawit and found that they were gone, they arrested Aster's third brother, Yohannes, even though he was only fourteen years old and had never been involved in politics. They told the family that they would detain him until the other two presented themselves to the authorities, and, if the other two did not show up, they would punish him for his brothers' political crimes. Aster's mother went to the police station and asked to be imprisoned in his place, but they would not take her. Aster and her mother went every day to the police station to try to see him. They left food, but they did not know if he received it.

One day, about three months after Yohannes had been arrested, the authorities would not take the food that Aster left for him. A few days later the police sent the family Yohannes's clothing, meaning he was dead. They never received his body and so could not perform the traditional funeral rites. Aster still weeps when she remembers Yohannes, more than twenty years after his death. "He was only a child," she told me, "and he had done nothing—why did they have to kill him?" Some time after Yohannes's death, Aster and her mother learned from farmers in a rural area away from the town that bodies from the prison were commonly brought to this area and buried in the woods. Aster and her mother visited this forest as one would visit a gravesite, as a way of paying homage to Yohannes's memory. A few months later, Aster's mother died of an illness brought on by severe grief. Aster, who was now about fourteen years old, went to live with her grandmother.

With the EPRP completely destroyed, the government relaxed its persecution, and Dawit felt safer. He had been working in the capital, Addis Ababa, under an assumed name, and now felt secure enough to enroll in the university there using his new name. He also brought Aster to live with him. She worked full time during the day and completed high school by attending night classes.

Dawit graduated from the university with an honors degree in economics and began working as a civil servant in the Ministry of Finance. Aster found a job at a luxury hotel, working as a chef and food service manager for their banquet hall. From her work, she learned some English and came into contact with many foreign businessmen and diplomats. Her brother continued to rise in the civil service and in the late 1980s was sent to Europe to continue his education.

As the years passed, the political situation in Ethiopia changed as well. For decades, guerrilla soldiers in the province of Eritrea had been fighting a war of secession. Eritrea had been an Italian colony at one time. When Eritrea was taken from Italian control after World War II, the allies made it part of Ethiopia. An Eritrea independence movement and guerilla army arose. They almost won independence in the 1970s, but the Dergue government managed to acquire military aid from the Soviet Union and Cuba and regain control of the province.

Through the 1980s, the Eritrean forces slowly won back control of their province, and by the end of the decade the Dergue government was in serious trouble. The Soviets had cut military aid to Ethiopia with the end of the Cold War, depriving the government of most of its foreign support. The Dergue government was also beginning to weaken due to its corruption and inefficiency.

The final defeat of the Dergue came about through a second revolutionary movement, allied to the Eritreans. The Ethiopian province of Tigre lies between Eritrea and the capital. The Tigreans speak the same language as the Eritreans and share a similar culture. In the 1980s, using the rebel-controlled areas of Eritrea as a base, a Tigrean revolutionary movement gained control of large parts of Tigre province and by 1990 had begun to expand its war to the rest of Ethiopia.

In a last-minute effort to win the support of the Ethiopian people, the Dergue government encouraged the growth of "popular" organizations, which would mobilize the Ethiopian people in support of the war. One of these organizations was a system of "Neighborhood Women's Associations." Far from being a real people's organization, its main function was to hold weekly meetings, at which attendance was mandatory, where the members would listen to government propaganda read by the association's officers.

Aster was elected to be vice-president of this organization, probably because the neighborhood knew that she was not pro-government and could be relied upon to be lenient in the prosecution of her duties. When I asked her if she had to campaign for this office, she laughed. "I didn't want to be vice-president—nobody wanted to be vice-president. They tell you, and you do it. I wasn't even there when they picked me."

She served as vice-president for two and a half years. When I asked her what she did as vice-president, she said that the job only occasionally involved politics. "We talked to the people about the war, about the government, what they told us to say." She spent most of her time resolving disputes and helping other women in the neighborhood, a role that she enjoyed. "If two women got into a fight, we would try to solve the disagreement. We also helped with women's problems—we would try to talk to the government and get them to fix things." She was not very successful with this part of the job, however, because at this point, with the war against Eritrea going very badly, the government had little money to spend on development, health care, education, housing, and other human needs.

In May 1991 the Dergue government was finally overthrown by the Tigrean and Eritrean revolutionaries. The new government undertook two main policy changes: to end the domination of Ethiopian society by ethnic Amharas and to allow the province of Eritrea to secede from Ethiopia.

For centuries, Ethiopia's political, economic, and cultural life had been controlled by members of the Amhara ethnic group, the second-largest in a country that has over seventy different ethnicities. The Amharas ruled as feudal warlords, and Amharic dominance had continued under Haile Selassie and the Dergue. The new government's stated policy was to replace the Amharas' domination of Ethiopian life with a more egalitarian system. But as time went on it became clear that the government was not truly interested in bringing about ethnic equality but sought only to replace Amharic dominance of national affairs with Tigrean dominance.

The other primary decision of the new government was to allow Eritrea to secede and form a new country. It was obvious that the new government would do this, since the Tigrean revolutionary movement was an offshoot of the Eritrean revolutionary group. The province of Eritrea was now controlled by the Eritrean rebel group and in effect became an independent country in 1991, though it did not achieve official status until later. The new government of Ethiopia announced that a referendum would be held in the province of Eritrea in which the Eritrean people could decide through a popular vote whether they wished to form their own country. The Eritreans themselves were ecstatic, and in the 1993 referendum more than 95 percent of them voted in favor of independence. The country became officially independent the same year.

The new, Tigrean-dominated government began to dismiss Amharic government employees and to replace them with Tigreans. If the new government had allowed dissenting opinions a voice, it is possible that Amharic dissenters such as Aster could have been accommodated. Instead the new government used the same violent methods that the Dergue and Haile Selassie's governments had used before them. The Tigrean government imprisoned opponents, censored the media, and tortured people into silence. They outlawed some opposition political parties and harassed and restricted the others so severely that they effectively ceased to function.

Aster opposed the government's new policies and encouraged other people to oppose them as well. She began recruiting neighbors to participate in political meetings, and these meetings later became a source of recruits for a new political party, founded in 1992, called the All-Amhara People's Association.

In August 1991, four months after the new government took power, soldiers began to call in suspected supporters of the old government for questioning. Aster was called in late in the month. She was first taken to the office of the neighborhood government association to speak to a local official. This official told her that she had to explain her political background and history, and gave her a piece of paper to write on. He told her to write her life story on it, including any political activities in support of the Dergue regime.

Aster refused to do this. "I told him that he had no business asking me my life story. I have nothing to hide. I have done nothing. Everyone knows me. Why does he arrest me? He has no right." The local official threatened her with imprisonment, but she still would not cooperate. He detained her for a week, then ordered her transferred to a police station in the town of Nazareth, about forty miles from Addis Ababa. She was kept in a cell crowded with women, in unsanitary conditions with inadequate food.

The first night she was there, she was taken out of the cell in the middle of the night and brought to an interrogation room for questioning. This time there was no piece of paper for her to write on. The interrogator asked her questions and insisted that she answer him. Aster argued with him instead. "I told him that he had no right to question me. I told him the new government was not a real government, because a real government brings people together, and all his government did was split people apart. It split people apart by dividing everyone by ethnic group, and it split people apart by letting Eritrea leave the country. Even in Eritrea," she told him, "there are some ethnic groups that want to stay in Ethiopia. Your government doesn't listen to them."

The interrogator became furious at her opposition. He punched her in the face, and she fell down. "Then I heard a noise, and it seemed like the lights went out. I felt this strong pain, a weird feeling, all through my body. Then I passed out." When Aster came to, she was in a prison cell with the other women. She was bleeding from her left arm and her leg, and when she described what had happened the other women told her that she had been given an electric shock.

The same interrogator called her back about a week later. He asked her questions again, and this time she refused to answer or say anything. When she continued to be silent, he called in two guards and told them to take care of her. He said that Mengistu, the leader of the former government, was her uncle and that she deserved whatever they could do to her. He left, and the soldiers raped her. As they did so, they told her that she deserved it, since Mengistu's soldiers had raped their women. After raping her, one of them stabbed her in the groin with a knife.

They dragged her back to the cell, and left her with the women there. She was bleeding profusely, and after the bleeding stopped she became ill and feverish. She was too sick to torture further and was left alone for a few weeks. The prison officials gave her no medical treatment, but the other prisoners helped nurse her back to health.

Aster probably would have died in prison if she had not had help from someone in a position of power within the new government. Her brother, Dawit, had actually benefited from the change in the government. Most of his superiors had been arrested, leaving few qualified people in his department. He had no political links with the former government, so the new rulers relied on him to manage his department of the government. Within a few months he had been promoted to vice-minister.

From the time of Aster's first arrest, Dawit had begun to contact different people within the government to learn where she had been taken and to try to get her released. It took him some time to find out which prison she had been taken to, and he had to move cautiously as he inquired among different officials to see how he could arrange for her release, either through bribes or personal appeals. He had also tried to arrange for her to get a passport and exit visa so that once she was released from jail, she could leave the country for safety elsewhere.

3

⊓⊔⊓⊔⊓⊔

Escape

Adele and Philippe Fontem

While Adele was detained at the "Americanos" prison, she had some contact with her family and friends, who brought her food and bribed the guards to prevent her from being raped. She did not know it, but they were also working behind the scenes to arrange for her to escape from prison and flee the country. When the day of her release finally came, it was a surprise to her.

Adele was in her cell, as usual, when a guard came to take her away. He did not say where they were going, and she assumed she was again being taken to the torture room. But he took her down a different hallway. "Now I was really scared," she remembers, "because I didn't know where we were going. Maybe they were going to transfer me to a different prison. Maybe they were going to kill me, or worse."

Finally they arrived at a door which led outside. He told her, "Go through this door—and you don't know me," meaning that she should never tell anyone the identity of the person who allowed her to escape. Adele went through the door and found a taxi waiting for her on the street. The driver motioned her inside, and when she entered he told her that he was from her political party, the SDF, and that she should not worry. The party had arranged for her to be allowed to "escape" from jail, and her family had provided the money used for bribes.

The taxi driver took her to the house of one of the local SDF leaders. He gave her clothing and something to eat. After a rest of about five hours, they drove her to Douala, her home town, which is about four hours away by car from Yaoundé, where she had been detained.

Adele's parents lived in Douala, but she did not go to their house as she was afraid the government might be looking for her there. Instead she went to the house of one of her father's friends. After waiting two days, the SDF agents judged that the search for her had become less intense, and it was safe for her to go out. She went to the hospital to get treatment for the injuries she received from torture while in prison. The SDF agents took her to a doctor who they trusted, and he treated her without making a formal record of her admittance. He cleaned the wounds on her feet and gave her antibiotics for the pains she was having in her abdomen. Adele was three months pregnant and had been having contractions while in jail. The doctor was afraid she would miscarry because of the torture, but he could do little else for her. He advised her to rest, eat well, and try to regain the weight she had lost in prison.

After seeing the doctor, she went to stay at a house that belonged to one of her father's relatives in a small village near Douala. The national elections were to be held soon, and she hoped that government security forces would be too busy with the election to search for her. About six weeks after she came to the village, she heard from relatives that Philippe had gotten out of prison, too, and that he was safe, but she could find out no more about him. After about three months, some of the SDF leaders came to Adele's hiding place and gave her a passport that she could use to escape the country. The passport was genuine but belonged to someone else, a Cameroonian student who was about her age and who looked like her. This woman was a university student in Canada and had a valid student visa in her passport.

Adele was worried that she would get caught while trying to escape, but the SDF party members assured her that they had helped many other people escape in this way. They had developed a network of sympathetic officials within Cameroon who were willing to accept bribes to allow people to escape. They had used contacts with SDF party members in Canada to develop a list of people with valid passports and student visas who were willing to let their passports be used by other people trying to escape Cameroon. Everything had been arranged for her by the party, and her family had contributed money for the officials at the passport ministry and at the airport. Everything was ready for her to go.

Adele was nervous throughout the trip from her village to the capital city and even more nervous when she arrived at the airport. The SDF had bribed the right people, however, and she made it through the security checkpoints at the airport without problems. She also passed through Canadian immigration without any problem.

An SDF party member met her at the airport and took her to his house to spend the night. The next morning he put her on a bus for the United States. She crossed the border at Plattsburgh, New York, still using the student's passport, and made it through this passport check easily as well. At the border the passengers had to get off the bus and show their passports and luggage to U.S. immigration and customs officials. Adele should have been nervous, but she was so exhausted and depressed from travel and from worrying about Philippe that she was barely even awake when she went through the border crossing. Her sleepiness and indifference actually helped her get through the crossing point, since border inspectors look for nervousness as a sign of possible fraud.

She continued on the bus to Washington, D.C., and after she arrived she mailed the passport to an SDF party member in Europe, as she had been instructed to do. She was safe for the moment, but still had to figure out how to survive in this new country, how to gain legal status there, and how to get in touch with Philippe again. She was also four months pregnant at this point and just starting to show. Her family had assured her that Philippe was alive and safe, but she did not know if this was true or if they were only trying to keep her spirits up. She wondered if her baby would ever know its father.

Philippe had escaped prison and Cameroon in a similar way. After three months of interrogation and torture at the "Mobile Mixe Brigade" prison, he was scheduled to be transferred to the "Americanos" prison for long-term detention. Shortly before his transfer was due, one of the guards came up to Philippe and began punching him and insulting him, telling Philippe to come with him. "I knew this guard," Philippe said, "because he was Bassa, like me. One time I even asked him, in Bassa, why he kept treating me so badly—a fellow Bassa. He told me to stop bothering him, that he was just doing his job. I didn't see him much after that."

The Bassa guard took Philippe out of the main cell to another part of the prison. As soon as they left the main cell area, the guard stopped punching and shoving him. The guard took Philippe to an open door and told him to go through it. He told Philippe never to tell anyone who had helped him escape. When Philippe went through the door, he saw one of his friends waiting for him outside in a car.

The guard had not helped Philippe out of jail from motives of kindness or feelings of solidarity with a fellow Bassa, he had been bribed. The SDF had been working to make contacts with the prison guards, and they had succeeded with this one guard. A friend of Philippe's family had paid the money and had helped make the arrangements to pick him up at the jail.

Now that Philippe was out of jail, he had to leave the country, because he might be arrested again at any time. He first went to his father's house, but he couldn't stay there long. He went to the house of another family member and waited while his friends got him a passport, a plane ticket, and an entry visa to Canada. After two weeks his friends drove him to the airport and took him through the terminal. When he was about to get on the plane, they gave him his ticket and his passport. The passport was from Cameroon but belonged to another man, a student in Canada.

Leaving Cameroon was difficult and dangerous, but entering Canada and the United States was easy. At the airport in Canada, the inspector just glanced at the passport and waved him through. His friends had given him the name and phone number of a woman who lived in Canada, and Philippe called her for help. Philippe had never met her before, and she was not even from

Cameroon. Still, she came to the airport to pick him up and took him to her house, where he spent the night. The next day she put him on a bus for the United States.

Philippe's border crossing into the United States was without incident. "Nobody believes me when I tell them," Philippe remembers, "but I don't even remember when we crossed the border. When we left, we were in Canada, and then the next thing I knew we were in the United States. I don't remember stopping or talking to any immigration people." It is likely that Philippe fell asleep during the trip and slept through the border stop. The number of people who cross the United States–Canada border each day by land is so great that the INS does not check everyone's passport. Usually an INS official comes onto the bus at the border stop, looks for anything suspicious, and perhaps spot checks the documents of some of the passengers. The INS official at the border, seeing Philippe asleep in his seat, probably assumed he was a U.S. citizen and did not bother to wake him up.

The bus took Philippe to New York City, where he called an old friend from home. He had gone to college with this man, who had lived in the United States for more than ten years and was now a U.S. citizen. Philippe's friend took him in and arranged for him to travel to Washington, where Philippe could stay with another friend. Philippe knew that Adele had also left Cameroon and was in the Washington area.

Therese Kabongelo

After being left for dead by the soldiers, Therese was taken to a Catholic mission in Uvira, where she remained for weeks, resting and trying to regain her health. The priests at the mission made all the arrangements for her to go. One day a priest entered her room at the mission and told her to get ready to leave the next morning. There was no international airport in eastern Congo, and it was too far and too dangerous to go to Kinshasa, the capital of Congo, so they would have to cross the border to Burundi in order to get a plane for the United States. The government of Burundi is a military dictatorship, controlled by Tutsis, and Burundi had sent troops and money to support Kabila's war against Mobutu. Going to Burundi was even more dangerous than staying in Congo, but Therese had no choice but to take this risk. The priests set out early in the morning in September 1997. To make things easier at the border, they had Therese hide in the trunk of the car. They had already arranged things with the border guards, but to be safe they wanted Therese out of sight.

The city of Uvira is on the far eastern edge of Congo, where the country borders Burundi, so the trip lasted less than an hour. Soon, from the trunk, Therese could hear and feel the car slowing down and finally stopping at the border post. Therese could hear the priests talking to the border guards, but she could not hear what they were saying. She kept silent and prayed. After a few minutes the car started up again and passed across the border. After traveling a few miles, the priests pulled off the main road, stopped the car, and let Therese out of the trunk.

The priests drove her straight to the airport and went through the gates to the plane. Therese does not know which airline the plane was from, but all the flight attendants were white. The priests talked to one of the flight attendants for a long time in a language that Therese did not understand. They had already obtained a French passport for Therese, one that had been issued to a Congolese woman who was married to a French citizen. The priests had replaced her photo with Therese's, but the passport itself was genuine. They gave Therese's passport and plane ticket to the flight attendant and told Therese that she would be taken care of.

Therese boarded the plane first and sat in the back. The flight attendant told everyone on the plane that Therese was sick and should not be bothered. Therese was still injured from the rapes and the beating, and she was feeling the effects of medications that the priests had given her. The plane flew to Moscow, and the flight attendant helped Therese change planes there. She gave the passport and ticket back to Therese after the transfer and told her to ask for someone who speaks French when she got to New York.

In New York, Therese got off the plane and went through the line at immigration. She felt terrible and must have looked terrible—her face was swollen from crying and from the effects of the medication, and her voice was faint and hoarse. "I wasn't worried about the false passport," she remembered, "I was so sick I didn't care. The immigration person just looked at it and gave it back to me. She didn't ask me any questions—just my name and where I was from. And if I needed a wheelchair."

After going through the immigration line, Therese threw away the ticket and passport, as the priests had told her to do. She then considered what to do next. New York was a big city, and the airport itself was overwhelming. She knew no one in the United States and did not know where to begin. She was safe from Tutsis, but she did not know where she would be sleeping that night or where her next meal would come from.

Aster Cheru

Aster's release from jail came about in the same way that Adele's release did. Late at night a guard called her from her cell. She was afraid, thinking that she would be interrogated and tortured again. Her fear grew when the guard took her down a different hallway from the one that led to the interrogation room. To her surprise, the guard took her outside where her brother was waiting for her in his Land Rover.

Her brother, Dawit, had been working to bring about her release for months. While his high position in the civil service helped him make contacts with people who could effect Aster's release, he also had to be careful. He had worked in the civil service under the old government and was still viewed with suspicion. But he eventually found where Aster was being held. He then contacted the guards at this prison and bribed them to release her. This was not an "official" release, and she would be treated as an escapee if she were found again. It was not safe to return to Addis Ababa, and wherever she hid she was in continual danger of being arrested again by government security agents. To prevent her from being found, Aster's brother took her to a town far from Addis Ababa, where she went to live with a friend and business associate of his. She had never met this man before and had never been to this town before, so government agents were not likely to look for her there.

Dawit went back to Addis Ababa to arrange for her escape

from the country. He already had her passport, but Aster needed to have it stamped with permission to leave the country, and she needed a visa to enter some other country where she could apply for asylum. Getting the exit visa was not difficult, especially given that she already had a passport; Dawit just had to bribe the right people to stamp her passport with permission to exit.

Getting a visa to enter another country was more difficult. Dawit decided to send her to the United States, where he knew it was possible for refugees to gain asylum. There was a large Ethiopian community in the United States, and there were friends of his who could give Aster a place to stay when she first arrived. He took her passport to the U.S. embassy and applied for a visitor's visa for her. Of course he could not tell the embassy that she wished to apply for asylum, since they would certainly not have granted her a visa if they thought she was going to stay permanently. Instead he told the embassy she was just going as a tourist and to visit friends. He brought evidence of her job at the luxury hotel and the salary that she received there. Since Aster had a good job to return to, the embassy decided that it was not likely she would stay in the United States illegally. The embassy gave her a visitor's visa, which gave her permission to enter the United States and to stay for six months, but did not authorize her to work.

Aster left Ethiopia in March 1992. Like Adele and Philippe, she was nervous about being arrested at the airport. Security officials keep a list of people who were to be arrested if they tried to leave the country, but Aster's name was not on the list. Her brother had bribed people at the prison so that they had not reported her escape, and he had also bribed the security officials at the airport to make sure that her name would not be on their list. Aster got on the airplane and took her seat, but she did not relax until the plane was actually in the air. She spent one night in London and flew to Washington, D.C., the next day. She went through the passport line with no problems and called a friend of her brother's who had agreed to pick her up and give her a place to stay.

4

ΠΠΠΠΠΠ

America

Adele and Philippe Fontem

After leaving prison, hiding in Cameroon, traveling to Canada, and crossing the land border into the United States, Adele and Philippe had finally arrived in the country where they intended to find safety. They still had not located each other, but both of them were in the Washington, D.C., area, where they had friends and contacts from the SDF party.

Adele went to stay with a family friend who lived in a Maryland suburb of Washington. He was a legal permanent resident and had lived in the United States for ten years. He had a job and a house and was financially secure, so he did not mind giving shelter to a friend of the family for a few months until she found her own way. Two weeks after her arrival in Maryland, Adele found Philippe, who had been living with a friend of his. They decided to try to find work so they could earn enough money to rent an apartment and live together.

At first, Adele and Philippe were overwhelmed by America and spent all their time trying to find their way around and arrange for their basic needs. They were impressed with the roads and the buildings, but most of all, remembers Adele, "we were impressed with the way everything works. You come from Africa, you're not used to everything working the way it's supposed to." They were also impressed with how friendly everyone was. "People really try to help strangers—they will spend lots of time, telling you where something is, explaining how things work. Even if you don't speak English well, they will spend time with you and try to understand. If you ask them where something is, they take your hand, and they walk with you."

Adele and Philippe had two problems—making themselves understood in English and finding jobs. Adele spoke English well even before she arrived in America, but she spoke with a heavy accent, and Americans had a hard time understanding her. Philippe began to learn English, but his accent was so strong that most people couldn't understand him either. Laughing, he remembers, "I would ask them a question in English, and they would look at me and say, 'I don't understand. Stop speaking Spanish.'"

Finding employment was also a problem. They soon learned that, without a work permit, few employers would be willing to hire them. They would apply for jobs, be offered one, and then refused when the employer discovered they did not have the right documents. After a few experiences like this, they stopped looking for regular jobs and began asking friends and acquaintances if they knew of any jobs where a work permit was not required.

Adele managed to find a job in a place where she had not even been looking for one. After searching for a job without success, she decided to try her luck with a small, informal business. She asked her family to send her some African art pieces from Cameroon, and she tried to sell them to stores and dealers in the United States. At one of the stores, the owner, an American man, asked her about the different pieces and was impressed with her knowledge of the art. He was so impressed that he asked her if she wanted a job at his store.

Adele explained that she did not have a work permit and told him her story. He was sympathetic and offered to arrange things so that she could work there without documents. Adele was again impressed with the kindness of American people. "He gave me a job even though I didn't have the right papers, and he helped me learn it. I didn't know the right things to say to customers, and he helped me with my English. Later, when we had problems with our case, he asked me how things were going. This is the American spirit—they give you a chance."

Adele's job was nearly full-time, but the pay was low; she brought home about $800 per month. Philippe could not find a full-time job, so he worked part-time as a valet parking attendant and occasionally as a taxi driver. He worked two to four nights a week, and brought home $20 to $30 each night, more when he drove a taxi.

They found a small apartment, and Adele's friend took out the lease in his own name, with the understanding that Adele and Philippe would pay the rent each month. The rent was $600, so Adele's salary was taken up almost entirely with rent and groceries. Philippe's earnings paid for any other expenses. They had no money for anything but necessities, and they could not even pay for all of those. Still, they had a place to live and enough to eat, and they were safe for the moment.

Adele and Philippe were feeling more confident about their own future, but they were worried about their baby. Adele was now six months pregnant, and her torture and imprisonment had caused some health problems. She was feeling better now and gaining weight, but she was still worried that there might be something wrong with the baby. If there was, how would they go to the doctor? They had no health insurance, no legal status, and no money to pay for medical treatment.

As they arranged for employment and a place to stay, they also looked for a lawyer who could help them with their legal status. They were well educated and knew that it was possible to apply for refugee status in the United States. They found a lawyer, also a native of Cameroon, who agreed to represent them. He had experience with asylum cases, and friends had recommended him. He charged $2,000 to prepare their case and to represent them at the asylum office, but he agreed to let them pay $400 up front and the rest later.

Their lawyer spent only a few hours with them, hearing a basic summary of their experiences. He typed up their asylum applications and read the contents to them, then made corrections by crossing out and writing over the typed application by hand. He then had them sign the applications, and he mailed them to the INS. Adele and Philippe were not impressed with the final product—it was badly typed, messy, and had little supporting documentation—but they appreciated that the lawyer was willing to help them at all, given that they could not pay his fee. He told them they would get an interview with the INS within two months, so they continued to work and waited.

Therese Kabongelo

After leaving the airplane in New York City, Therese tried to decide what to do next. She had about $200 which the priests had given her. They had told her to find a Catholic church once she arrived in New York and to ask for help there.

Therese did not even know how to find a Catholic church, so she went out to the taxi stand to try to find someone she could ask. Some of the taxi drivers were African, and after talking to a few of them she found one who spoke French. She told him that she had just arrived from Congo and had nowhere to go; she asked him to take her to any Catholic church. He took her to a convent in the city and translated for Therese when she asked the nuns for help.

The nuns took Therese in, but they did not speak French and thus looked for a more suitable place for her. They learned about a large community of Congolese immigrants and refugees in Washington, D.C., and contacted a Catholic church there. After a week or so they sent Therese to Washington, where she met with a priest who was also a native of Congo. The priest arranged for her to live with a Congolese woman, a member of his church who had legal permanent resident status in the United States.

This woman was married and had one child. She operated a child-care business out of her home, and she was glad to have Therese living with her. Therese, with her experience as a teacher and a mother, was good with children and anxious to help. She stayed at this house for a month, helping her host with her child-care business while she tried to figure out what to do next.

Therese had an idea that it was possible to gain "refugee" status in the United States; some of the other Africans she met at church had refugee or asylum status. She did not know exactly how to go about this, however, and the other refugees told her that she needed a lawyer to apply for asylum and that lawyers were expensive.

Finally she met a Burundian woman at her church who was also an ethnic Hutu. This woman worked for a refugee assistance agency, Lutheran Social Services (LSS). She told Therese that a legal worker at her agency had helped people like Therese and did not charge a fee. She gave Therese the phone number. Therese called me, and we set up an appointment in a week's time.

The first time I talk to a potential client, I try to get an overall sense of the person's story. I make an initial assessment as to whether the story is true, whether the person qualifies for asylum status, and whether the person has the financial resources to afford an attorney. I explain how the asylum system works and answer questions about the process. Every asylum applicant who calls my agency is given at least an initial interview, but because there is such a demand for legal services, I can only agree to represent about one-third of the people who ask me for help. I give priority to people who have no family or friends in the United States and to those who have suffered severe trauma or torture.

In the first interview I was struck by how tired and sad Therese seemed. She smiled warmly and shook hands firmly at the beginning of the interview, but after the interview began her demeanor changed. She recounted the facts of her story in a quiet, unemotional voice. Withdrawal is common among survivors of severe trauma, and it indicated that she was most likely telling the truth. I told her I would take her case and explained the process of applying for asylum.

It took a few more interview sessions to complete Therese's application. Meanwhile she needed a great deal of assistance. Therese was having problems with the family where she stayed. They were using her as a source of labor and giving her only room and board in return. While she had accepted this arrangement at first, it had begun to seem to her like an exploitative relationship. The woman who was letting her stay there had also begun to pressure her to find somewhere else to live. The woman's home-based child-care business was in the process of being evaluated by state regulators, and she was afraid that if the regulators found an "illegal alien" living in her house she would be in trouble.

Therese had made a few contacts in the Congolese community, mostly through her church, and could turn to them for help. Another family at the church—Hutu refugees from Rwanda—agreed to let her stay with them. LSS provided her with some donated furniture, housewares, and linens for her new home. Another local church, which operated a thrift store, agreed to let Therese take all the clothing she needed for free. I convinced my supervisors at LSS to give her $200 each month to help her survive until she won her case and received a work permit.

Two-hundred dollars per month was not enough to pay for both food and expenses, but it was all that LSS could spare. I tried to get more food for her by asking for help from local food banks. Unfortunately, most food banks will not allow clients to take food more than two or three times in the course of a year. This policy makes sense where U.S. citizens are concerned, since they have permission to work and should not have to depend on a food bank for long-term needs. It did not, however, make sense in Therese's case. Although I explained Therese's situation to the food banks' managers, they would not change their policy for her. I called other food banks but found out that one had to be a resident of a certain county or area in order to receive assistance from them. The solution to these problems was simple but dishonest: we went to a different food bank every two weeks and gave out a different address at each one.

This took care of Therese's immediate needs for food, clothing, and shelter, but she also needed medical attention. She had never been examined by a doctor after being raped, and she had an infection that needed treatment. She was also feverish and weak, had a chronic sore throat, and often felt nauseated. These could be just symptoms of a cold, or could be a sign of something more serious. She was depressed about her own situation and anxious about her children. Because of her mental state she had insomnia and slept only a few hours each night, if at all. The sleeplessness aggravated her physical condition, which in turn contributed to her depression.

Finding health care for an undocumented person is difficult, and Therese could not wait for six to twelve months until the INS gave her a final grant of asylum to make her eligible for government services. Many asylum seekers and other undocumented people simply go to the emergency room for health care, since emergency rooms at public hospitals are not allowed to turn people away. I considered recommending this, but it seemed better to find a free health clinic that served undocumented people, so that Therese could get a referral to a gynecologist and receive follow-up care.

I called the local free clinics that are administered by each county. Therese lived in Fairfax County, Virginia, so we tried this clinic first. The Fairfax clinic was open by appointment only, but the appointments line was an answering machine, and no one ever called back. We gave up and called the Arlington free clinic, which gave us an appointment right away. This time we had to give a false address, but at least we did not have to invent one; I live in Arlington, so I just told them that Therese lived at my address.

The Arlington clinic examined her and found that she had no serious health problems. She did have a cold and severe allergies to pollen, mold, and other airborne pollutants, so they gave her medicine to alleviate her symptoms. The clinic also referred her to a gynecologist for a complete exam, which confirmed that she had an infection but no serious illness. The gynecologist gave Therese antibiotics for her infection.

I also tried to find a mental health counselor who could help Therese. I contacted several different agencies, and the most helpful one was the Victim's Assistance Network of Northern Virginia. This agency, staffed mainly by volunteers, operates Northern Virginia's sexual assault crisis line and provides counseling services for sexual assault victims. They do not require clients to have legal immigration status to receive services. I called the crisis hot line and explained Therese's situation, and within a week they had arranged for Therese to meet with a psychologist and a volunteer interpreter.

Therese's first appointment led to weekly visits with the psychologist, which helped her a great deal. The counselor immediately referred her to a psychiatrist, and he prescribed both anti-depressants and sleeping pills. He recommended that she not take these drugs over a long period of time, but he thought the sleeping pills were necessary to allow her body time to sleep and heal, and that after two or three months her mental health would improve to the point where she would no longer need them. Similarly, he recognized that Therese's depression was caused by events rather than an underlying mood disorder, but recommended anti-depressants because they might alleviate her symptoms while she underwent counseling for her trauma.

The psychological counseling that Victim's Assistance Network provided was highly effective. Therese's counselor, Sandy Berger, had had years of experience counseling rape victims and some experience counseling other African refugees who had been victims of politically motivated rape. The translator, Katherine Darke, had worked as a volunteer counselor for several years. Neither the counselor nor the translator charged Therese a fee for their services, and they continued to provide counseling to Therese as long as she needed it—almost six months in all. After the formal counseling sessions ended, both of them kept in touch with Therese informally. Katherine was particularly supportive, acting as an English tutor, helping Therese learn how to use a computer, and spending time with her as a friend.

Therese's counseling sessions were confidential, so Katherine and Sandy never told me what they talked about. In any case, I did not want to know; I was so involved with every other aspect of Therese's life that I thought she should have some privacy from me. A few times, however, Therese volunteered information about the counseling and told me what she talked about there.

Therese was unable to sleep or to concentrate because she was constantly replaying in her head the events of her rape and the death of her husband. She was also extremely anxious, her mind spinning with worries about her children. Sandy told her to write down her thoughts in a journal, both in order to analyze them and to help her stop thinking about them. Therese told me that this strategy actually worked, and she began to feel calmer.

Therese also felt a lot of anger, which she kept pent up inside her. She was ashamed to find herself thinking violent, hateful thoughts about the people who had hurt her, and her anger included not only Kabila's soldiers but all Tutsis. She told me once,

"If I meet a Tutsi here in the United States, I don't know what I will do. I should not hate them, but I do. If I see one, I might do anything—I might fight him, I might try to kill him." Sandy reassured her that it was normal to feel this way, and taught her different ways to channel and deal with her anger when she felt it.

Finally, Therese's experiences had challenged what had once been a strong faith in God. When she turned to religion for comfort after her experience, she had found herself angry at God and doubting that God even existed. Sandy suggested that she write a letter to God, telling God why she was angry and asking the questions that she wanted answered. Therese, a Catholic, also wrote to the Virgin Mary, asking her many of the same questions. "Mary," she asked, "you are a mother too—how could you let me suffer so?" The process of writing down her questions and angry thoughts helped console her. She began to feel less angry about events, and as her anger dissipated, so did her depression. The medication helped with her anxiety and insomnia, and as she slept better she began to feel better during the day.

As time went on, I saw a wonderful change in Therese. When I first met her she seemed barely alive. She talked in a low voice with no emotion, she was physically ill, and she always seemed exhausted. Within a couple of months she was healthy again, sleeping regularly, and interested in the world and people around her. She still had sad days and still worried about her children, but she smiled and laughed now, and had become talkative and outgoing. We began to see the real Therese, the happy, aware, friendly person that she had been in Zaire.

As time went on, my fiancée, Ashley Spell, and I began to spend time with Therese socially. We invited her to our house, and we took her out places. We also became friends with Katherine and Sandy, and all five of us went out a few times. It was always a pleasure to spend time with Therese. She was always polite and considerate, and while she had many needs she always tried to do things for herself before asking for help. She was an intelligent, sophisticated woman, who had seen a lot in her own country; at the same time she was new to the United States and excited by many of the things she saw here. Many of her observations were interesting and insightful; others were wonderfully funny.

When she moved into her new apartment, Therese was impressed with how green the neighborhood was and how many trees and plants there were around her building. Her apartment was in an old low-rise building in the Virginia suburbs and was not in good repair. It was located in a reasonably safe area, and the rent was low by Washington standards, but it was not a particularly nice building. She was pleased with her new home, though, until one day she noticed that the back yard was full of rats. There were rats on the grass, running from bush to bush and, worst of all, crawling up the trees. "Rats!" she said, to her roommate. "This area is full of rats! On the ground! In the trees, even! We can't live here." Her roommate explained to her that the "rats" were only squirrels and that they did people no harm.

Ashley and I once went to dinner with Therese, Katherine, and Katherine's husband, Yann. Everyone spoke French, and we had a good time. On the way home, Katherine asked Ashley if we did anything special for Valentine's Day. Therese asked what Valentine's day was. Ashley explained who St. Valentine was, how the day was named after him, and how it had changed from a saint's day into a secular holiday celebrating romance. Katherine then told Therese about the "St. Valentine's Day massacre," when Al Capone had lured his enemies into one place and had gunned them down. "So who was Al Capone," Therese asked, "a politician?"

Aster Cheru

Aster arrived in the United States in March 1992. Her brother had arranged for her to live with an older woman, an old friend of the family, in Washington, D.C. This woman's son took an interest in Aster, showing her around the city and introducing her to other Ethiopians. He encouraged her to apply for asylum as so many other Ethiopians had done.

In late 1992, Aster's brother Dawit came to the United States on an official visit. He was glad to see that she was doing well. He had recently been promoted again, and he was optimistic about his future. Aster asked him not to go back to Ethiopia, and in light of later events she regrets that she could not convince him. "I told him not to go back—that it was still dangerous there. Even though it is good now, everything can change. You can't trust those people." She was worried that the government would discover that Dawit had once been a member of the Ethiopian People's Revolutionary Party, which had started up again after the fall of the Dergue and was now fighting a military campaign against the new government. She was also afraid that the government would discover that her brother had helped her escape. Dawit told her not to worry. "He told me it was always at least a little bit dangerous, but the worst part was over. The government had confidence in him now. And he wanted to stay and help rebuild the country." After a two-week visit, Dawit went back to Ethiopia.

The son of a woman with whom Aster was living began to come to see Aster more and more often. They became romantically involved, and in early 1993 they became engaged. She became pregnant shortly after their marriage and in 1994 gave birth to a son, Joseph. In 1996 they had another child, John.

Before their marriage, Aster's husband had helped her file for asylum, and they went to Lutheran Social Services for legal representation. At that time I did not work there, and LSS had two staff members working in the immigration law program, a lawyer and a legal assistant. They prepared a large number of asylum cases and did not devote much time to each one, in large part because it was unlikely that the applicants would be called for an interview. Under the system in place at that time, most asylum applicants received a work permit shortly after applying for asylum, but had to wait for years before receiving their first asylum interview. The lawyer at LSS gave Aster the asylum application form to take home, which her fiancé filled out. The lawyer then interviewed Aster briefly, with her fiancé acting as interpreter. The lawyer wrote a one-page summary of her asylum claim, and Aster signed it, not knowing what it said.

Aster's fiancé told her not to worry about her asylum case. He already had his green card, and once they were married he would file an immigrant petition for her. The waiting period for this visa was about four years, but in the meantime Aster would be eligible to work in the United States because she had a pending asylum application. Her husband's petition for her would probably go through before she was scheduled for an asylum interview, so, according to Aster's husband, it didn't really matter what the asylum application said.

Aster received her work permit in early 1993. She soon found a job working in a hotel, as she had in Ethiopia, but here she was a member of the housekeeping staff. Like so many refugees, her standard of living actually went down when she came to the United States, because her lack of English skills prevented her from working at the same level of employment that she had enjoyed in her home country.

Aster heard more bad news from Ethiopia in late 1993. She talked often to her cousin and her daughter, Beth, who was living with her cousin and his wife. She could not reach her brother Dawit, and when she asked her cousin about him, he gave her only vague answers. He said that he did not see Dawit very often, since he lived in Addis Ababa and was always busy with work.

One day Aster's daughter mentioned on the phone that Uncle Dawit was dead, but refused to say any more. Horrified, Aster asked her cousin what had happened. Aster's cousin confirmed the story and said she had been keeping the information from Aster because they knew Aster had her own problems in the United States and they did not wish to worry her. Apparently he had died in early 1993 while on an official visit to an economic development project in a remote area. The official story was that he had died in an accident at a construction site, but the government had never given his body to the family for burial. Rumors circulated that he had been shot and his body buried secretly. Aster supposed he had been killed because his EPRP background had been discovered or because the government had learned that he had helped her escape from prison.

While she was absorbing this loss, Aster began to have problems with her husband as well. "When I first knew him, he was so nice. He took me everywhere, he helped me with everything. He was so good to me." After their marriage, while he remained attentive and involved in her life, his attentions became more threatening and controlling. He did not seem to like the fact that Aster was becoming self-sufficient in the United States and needed his help less and less. He grew angry with her when she went out on her own or asserted herself. He insisted on controlling the money in the household and making all of the decisions about other important things. Despite these problems, Aster stayed with him and hoped that things would improve. For the children's sake as well as their own, she thought they should stay together and try to make things work.

About two years after her arrival in the United States, Beth, Aster's daughter, came to live with her. After Dawit's death, Aster began to fear that it was dangerous for Beth to stay in Ethiopia. And Aster had only been waiting for her life to become more stable before she brought her to the United States. Aster's husband helped pay for her ticket, and Beth had a temporary status, as a dependent of her mother's, while waiting for her asylum claim to be adjudicated. Aster's husband also filed a family immigrant petition for Beth, and the INS granted her legal permanent resident status—or a "green card"—in 1997.

Beth turned twelve years old in 1996 and started to go through puberty. Aster's husband began to pay more attention to her than he had before. At first this seemed innocent, but then Beth told Aster that when she was away from the house, her stepfather had started trying to touch her and rub himself against her, and had even exposed himself to her. Aster had a hard time believing this at first, but Beth continued to complain. Beth seemed afraid of her stepfather and didn't want to be left alone with him. One day Aster found that Beth was wearing blue jeans to bed every night. She believed her daughter and confronted her husband.

He denied everything. Aster did not know what to do. She was afraid to leave him because he had told her that without his sponsorship, she would not be able to get a green card and would be deported. She also did not know where to turn for advice; she had few friends in the United States who were not also friends or relatives of her husband. Feeling as though she had no good options, she decided to continue to live with her husband while trying to protect her daughter from him. Aster slept in her daughter's bed at night and made sure that she was always home when her husband was there.

Her husband continued to pressure Beth to give in to his desires, and punished her for not cooperating. He withheld small privileges from her—watching television, using the computer, or even sitting on the living room sofa. He refused to buy her things she needed, such as new clothing for school. He also exercised more control over Aster's life. She had injured her back at work, so she was staying home from work and collecting workmen's compensation checks. He made Aster sign the checks over to him so that he could control all the money in the house. Aster became increasingly distressed and felt that she had no way out; she was afraid to leave her husband but was also afraid to stay. "I was thinking, Beth is a good girl, but she is young and she can't be strong. She wants clothes and things, like the other girls. Maybe she will stop saying no. What can I do?"

Beth was particularly upset about not having new clothes for school. She had outgrown some of her old clothes and was embarrassed at having them when all her classmates were wearing new clothing. Aster had no money of her own with which to buy her clothing, so she decided to steal clothes for her from the store. Aster went about this in the most foolish way possible. She went to a department store with Beth and her two infant sons. When Beth had selected a number of items, Aster simply tucked the clothing into a bag and walked out of the store. She was stopped by store security, who called the police. Aster was arrested, and the store pressed charges against her.

Aster's trial did not go well. She had stolen clothing valued at $550, which was a large enough value to classify her crime as "grand larceny," more serious than mere "petty larceny" and subject to a heavier sentence. The judge was horrified that Aster had committed theft with her children present and seemed inclined to give Aster a heavy sentence. Aster's defense attorney counseled her to plead guilty to grand larceny as part of a deal with the prosecutor, who would ask for only a one-year suspended sentence. Under this arrangement Aster would be sentenced to a year in prison, but this sentence would not be carried out, provided that Aster agreed to go to psychological counseling and did not commit other crimes.

Aster agreed to the plea bargain. She felt guilty and remorseful about her crime and was willing to admit that she had broken the law and accept punishment for it. When she remembers her crime now, she cannot explain why she did it. "I do not know what I was thinking. I was crazy. I couldn't think. It was wrong—I am ashamed to think of it, to talk about it. So much shame." At the time of the sentencing, Aster thought she deserved a guilty verdict and that she deserved punishment. She considered herself lucky not to have to go to jail, and she also understood that the court would send her to someone who would try to help her with her problems.

She began counseling shortly after the trial. Her counselor talked to her about her problems with her life, her family, and her adjustment to the United States. Aster did not mention the bad things that had happened to her in Ethiopia, focusing instead on her relationship with her husband and children. She talked about her problems with her husband but was afraid and ashamed to talk about her husband's attempted abuse of Beth. She did say enough about her own problems with her husband for her counselor to recommend that he come in for a joint counseling session. Aster asked him to come, and reluctantly he agreed.

In the counseling session her husband was sullen, defensive, and uncooperative. The therapist tried unsuccessfully to bring him out. Aster and he began to argue, and finally he became angry and told the therapist that Aster was bringing him to counseling only so she could accuse him of molesting his stepdaughter. He denied that he was doing this and left the room.

Aster's family secret had been let out. After her husband left the session, Aster told her story to the counselor: the history of her husband's attempts to molest her daughter and her attempts to protect her, as well as her fear that she would lose her chance for an immigrant visa and might be deported if she were divorced. The counselor encouraged her to leave her husband, but Aster hesitated. The counselor called Child Protective Services to investigate the matter, but they did not find enough evidence to start a case against Aster's husband.

This situation lasted only a few months, until a final confrontation forced Aster to make a decision. Her husband returned home late one night, after drinking with his friends. He began to argue with Aster about how she was feeding their youngest son,

John, who was only one year old at the time. She was holding him during the argument. Then her husband hit her in the face, and his fingernails grazed her cheek and drew blood. He also took John's bottle and threw it at her; it missed, hit the wall, and shattered, scattering glass everywhere.

The police came and arrested her husband and charged him with assault and battery. When he was released on bail, Aster went to live with a friend, and she remained separated from her husband. He pled guilty to the charge of assault and, like Aster, received a suspended sentence.

They went to family court and agreed to a joint custody arrangement for John and Joseph, with Aster gaining full custody of Beth. Aster was given primary custody of the two boys, so they lived with her most of the time and stayed with their father every other weekend and on alternate holidays. Aster moved into a place of her own, went back to work at the hotel, and once again had a stable life. She still had no permanent immigration status, and the possibility that she might lose her asylum case loomed over her head. Like the hundreds of thousands of other applicants who had cases in the asylum backlog, she had a half-legal, temporary status. She wanted to have her asylum interview, so that she could get permanent status, but she was also afraid that she might lose and be deported.

I first met Aster in 1997, about a year after her separation from her husband. She came into my office to ask what she should do with her case. I had never met her before, but there were many cases like hers in Lutheran Social Service's files—people who had applied for asylum in the early 1990s and who were still waiting for their first interview. Aster was upset because she had heard about the 1996 change in the immigration laws, which made it more likely that people with criminal records would be deported. She wanted to know what to do, because she was afraid that her ex-husband would tell the INS that she had a criminal record in order to get her deported.

I reviewed her file with Aster. She was surprised at what it contained. Her husband, apparently acting on the advice of friends, had not used Aster's real story but had written a story based on what he thought the asylum office wanted to hear. The application form had accurate information about Aster's family, education, and employment history, but it contained a fabricated story about Aster's political activities and persecution.

Given the fact that asylum applications do not always succeed, and the additional problems posed by the inaccuracies in Aster's application, I considered whether Aster would be eligible for some other immigration status. It occurred to me that, as the wife of a legal permanent resident who had abused her, she might be eligible for a green card under the provisions of the Violence Against Women Act.[1] One of the provisions of this 1994 act is that a woman who is eligible for an immigrant visa from her husband, but whose husband is abusive, may leave her husband and still request an immigrant visa and a green card. The woman must submit evidence showing that she has been abused and that the marriage is a valid one.[2] If she can prove these elements of her case, she can gain the legal permanent resident status for which she would have been eligible if she had stayed with her abusive husband.

Aster had asked for help from another nonprofit agency, AYUDA, Inc., whose staff attorneys have extensive experience with battered spouse petitions. I called the attorney there to whom she had spoken, and he warned me that the 1996 changes in the immigration law had serious consequences for Aster. The new law defined any crime of theft, with a sentence imposed of one year or more—even if suspended—as an "aggravated felony," which led to almost automatic deportation. The law stated that this classification was retroactive, meaning that even people like Aster, who had been convicted before the passage of the law, would be classified as aggravated felons and deported.[3]

The 1996 law provided that any type of sentence of at least a

1. Violent Crime Control and Law Enforcement Act of 1994, Pub. L. No. 103–322, 108 Stat. 1796, 1953.

2. From 1994 to 2000, women also had to prove that it would be an "extreme hardship" for them to return to their home country. This requirement was removed by the "Victims of Trafficking and Violence Prevention Act of 2000," (Pub. L. No. 106–386), signed into law on October 28, 2000. The 2000 law also eased a number of other technical and procedural requirements, making it easier for abused women to receive protection from deportation through a battered spouse visa.

3. Immigration and Nationality Act (INA), Section 101(a)(43).

year, including suspended sentences, counted in classifying her crime as an aggravated felony; it did not matter, in Aster's case, that she had never gone to prison.[4] The Board of Immigration Appeals ruled that post-conviction relief, such as the expungement of a crime, would not affect the status of the crime for immigration law purposes.[5] Many states would erase a crime from an offender's record, particularly for first offenders, if the offender committed no further crimes and participated in a program of counseling or community service. But, according to the BIA, the criminal conviction nonetheless counted for immigration law purposes and could cause the deportation of a noncitizen.

If Aster had known all this when she had gone to criminal court, she would not have accepted the plea bargain and would have fought for a sentence of less than one year, even if this had meant going to jail. Since the law had not even existed at the time of her sentencing, however, she had no way of knowing that her guilty plea would later cause her to be deported. Now that her conviction and sentence were in the record, there was nothing she could do.

I called Aster back and advised her that she could not apply for a battered spouse visa and that she was not even eligible for asylum due to her criminal conviction. Under the law in place at that time, she was eligible only for a status called "withholding of deportation," also called "restriction on removal." This status is similar to asylum but offers fewer benefits; its only advantage over asylum is that it is available to aliens convicted of minor crimes.

If Aster's criminal conviction was discovered by the INS, they would probably start removal proceedings against her. There was, however, no sign that the INS realized she had a criminal conviction, and the INS does not usually look into an asylum applicant's criminal record until an asylum interview is scheduled. It might be years before she was called for an interview, and in the meantime she could continue to live and work in the United States. By the time she was actually called in for an asylum interview, the law on criminal convictions might change, and she might become eligible

4. Immigration and Nationality Act, Section 101(a) and (48)(B).
5. *Matter of Roldan*, Int. Dec. 3377 (BIA 1999).

for asylum again. Even if the worst happened and she was eventually deported due to her criminal conviction, at least she was postponing this as long as possible.

Given these facts, I advised Aster to do nothing, to continue renewing her work permit, and to wait and hope that the law would change. If she were lucky, years would pass before the INS came to her case. Aster did not like this advice—she wanted to solve the problem, not continue to live with it hanging over her head—but there was nothing else for her to do.

Aster returned to my office about six months later and asked many of the same questions. She thought that, somehow, there must be a way for her to get around her criminal conviction and obtain legal immigration status. She was in tears this time, terrified that her husband would tell the INS about her criminal conviction. Her husband was trying to gain full custody of their sons, and having her deported would be the easiest way to do this. I gave her the same advice I had given her before. I also told her not to worry, assured her that the INS is not in the business of listening to angry ex-husbands, and that it was too busy going after real criminals to bother with her.

I was wrong. Six months after we spoke, Aster was arrested from her place of work by INS deportation officers. They took her to the INS district office, where they allowed her to make phone calls to arrange care for her children. From there they took her to a local jail, where she was to be detained until they deported her. There she was the only female INS detainee in a jail filled with American prisoners serving criminal sentences.

According to the INS's interpretation of the deportation provisions for aggravated felons under the 1996 law, Aster would be held in jail, with no possibility of parole, until she was either deported or granted permission to stay in the United States. She was placed in "administrative removal" proceedings, which meant that a low-level INS bureaucrat could decide her case and deport her without her ever having seen an immigration judge. If she asked to see a judge, the same low-level INS bureaucrat would decide whether to grant this request. There was no appeal from the INS officer's decision and only a limited provision for judicial review. The INS deportation officers did not know about her asylum application, which was on file at another office, and there was no formal mechanism for her to get her case in front of the immigration judge so that she could apply for restriction on removal. In short, there was a real risk that she would be sent back to Ethiopia, where she faced torture, rape, and death, without ever being able to see a judge to ask for protection.

Why did the INS arrest her at that time? Did they act on a tip from her husband? The Washington District Office declined my requests to interview them for this book, so I do not know their policy on placing aliens with criminal convictions into deportation proceedings. Another client that I represented was put into removal proceedings because her husband, who had abused her, called the INS and told them the marriage was fraudulent and that she should be deported. So it is possible that Aster's husband had some influence on the INS's actions. But many other aliens with old criminal convictions were arrested around the same time as Aster, so it may be that the INS was doing routine criminal background checks for a number of people and that Aster's crime was discovered in this manner.

While Aster tried to fight her deportation, she remained in jail, unable to intervene as her life outside of jail fell apart. Since she was not working, she could not afford to pay rent on her apartment. After three months of nonpayment, she was evicted and her possessions thrown into the street. She had no family in the United States and was ashamed to tell her friends or people from her church that she was in jail, so she did not ask anyone to collect her possessions for her. She lost almost everything she owned. She lost custody of Joseph and John, who went to live with their father. Beth had no one to take care of her, so the county government placed her in foster care.

5

⊓⊔⊓⊔⊓⊔

The Interview

Adele and Philippe Fontem

Philippe and Adele had mailed their applications on the same day, but Philippe's interview was scheduled first. He tried to meet with their lawyer before the interview, but every time he called, the lawyer said he was too busy to see him.

Entering the asylum office is a somewhat intimidating experience. Philippe's interview was at 7:45 in the morning. He left the house early to be sure that he would arrive on time, and he arrived at the INS office at 7:30. He entered the large office building where the asylum office was located and went to the office suite itself on the first floor. The office door was locked, and a line of people was already in front of the door. Philippe took his place in line and waited, looking around to watch for his lawyer.

At 7:45 the doors opened, and the line began to move inside. To get into the office, one must go through a metal detector operated by a security guard wearing a uniform and carrying a gun. The armed guard reminded Philippe of the security agents and policemen who had tortured him in jail. After going through the metal detector, Philippe took his place in line behind the other applicants, waiting to speak to a woman at a window at the front of the room.

Only a few people were ahead of Philippe in line, but each

person seemed to take a long time. At 8:00, Philippe's lawyer arrived with an interpreter. A few minutes later it was their turn at the window. Philippe gave the woman at the window his interview notice, and she gave the interpreter a form to fill out. She then told them to sit down and wait.

Philippe asked his lawyer what kinds of questions he should expect and what his strategy should be. The lawyer told him not to worry, to tell the truth, and to make sure that he listened to each question before answering it. They waited for a long time—more than an hour.

Finally Philippe's name was called. The asylum officer came out to meet them—he was a white man, about fifty years old. He introduced himself to Philippe, the lawyer, and the interpreter, and when he heard Philippe's accent he introduced himself in French also. He said something to the lawyer, and they all followed him out of the waiting room, through a door that had a combination lock. They then walked through a narrow corridor with many doors, until they came to the man's office.

He said something in English and motioned them to sit down. He spoke to the interpreter and the lawyer for a minute, then to the interpreter again. The interpreter began translating what the officer was saying. He told Philippe that he had to swear to tell the truth, so Philippe stood up while the officer recited to him an oath and the translator interpreted the oath to him. Philippe said he would tell the truth.

The asylum officer went over the form slowly, asking Philippe many questions: his full name, address, phone number, date of birth, and country of birth; whether he was married or single, and if he had any children; the date he left Cameroon, the date he arrived in the United States, and how he had entered the country. The interviewer asked him to list all the schools he had attended, his employment history for the last five years, and all the places he had lived during the last five years. Often he crossed out what was written on the form and wrote something else. It seemed to take a long time, and the officer seemed to be getting impatient about how long it was taking.

Finally they finished with the form. He then asked Philippe why he had left Cameroon. Philippe began to tell him about his political activities, his job at the pharmacy, and how he had been put in jail for his beliefs. "I began to think there was something wrong," Philippe remembers. "He kept asking the same question more than once. He was frowning, as though he didn't like the answers." The translator seemed to be having difficulties too. "The questions didn't always make sense, or they didn't follow. He would ask me about one thing, then the next question would be about something completely different."

The worst thing for Philippe was being cut off before he could finish answering a question. "The translator could remember only a few sentences at a time, so he asked me to stop and let him translate. I did this, but then I couldn't keep talking—the interviewer would ask another question." After spending so much time on the form, which asked questions about his education, residence, work history, and other things that seemed unimportant, Philippe was eager to talk about what he thought was important—the politics of Cameroon, his involvement in them, and how he had suffered because of his activism. He felt rushed, however, and could not fully explain himself.

The interpreter seemed to be having more problems as the discussion became more substantive. The interviewer became more and more frustrated as well. Finally he began asking Philippe questions directly in French. The interview seemed to go better this way than in using the translator, but the asylum officer did not speak French very well and seemed to be missing a lot of what Philippe was saying.

At the end, the interviewer asked if Philippe had anything to say that he had not been asked about. Philippe thought for a minute; he had not been able to say everything he wanted, but he had talked about everything at least briefly. Philippe said no. The lawyer then spoke for a few minutes, and the asylum officer nodded his head and took notes. The asylum officer asked Philippe to sign the form again, and he did so. He gave him another piece of paper to sign and told him to bring that piece of paper back in two weeks when he picked up his decision. They then stood up, the officer shook everyone's hand again, and he led them out of the office into the waiting room.

They left the waiting room and went into the corridor, and

Philippe asked the lawyer what he thought. The lawyer smiled, said that everything was fine, and said that he had another meeting that afternoon, so he had to go.

Adele's interview was scheduled for the next week. On the night before the interview, however, she went into labor. Philippe went to the asylum office on the day of her interview to tell them that she could not attend her interview, and Adele spent the day in the hospital. She left the hospital the same day without giving birth—her labor pains were premature. She went back to the hospital two weeks later, and this time she gave birth to a healthy baby boy. They decided to name him Richard, after Philippe's uncle.

Meanwhile, Philippe had received his decision from the asylum office. His case was referred to the immigration court for further proceedings. In such referral letters, the asylum office does not state the exact reason for the referral, but it does check one or more boxes on a list of possible reasons. The boxes checked for Philippe's case stated "Your claim was deemed not credible on the basis of material inconsistencies between your testimony and application and/or other evidence," and "Lack of detail(s) on material points."

Philippe was shocked at this result. He had explained everything to the interview, and he was telling the truth. It must be a mistake of some kind. He thought back to the interview and remembered how frustrated and angry the asylum officer had become, and how he had started avoiding using the interpreter. He also remembered how many changes the asylum officer had made on the form that the lawyer filled out.

Philippe and Adele decided they needed a new lawyer. They did not know how they would pay for one, because they had already gone through all their money paying their current attorney. They also did not know where to look. They had hired their current attorney because he was also from Cameroon and because their friends in the United States had recommended him. If they stopped using him, they had no idea how to go about hiring someone else. As a result, they continued to work with this lawyer until Philippe's first immigration court hearing and then began looking for a new person to represent them.

The referral notice had a piece of paper stapled to it that had a list of the names and numbers of organizations that provided free or low-cost legal assistance. Philippe and Adele called every number on the list. No one answered the phone at most of the numbers and they left messages with everyone. Only about half of these called back, but Philippe and Adele kept calling until they got through to most of them.

Some of the organizations did not represent asylum seekers. Many of the agencies who did take political asylum cases charged a fee for services but said that the fee scale was flexible and that if Adele and Philippe could not pay now, they could pay after they received work authorization. Most of these agencies, however, said they were too busy with their current caseload and did not have an open appointment for over a month. Adele and Philippe could not wait this long. Philippe had already had a problem at his first court hearing, and Adele's asylum office interview was coming up in a few weeks. Adele and Philippe did not think the asylum office would let them reschedule her interview a second time.

Finally, one organization, Lutheran Social Services, gave them an appointment the next week. Their office was in Virginia, far from where they lived, and as it turned out, the building was hard to find from public transportation. They arrived a half-hour late for their appointment and were anxious that the lawyer would be angry with them for arriving late.

It was at this point that I met Adele and Philippe. They explained to me their situation and showed me their paperwork so far. It was obvious that their lawyer had done almost nothing on their case. He had submitted the asylum application form with no supporting documents and only a one-page summary of their stories. The form itself was badly typed and contained many spelling errors. Many of the questions on the form were answered incorrectly or inadequately.

I counseled them first to get married as soon as possible. This way, if either of them won, he or she could file for the other as a dependent. The only way they could get deported was if both of them lost their cases at the asylum office and in court. Since they had been dating for a long time and had a child together, they could prove that their marriage was valid, not a fraudulent one undertaken only for immigration purposes.

Adele and Philippe tried to get married the same week that I spoke to them, but the county court office at first refused to perform the ceremony because neither of them had identification. After several weeks of negotiating with the county court, they finally convinced the court to let them marry by using the receipts from their asylum applications as identification.

While Adele and Philippe were trying to get the local court to allow them to marry, Adele and I began preparing her asylum case. Adele and Philippe's experience with their first attorney is a common experience among asylum applicants. Applicants for asylum usually do not speak English and do not understand the system, so they are forced to choose an attorney or representative to trust and to lead them through the process. Often, as in Adele and Philippe's case, this trust is misplaced, but the applicants have no way of learning this until their case is denied, and it is too late.

Bad representation had caused the referral of Philippe's asylum claim. There was so little written information on Philippe's case that the asylum officer had to elicit all of Philippe's story during the interview. The short time allotted for each interview, combined with the poor performance of the interpreter, made it impossible for him to find out enough about Philippe's case to approve it. The interviewer should have stopped the interview and told Philippe to come back with a better interpreter. Instead he referred Philippe's case to court for further consideration.

Philippe had already lost his case at the asylum office, but with Adele there was still time to fix things. The asylum office allows applicants to submit additional information on the date of the interview and even allows applicants to replace an erroneous asylum application and statement with a correct one. I helped Adele fill out a new asylum application, and we wrote a four-page statement that described her political activities in Cameroon and the persecution she suffered as a result. I did research on Cameroon and found a good deal of information about political conditions there and the persecution of members of the SDF party. I selected the most relevant country conditions documents and assembled them into a packet of information for the asylum officer to read.

In preparing Adele's asylum case, as with any case, I had to balance the need to include all the important information with the need to be brief. Asylum officers are allotted only about three a half hours for each case. They spend an hour reading the case before the interview and about one hour interviewing the applicant. After the interview they have one and a half hours to research country conditions, read the case again, review their notes, and write up their decision. Given this relatively brief amount of time allotted to each case, the case file must be written clearly and succinctly, leaving out nothing important but including nothing superfluous. It must be possible for the asylum officer to read and understand the file in an hour, so that the officer can use the interview time to clarify any misunderstandings and to establish that the applicant is credible. Since the law states that the "burden of proof" is on the applicant, if the asylum officer is still confused after the interview or does not find that there is enough proof the case will be referred to immigration court.

After writing the statement, Adele and I practiced for her upcoming interview. I pretended to be the asylum officer and asked her the kinds of questions she might be asked in the interview. Doing this helps clients get over their nervousness about the upcoming interview and gives them confidence. The practice interview also acts as a final check for errors. Before filing a case, I always have the client read over the application form and the statement, or I have an interpreter read these to the client. Even with this, it is still possible to overlook errors in the form or the statement which could cause problems during the interview. These errors often become evident during the practice interview, in time to be corrected before the real interview.

We submitted the new asylum form, statement, and supporting documentation on the day of Adele's interview. Her interview went much better than Philippe's, both because she was better prepared and because she was assigned one of the asylum office's best interviewers. This asylum officer has a law degree from a prestigious university, he could have taken a high-paying job in private practice but chose to work as an asylum officer to help refugees.

Adele spoke English well enough to interview without an interpreter. The officer had already read and understood her case, so she did not ask Adele to retell her entire story. Instead she asked Adele detailed questions about individual aspects. This is an effective way to see if an applicant is telling the truth. If an asylum applicant has simply memorized a story written by someone else, she cannot provide any more details than what is written in the application. If an applicant is telling the truth, she should be able to elaborate on each point.

Adele is articulate, and she actually seemed to enjoy answering many of the questions. She explained the political party system in Cameroon, the platform of her own party, and the technical points of the issues at stake in the most recent election. She went into detail about Cameroon's new constitution and how it gave the ruling government an unfair advantage in the elections. She explained how her party had decided to boycott the elections and how difficult it was to break this news to party members in the village.

The asylum officer also asked her to talk about her escape from prison and from Cameroon and her arrival in the United States. Again, she wanted detailed information to establish that Adele's story was her own and not one that she had memorized. She had Adele narrate in detail each event of her escape, starting with her leaving her prison cell. She then asked her the exact location of each place where she stayed in hiding and had Adele tell her exactly how she had obtained a visa for Canada and how she had crossed into the United States.

The interviewer asked only a few questions about Adele's treatment in jail and her torture there. Since the interviewer could ascertain Adele's credibility by asking her for details about any part of her story, she chose to focus on the less traumatic aspects of her case. She did ask Adele if her newborn baby was the result of "something that happened" while she was in prison. Adele realized that this was a sensitive way of asking if she were raped in prison, and she explained that the baby was the son of her husband. While many women were raped in the prison in Cameroon, she said, the bribes that Adele's family had paid the guards had protected her from rape.

Since the interviewer was so good, there was little for me to do during the interview, and I did not need to make a statement at the end. It was obvious from how the interview had gone that the interviewer would grant Adele asylum, and I did not wish to waste her time making unnecessary arguments on Adele's behalf.

Two weeks later, Adele went to pick up her decision, but she was told that it was not ready. Then I received a call from her asylum officer, who told me that Adele had to return to the asylum office for another interview. The asylum officer would not say why, but she did say there were "questions of identity" which needed to be resolved.

When we arrived at this interview, we found that the INS had entered Adele's name and date of birth into their computer and had discovered that there was another person named Marie Adele Fontem, with the same birthdate, who had entered the United States as a visitor from France two years earlier. Since Adele's middle name was Marie, it looked as if this was the same person. The asylum officer asked Adele if she had ever previously entered the United States. She said she had not. The asylum officer asked a number of questions along this line, and Adele repeated her contention that she had entered the United States for the first time six months earlier.

The asylum office took the previous entry date as a reason to suspect fraud. Adele had stated that she entered the United States illegally, without going through the usual passport controls. The Marie Adele Fontem who shared Adele's last name and birthdate had entered two years earlier on a visitor's visa. The asylum office apparently suspected that Adele and this Marie Adele were the same person, that she had been in the United States for two years and had made up her entire story as a way of gaining asylum and permission to stay. Since the persecution she claimed to have suffered happened only eight months ago, if she had been in the United States for two years, it had obviously never happened.

The asylum office's suspicions were more reasonable than it might seem. Immigrants do sometimes try to take advantage of the asylum system by making fraudulent applications. Aliens sometimes come to the United States on a temporary visa, or with no visa, and decide to stay for economic reasons. If they are from a country where others have won asylum, they may consider this a good way to get a work permit and permanent residency. Fraudulent applicants typically use the asylum application of a friend or relative and try to memorize the story, or pay someone to write them a story and help them memorize it. The asylum office apparently suspected that Adele had done this and had invented a story about entering the United States recently on a false passport in order to cover up the fact that she had been here for two years.

I was given the opportunity to ask questions or to comment. Adele had pointed out that her middle name, Marie, is not an "official" name but a name she was given at her baptism. While the interview was going on, I looked at her birth certificate and her Cameroon identity card, copies of which were in her asylum file. Both documents listed her name only as "Adele Fontem," with no middle name. I pointed this out to the asylum officer, and Adele showed her the original documents, which she had brought with her. Adele stated that none of her official identification, including her passport, had the name "Marie." I also asked Adele if Fontem was a common name in Cameroon, and she said that it was.

At the end of this second interview, the asylum officer gave me a few minutes to speak. I pointed out that the only similarity between the two persons was in their dates of birth; their names were in fact different. Having the same last name and same birthdate as someone else is not that unlikely a coincidence, particularly if one has a common last name. Given the fact that Adele had already offered detailed, credible testimony to her identity and manner of entry, the asylum office should not count this minor coincidence as evidence strong enough to justify a denial of her asylum claim.

The asylum officer could not say anything that day, but she thanked us for coming. A few days later we received her recommended approval notice in the mail. This was great news for Adele, and it meant that she could file for Philippe to gain "derivative" asylum status as soon as her final paperwork came through.

Therese Kabongelo

I went through a similar process in preparing Therese's asylum application. I interviewed her about her life in Congo, asking her questions about her political activities and the activities of her husband and sons, and about the attacks of Kabila's soldiers on her and her family. My French was not fluent at that time, so I asked my fiancée (now my wife) Ashley Spell to help interpret.

Ashley and I interviewed Therese several times, for several hours each time, before I felt that I understood her story completely. The sessions took a long time because it was difficult for Therese to talk about what had happened; we had to stop at times because she was crying too hard to continue. For the last session, I wrote down her story and Ashley translated it back to her so that Therese could correct any errors. I also did research to find documents about human rights conditions and political events in Congo and assembled them into a packet with a summary and quotes of important information from each document.

We mailed the case to the INS and waited for Therese's interview to be scheduled. Normally it takes the INS six weeks to process an asylum case and set an interview date. In the meantime, I arranged for Therese to see a psychological counselor. On the day of her interview, we brought a report from the counselor, attesting to the truth of Therese's story and reporting the counselor's diagnosis that Therese suffered from post-traumatic stress disorder, which we submitted as new evidence.

Ashley came with us to Therese's interview as the interpreter, and we signed in at the front window as usual. Because Therese had been a victim of sexual violence, we asked to be assigned a female interviewer. The asylum office complied with our request, but, unfortunately, they assigned us one of the least competent officers. She had been transferred into the Asylum Corps from the inspections branch of the INS, where she had worked as an airport inspector, questioning newly arrived foreigners about their passports and visas and looking for fraudulent entry documents. While she had gone through the asylum officer training program, she had not changed the suspicious, interrogatory interviewing style that she had learned in her previous assignment. She had worked in the asylum office for only a few months, and she was not well informed about the political background of many countries. Since both Therese's individual story and the politics of her home country were complex and difficult to understand, I was afraid that the officer would not be able to understand Therese's story and would find her testimony to be noncredible.

The asylum officer introduced herself to Therese, explained the nature of the interview, and had her swear to tell the truth. She also had Ashley swear that she would translate honestly and accurately. She began the interview by going through the information on the asylum form, checking each entry for accuracy.

She then asked Therese why she had left Congo. Therese began to tell her story, but the asylum officer interrupted her many times to ask questions and clarify details. Much of the time was spent having Therese explain the political background in Congo and Rwanda, not leaving much time for Therese to explain her own situation.

Even though the asylum officer was relatively new to her job, her ignorance of the events in Congo was striking. At one point she asked Therese which of the two Zaires Therese was from. (There are two countries in Africa called Congo, but only one Zaire.) She also asked insensitive questions, such as, "Now at this point, was it the Hutus killing the Tutsis, or were the Tutsis killing the Hutus?" She even mixed up the names of the two ethnic groups, calling them the "Hutsis" and the "Tutus." This would have been comical had Therese's life not been at stake.

The asylum officer evidently found the issue of ethnicity too confusing, because she abandoned this line of questioning and began to ask about Therese's husband's activities in politics. Therese was able to explain his political party participation and the nature of the party to which he had belonged. The asylum officer seemed more comfortable with this.

When Therese told how she was left by the soldiers and rescued by priests, the asylum officer became noticeably skeptical. Asylum officers evaluate the credibility of stories on their plausibility, and I have noticed that at times, when applicants have suffered extreme persecution yet escaped through good fortune or mercy on the part of their captors, the asylum officers are reluctant to believe them. In Therese's interview, the officer asked many questions about the assistance given her by the priests and her eventual escape from Africa.

"What were the names of the priests who took care of you?" Therese could give only their first names. "What is the name of the church or monastery where you stayed? Where was it?" Therese didn't know and explained that she had been taken there while she was unconscious. "How long, exactly, did you stay there?" Again, Therese didn't know—she had lost track of time while she was staying there, because of her illness and depression.

The asylum officer also asked her for details about how she was able to make it through immigration once she arrived in the United States. The interviewer said she found it hard to believe that the immigration officer at the airport had waved Therese through, after just glancing at her passport, because she was ill. She even told Therese, "When I was an airport inspector, I didn't let people through so easily."

The officer also asked many questions about Therese's rape and the death of her husband. "How did the soldiers know where you and your husband were hiding?" Therese didn't know. "When they found you, how did they know you were married to the man they were looking for?" Therese didn't know. The asylum officer began to ask questions about the rape itself, but I interrupted and protested that it was not necessary to make her relive the experience by recounting it. We had already submitted a statement from a rape crisis counselor that documented the fact that the rape had actually happened, and this evidence should be enough to prove the point. The asylum officer backed off from this line of questioning, but she did ask Therese, "Why didn't the soldiers kill you after they raped you?" Therese could only say that she did not know.

The asylum officer finished her questioning, and I was given the chance to make final comments. I emphasized the importance of understanding the ethnic character of the violence in eastern Congo, and I urged the asylum officer to read carefully the supporting documents about events there so that she would be able to make an informed decision about Therese's case. I said it was true that the events in her case were improbable, but that we also knew that most people in Therese's situation did not escape. Therese was simply one of the few people for whom a series of lucky accidents had allowed her to escape alive. Even though her story was a remarkable one, the clear, consistent, and detailed nature of her testimony, along with the supporting testimony of her rape crisis counselor, should establish that she was telling the truth.

After the interview was over, I thought about what I could do to make sure Therese would win her case. The interview had gone badly, and the fault lay with the asylum officer. I was concerned because another of my clients, who was also from eastern Congo and had a similar story, had recently been referred to immigration court for similar reasons. In that other case, the asylum officer had also not been well informed about the political situation in Congo and had seemed skeptical and unconvinced during the interview. The officer had found the case not credible because she had found her story to be implausible and because the events described in the story were not consistent with information about current country conditions.[1]

To try to fix things with Therese's case, I called the asylum officer's supervisor and asked her to take a look at the case and make sure that the asylum officer spent an adequate amount of time on it in order to make a good decision. I mentioned what had happened with the other case, and I stated that it was likely that officers were having trouble with cases of applicants from eastern Congo, which was understandable given the complex history of events there and the many recent changes in country conditions. I was trying to make it sound like a general request to be fair and careful in all Congolese cases, not like a plea for favoritism on behalf of my client. I did, however, complain about the asylum officer's lack of knowledge and lack of sensitivity in conducting her

---

1. This other applicant won her case in court but had a difficult time doing so. I helped her get representation from the Lawyer's Committee for Human Rights, a non-profit group that recruits large law firms to take on asylum cases and not charge a fee. To win the case, the law firm decided to pay an expert witness, a development consultant who had lived and worked in Zaire, to testify that the applicant's story was plausible and credible according to his expert knowledge of current country conditions.

interview, and I asked that Therese be called back for a second interview with another officer if the supervisor deemed it necessary.[2]

Therese and I went together to pick up her decision two weeks later. The asylum office calls everyone to pick up their decisions at the same time, 1:00 p.m., so it is good to get there early because there are usually twenty or more other applicants called each day to pick up their decisions. The asylum office is closed from 12:00 to 1:00 for lunch, so when we arrived at 12:45 we had to wait in a line with other applicants, in the hallway by the elevators. When the door opened at 1:00, we went in and signed in at the window. Only two people at a time are given their decisions, and there were ten other people ahead of us, so we had about thirty minutes to wait until we heard the result.

Two asylum office clerks deliver the decisions at tables in the main waiting room, which is separated from the rest of the building by two locked doors. When you pick up your decision, you do not speak to the asylum officer who adjudicated your case, and there is no way to reach the locked part of the office where the asylum officers work. The office is designed this way so that angry applicants cannot argue with or attack the officers who denied their application.

After about a half-hour the clerk called Therese's name, and we went to the desk to hear the decision. He handed the decision across to us—a long letter, with the words "Recommended Approval" at the top—and began to explain in a neutral tone of voice that "this letter represents a recommended approval. Final approval of your asylum case is still undecided pending a criminal background check. . . ." Therese stared at him, not understanding what he was saying but trying to guess from his tone of voice whether this was good news or bad news.

I told Therese, in French, that we had won. She shouted,

2. Other representatives also complained about this officer, and the asylum office's supervisors take complaints about the behavior or decisions of officers seriously. Since the time of Therese's interview (January 1998), the asylum office has worked with this officer and has given her additional training, and she has greatly improved both her interviewing technique and the fairness of her decisions.

"Merci à Dieu!," hugged me, thanked me, thanked God again, thanked the asylum office clerk, and shook his hand—she would have hugged him too if he had not been seated on the other side of the desk. She then relaxed, sat back in her chair, and smiled, no longer listening to the clerk. The clerk smiled, congratulated her, and went on reading the decision letter to her, as he is required to do.

The decision letter explained in technical detail the steps necessary to apply for a work permit, how to file for visas for immediate relatives, and what would have to occur before a final approval would be issued. I did not translate this directly, since Therese was too happy to pay attention anyway, but we did go over all this information together later on, when she was able to listen. We both thanked the clerk, left the building, and went immediately to a photo studio to get photographs for her application for a work permit.

Aster Cheru

After Aster had been imprisoned by the INS because of her former shoplifting conviction, she tried to find an attorney to prevent her from being deported. She did not contact me initially but saw a private attorney at a small law firm. This lawyer agreed to take her case and agreed to charge a greatly reduced fee for the work. The lawyer was not expert in immigration law but was willing to work hard on the case. She called me to get some of the information she needed. Since she was obviously committed to the case and had put in a lot of time on it, including some that was not paid, I was glad to help her. After two months, however, she left her firm, and her supervisor, the principal partner of the firm, took over the case. He was not as committed to the case as the first attorney, and he did little work on it. After waiting a few weeks and attempting unsuccessfully to reach him on the phone, I decided to take the case back from the firm.

I visited Aster in jail and told her that I would be willing to represent her if she wanted me to. She was glad for the help. After the first attorney had left, the law firm had done nothing on her case and had not called or written to her to keep her informed on her case's progress. She signed the form making me her representative, and I went to work.

I helped Aster apply for "withholding of deportation" status and protection under the U.N. Convention Against Torture. As an alien convicted of a crime considered by immigration law to be an "aggravated felony," Aster was not eligible for asylum, but she was eligible for these two forms of protection. Her case was currently being processed under administrative removal proceedings, a new procedure which was introduced with the 1996 immigration reform law. It provided that aliens with aggravated felony convictions could be deported by order of an INS official, without ever having a judicial hearing.

To get her case before a judge, we had to apply for restriction on removal and Convention Against Torture protection, and then pass a screening interview called a "reasonable fear" interview. When the INS made regulations interpreting the 1996 law and the law implementing the U.N. Convention Against Torture, it introduced the "reasonable fear" screening interview process as a way of preventing aliens with criminal convictions from using the convention to delay their deportation. The "reasonable fear" interviews are designed to screen out those claims that have no basis; only those aliens who can demonstrate that they are credible, and that there is a "reasonable possibility" they will be persecuted or tortured in their home country, are referred to an immigration judge.

Aster first requested a hearing before a judge in February 1999, but at that time Congress had just passed the legislation implementing the Convention Against Torture, and the INS had not yet formulated regulations to implement it. These regulations were published in March, but the INS was slow in putting them into effect. Aster did not get her "reasonable fear" interview until July, six months after she had first been imprisoned.

Aster and I spent hours preparing for this interview. I was not worried that she would not pass the interview, since her case was very strong. I was, however, concerned about the possibility that incorrect information would be placed on her case record. Since the asylum officer's notes from the reasonable fear interview would go into the court file, any mistakes or discrepancies in his notes would undermine Aster's credibility in court. For this reason I made sure that Aster was fully prepared to talk about the persecution she had suffered in Ethiopia. Preparing for this interview was difficult, given the restrictions on access to the jail. Aster was being held in a state prison about fifty miles from Washington. Most of the other prisoners in the women's section had been convicted of drug possession, theft, or other minor crimes. Aster was the only Ethiopian and the only immigration detainee in the women's section.

I was surprised to find how difficult it was to arrange visits with prisoners at this facility. Prisoners were allowed only thirty minutes' visiting time per week, and during this time they talked to friends and family members through speaking holes in a Plexiglas wall. Many prisoners were scheduled for visiting hours at the same time, and there was only one large visiting room, divided into two halves, so the visitors all lined up down the length of the wall and tried to shout over one another to the inmates they were visiting. The noise from the echo in this small, cinderblock-lined room made it almost impossible to hear.

During my first visit to Aster, we spoke in this way. It was difficult for us to understand each other, as she had to strain to understand my English, and I had to listen carefully to hear her quiet voice and to follow her meaning as she tried to express herself in English. She had been in prison for three months, she was frightened, and she despaired of ever getting out. She had not heard anything from the immigration authorities for over a month, and she had no idea about the status of her case.

Aster was most concerned about her children. Having spent several months in prison with women convicted of drug offenses, she was worried about her fourteen-year-old daughter. She was convinced that Beth would end up as a drug addict if she were allowed to grow up in the United States without her mother's supervision. She also was worried about her two sons, who were living with their father again. She knew that if she were deported to Ethiopia, she would lose her right to return to the United States and would never see them again.

After I spoke with her, I asked the prison guards if I could send her anything—food, clothing, toiletries, or other necessities. The rules on sending such items were strict, apparently to prevent the smuggling of drugs and weapons into the prison. Prisoners could not receive any items through the mail except books, and books could only be accepted if they were mailed directly from the publisher. If prisoners needed personal items, they had to buy them from the prison commissary. One could not give cash to prisoners, but one could give them money by sending a money order to the jail to be deposited in the prisoner's commissary account. The jail gave prisoners writing paper, one stamp, and one envelope each week for free; any other stationery and stamps the prisoners had to buy from the commissary.

Apparently Aster had no money in her account and no friends who would send her money, so I mailed a little bit of money to her so that she could buy things she needed and she could write me. I did not have time to visit the prison every week, and it was not possible for us to communicate by phone. Aster could call people only by placing a collect call, but the phone system at my office did not accept collect calls, and the prison did not allow prisoners to receive phone calls. We did communicate sometimes through a third party, a domestic violence counselor named Katherine Anderson, who visited the jail regularly to counsel the women prisoners. Aster talked to her every few days, so we could send messages to each other through her.

I returned to the prison several times, with a volunteer translator, to prepare Aster's case. She told me many things about her life that she had not told anyone else before. Her original application contained many errors, and it also greatly understated the amount of suffering she had undergone in Ethiopia. It also understated Aster's political activities and commitment. Her case was much stronger in reality than it appeared to be on paper.

It took a while to develop a rapport of trust and to get Aster to talk about what she had experienced, but after several interviews Aster finally told me everything that had happened to her in jail in Ethiopia. She found it difficult to talk about how she had been beaten and given an electric shock, but she did not try to hide these facts from me. She did not, however, tell me about the rape she had experienced in jail. In Ethiopian culture, as in many others, a victim of rape is viewed as being shamed and disgraced, despite the obvious fact that the victim is not to blame.

Since I knew that sexual torture is commonly inflicted on female prisoners in Ethiopia, I asked her directly if she had been raped or sexually assaulted in jail. She began to cry and, slowly, told me what had happened. What she had experienced was particularly brutal and thus even more difficult to talk about. Aster had never told anyone about the rape until the day she told me.

Fortunately the domestic violence counselor already had an appointment to see Aster that day. With traumatic events, the more time that passes before the victim is able to talk about the experience, the more psychological damage the trauma does, and the more difficult it is when the victim finally tries to recover. A prison is the worst possible environment to try to recover psychologically from torture and rape, particularly when they took place in a prison. With Katherine's help, however, Aster was much better able to cope with her memories of trauma and work through them while in prison.

Aster had a difficult time in prison, and her difficulties were compounded by the tough treatment she received from the prison authorities. They were used to dealing with American criminals, not with asylum seekers from other countries. They did not have the patience to try to understand Aster's English, and many of her complains and requests went unheard. Because she did not understand the rules, she often inadvertently broke them and was labeled a troublemaker.

At one point she asked for a more comfortable bed or bunk than the ones normally offered in the prison, which she found uncomfortable. She had hurt her back in an accident at work in 1994, and she had had to have surgery at that time. At first the prison officials complied with her request, but toward the end of her prison stay she was transferred to another cell block and put back in a regular bunk. She complained of back pain again, but this time the prison medical officers did not believe her, and they told her she would have to prove that she had a back condition in order to get a different bunk. She could not obtain her medical records while in jail, so she could not prove this to them. Aster lost sleep and walked stiffly from the pain in her back, but the prison authorities decided she was only doing this to cause trouble.

She also wanted a Bible written in her native language, Amharic. I also wanted to give her an Amharic/English dictionary so that she could better understand the papers related to her asylum case. I had a difficult time getting these books to her because of the prison's policy of not allowing books into the prison unless they were shipped directly from the publisher. Since these books were published in Ethiopia, it was not possible to have them shipped directly to the prison. The prison's director of security allowed her to receive an Amharic/English dictionary directly from me, but he refused to let her have a Bible because the one that I tried to give her was used. Later I found a new Amharic-language Bible, but the security director would not let this in at all. I do not know why he allowed her to have a dictionary but not a Bible; I suspect he was trying to punish Aster for something else that he thought she had done. I had to appeal directly to the prison warden, who finally allowed her to have a Bible written in her own language.

Aster was granted only thirty minutes each week to see visitors, and there was not always someone to transport her daughter to see her, so she saw Beth only once every few weeks. She did not want her youngest children even to know she was in jail, because she was afraid they would not understand. She did not want them to visit her because she thought they would be frightened and confused if they could see her but could not touch her through the glass and could not stay with her. During her entire stay in prison, she saw her daughter only four or five times, and she never saw her sons.

Another problem arose in working with a translator. A former client of mine volunteered to translate and accompanied me to the prison. The security director there refused to let us have a contact visit because he suspected that the interpreter was actually a family member, and that we were trying to arrange a personal visit outside of visiting hours. He wanted an official interpreter's identification or some proof that the interpreter and Aster were not related. Since the interpreter was a volunteer, she could not give them anything like an employee identification card, and they would not take my word that she was a volunteer employee. She had a different last name from Aster, and they did not look alike, but I suspect that in the eyes of the white prison security director all Ethiopians looked the same. We conducted our interviews in a noncontact visiting room, shouting at each other through the glass divider and passing papers back and forth through a slot.

Aster's interview took place in the office of one of the prison officials. The INS uses telephone interpreters provided by AT&T, so we had to use this office because it was one of the only rooms within the locked area of the prison that had a phone line. When the interpreter came on the phone, he began to read from an information sheet written by the INS that describes the nature of the "reasonable fear" interview. Aster stopped the interpreter after a few minutes and began asking him questions in Amharic, and they began to converse in Amharic, without him translating what they were saying. The INS officer soon stopped them and asked the interpreter to explain what was happening.

Aster had ascertained from the interpreter's accent that he was from the Tigre ethnic group, and she told the asylum officer that she was afraid to have him interpret because of this. The leaders of the current government of Ethiopia are Tigreans, while Aster is an Amharan, whom the Tigreans have traditionally considered to be enemies. The men who arrested, tortured, and raped Aster were all Tigreans. Aster refused to continue with the interview using this interpreter because she was afraid that he might intentionally mistranslate her testimony. She was also afraid that, because he was from the same ethnic group as the current rulers of Ethiopia, he might somehow be a spy for the Ethiopian government. AT&T offered to change interpreters, but the only other interpreter available was a member of the Oromo ethnic group, another group which is traditionally antagonistic to the Amharas.

Aster refused to go on with the interview using a telephone interpreter. I had brought a volunteer interpreter with me, but the government's regulations stated that Aster could use her own interpreter only if the AT&T interpreter also listened in, to make sure the interpreter was translating correctly, and Aster would not agree to this. The asylum officer conducted the interview in English. Aster's English is good but not fluent, and the interview went slowly. The asylum officer was careful to speak slowly and repeat himself when necessary, and he was patient with Aster's imperfect English.

Aster's fears may seem unreasonable, even paranoid, but they are common fears among asylum seekers. Both the current government and the former governments of Ethiopia were totalitarian states where human rights were not respected. Many Ethiopians are afraid to talk about politics to strangers, since any stranger might be a government supporter or informer. AT&T requires its interpreters to promise to keep information confidential, but it would be possible for one of them to pass information to the Ethiopian embassy without AT&T being aware of it.

The asylum officer began the interview by giving Aster a series of written statements to read, which explained the nature of the interview, and asked her to sign the statements indicating that she had read them and understood them. She did not understand them, of course, given that they were written in a legalistic style of English, but she signed anyway. The information they contained was what I had already explained to her about the interview.

He then asked her about her life in Ethiopia, the persecution she had suffered there, and her fear of return. He went through all of this slowly and was very patient with her poor English. He frequently rephrased questions so that she could understand them, and he asked her to clarify her statements whenever he did not understand her answer.

The interview took six hours. It took Aster a long time to articulate the events of her life in her limited English, and the asylum officer took his time and made sure he understood her completely. At the end, he printed out his notes for her to look over and review, so that she could correct any errors or misunderstandings before it went into her file. I too read the statement, and while Aster found a few mistakes, I found no significant errors.

A week later he sent the official decision to us. He found Aster's testimony to be credible and her fear of persecution strong enough to qualify as a "reasonable" or a "well-founded" fear, the same standard used in asylum claims. If it had not been for Aster's criminal conviction, meeting this standard would have been enough for her to be granted asylum. Instead, since her criminal conviction made her ineligible for asylum, she was referred to an immigration judge for a determination as to whether there was a probability that she would be persecuted if she were returned to Ethiopia. It is more difficult to prove that there is a "probability of persecution" than it is to prove that an applicant has a "reasonable" or "well-founded" fear, so the court hearing would determine if Aster's claim met this higher standard of proof. If the judge ruled in her favor, she would be granted withholding of deportation, a status similar to asylum.

The asylum officer's written decision was the best possible one for Aster. Because he found her story credible, we could use the finding in support of Aster's claim in court. His written notes about the interview were accurate but lacked specifics, so it would be difficult for the INS trial attorney to use these notes to try to trick Aster into making contradictory statements at her court hearing. He wrote a summary of her case and cited human rights reports, including the U.S. *Department of State Annual Report on Human Rights,* to show that Aster had a well-founded fear of persecution based on current country conditions.

Shortly after Aster's interview, the INS headquarters changed its policy on parole and began allowing some people in her situation to be released from detention. Over the course of the year that mandatory detention for aggravated felons had been implemented, thirteen different federal district courts had ruled that the INS's mandatory detention policy amounted to prolonged unlawful detention and violated the Constitution. While these rulings were binding only in these judicial districts, the INS finally decided to change its policy for the entire United States and began releasing some aliens detained because of past criminal records. The INS made its own decisions about parole on a "discretionary" basis, however, and if local INS official decided to keep someone in jail, no immigration court could overturn their decision.[3]

Aster became eligible for parole after she was found to have a "reasonable fear" of persecution and was referred to immigration court. To have her parole request approved, she had to show that she had a place to stay if she were released. The women's shelter in

---

3. "INS Reinterprets Mandatory Detention Provisions, Proposes Other Detention Changes," *Interpreter Releases,* July 19, 1999, pp. 1082–1085, 1099–1101.

the town where the prison is located agreed to let her stay there for two months, until she started working again and could afford an apartment.

We asked for parole immediately after her "reasonable fear" interview. The INS officer assigned to her case assured us that she wanted Aster to be released and said she thought Aster had a good case for parole, but she warned us that many people would have to approve the request, including the head of the entire office, the district director. The parole policy was new, and the INS wanted to take no chances about releasing someone who might later commit a crime and create bad publicity for the INS. Weeks went by, and despite my frequent calls to the INS detention officer, there was no sign that her parole request was any closer to being approved.

While this was going on, the *Washington Post* was putting together a story about the detention and deportation of "aggravated felons." The *Post*'s reporter, Philip Pan, interviewed Aster about her prison experience, and three weeks after the parole request was submitted, he called the INS district office to ask about her situation. A few hours after Pan called the INS approved her parole, and she was released the next day.

Once released, Aster was quickly able to get her life started again, although her upcoming court hearing still caused her anxiety. The INS issued her a new work permit, and she started back at her former job. She began the legal process to get her daughter out of foster care and to regain permanent custody, and she requested that her two sons be returned to her. All these requests were denied, however, pending her permanent immigration status. Her husband had been granted primary custody of her two young sons, and her husband's lawyer was able to use her immigration problems against her in the custody hearings. Her domestic court lawyer advised her to wait until her immigration case was settled before she requested that her sons be returned to her primary custody. Likewise, her daughter, who was living with a foster care family, continued to live with that family; the child welfare authorities were unwilling to let her go home until Aster had a permanent immigration status. Aster waited, impatiently, for her day in court.

6

ⅉⅉⅉⅉ

Court

Adele and Philippe Fontem

Philippe's first court hearing was scheduled for June 1998, before the date of Adele's asylum office hearing. At this point I had not yet met Adele and Philippe; Philippe had continued to work with the private attorney who had represented him at the asylum office.

All Maryland residents go to the immigration court in Baltimore, even those, like Philippe, who live in the suburbs of Washington. Philippe did not know where the court was located, so the attorney agreed to meet him at the train station in Baltimore. Philippe left his home very early in the morning and took the bus to the commuter train station. He then took the train to Baltimore. His hearing was scheduled for 9:00, and he arrived at the train station in Baltimore at 8:00. He looked for his lawyer, but did not see him, and sat down to wait.

Time passed. Around 8:30 he began to get nervous, and he grew more and more nervous as it got closer to 9:00. Finally at 8:55, he decided to try to find the court on his own. He had no money for a taxi, so he walked and asked directions. He did not find the courtroom until 10:00.

When he entered, he saw that there were many immigrants waiting to be called by the judge. His lawyer had explained to him that this was the first of two hearings. Called the "Master Calendar" hearing, it lasts only a few minutes: you admit that you are not a U.S. citizen or legal permanent resident and state that you intend to apply again for asylum. The judge then sets a date and time for the second hearing, called the "individual" hearing. At the second hearing, which usually takes about two hours, the judge hears your testimony about your fear of returning to your own country, and decides whether to approve or deny your asylum case.

Philippe sat and waited as the judge called out the names of the people waiting for their hearings. They were from many different countries. Most of them had lawyers, but a few did not, and from time to time the judge would call a name and no one would answer. By 11:30 the judge had called everyone, but Philippe was still waiting. He asked the court clerk what was going on, and the clerk told him that a decision had already been made in his case. He picked up the decision, a computer printout with some boxes checked and some notes written on it by hand. He could not read it, but it seemed that his case had been decided against him.

When Adele and Philippe first talked to me, they brought in this piece of paper and asked me to explain what had happened. If you do not attend an immigration hearing, the judge can decide the case in your absence and order you deported "*in absentia.*" Many judges apply this rule to people who arrive late for their hearings, treating them as if they had not arrived at all, and they have been supported in this practice by rulings of the Board of Immigration Appeals. There is no appeal to *in absentia* orders of removal, and aliens ordered removed in this way can file a motion to reopen their cases only in limited circumstances.

If someone has never received notice of the hearing, he can file a motion to reopen at any time, even years after the hearing. If he can prove in his motion that he was not notified of the original hearing, he can reopen his case and get a new hearing. If he did receive notice but was prevented from attending the hearing, he can file a motion to reopen within 180 days of the judge's decision. He must prove, however, that his failure to appear was due to "exceptional circumstances."

The Immigration and Nationality Act does not define "exceptional circumstances" but says that this includes "serious illness of respondent, or serious illness or death of a spouse, child, or parent." Other circumstances may also be "exceptional" but must not be "less compelling" than those listed above. The BIA has ruled that "ineffective assistance of counsel" counts as an "exceptional circumstance,"[1] but lateness due to heavy traffic does not.[2]

In Philippe's case, I looked for some way to justify a motion to reopen. The real reason for Philippe's lateness—that he depended on others for transportation—would not qualify as an "exceptional circumstance" under the precedent set by the BIA. I thought of blaming his nonattendance on his lawyer, but he had not filed notice to the court that he would be representing Philippe. While Philippe had understood that this attorney would help him, there was no written evidence of this agreement, and we could not prove that it was Philippe's lawyer's fault that he was late to court.

Because there were few other options, I recommended that Philippe and Adele get married and that she add Philippe to her asylum application as her dependent. This way, if Adele won her case, he would be granted derivative asylum status as the spouse of an asylee. It was a shame that he never had a chance to have his asylum claim heard by the judge, but at least Adele had a strong case. She was likely to win, either at the asylum office or in court, and then Philippe would be safe as well. They followed my advice and were soon married by a justice of the peace. Their marriage took place two weeks before Adele's asylum interview and two months after the birth of their son.

I also recommended that Philippe find another attorney to represent him, since the INS might still try to enforce the judge's removal order against him. At that time I was accredited to represent only those applicants whose cases were at the asylum office, not someone whose case was in court. I asked Joe Berra, an attorney at AYUDA, a nonprofit legal services agency in Washington, D.C., to take the case. I explained the situation to Joe, and after speaking to Adele and Philippe in person he agreed to represent Philippe.

1. *Matter of Grijalva,* Int. Dec. No. 3284 (BIA 1996).
2. *Matter of S-A-,* Int. Dec. 3331 (BIA 1997).

Since Philippe had been ordered removed from the United States, his file went to the INS Baltimore district office, and the Detention and Deportation division of that office began the process of deporting him to Cameroon. The INS sent Philippe a letter telling him to come to the INS district office in Baltimore at a specific date and time, ready to surrender himself so that he could be jailed while they arranged for his removal from the United States. Joe sent the INS a copy of their marriage certificate and Adele's asylum case and asked for a temporary stay of removal of Philippe's deportation while Adele's asylum case was being decided. The deportation officer insisted that he turn himself in anyway.

As it turned out, the day that Philippe was supposed to turn himself in was the same day that Adele's asylum interview was scheduled. He was supposed to come in the morning, but Joe told the deportation officer that he was needed as a possible witness at Adele's hearing and that he would have to come in the afternoon.

After Adele's interview, Joe came to the asylum office to drive Philippe, Adele, and the baby to the Baltimore INS office so that Philippe could turn himself in. By law, Philippe had to comply with the INS's requests, but Joe was hoping to convince the deportation officer not to detain Philippe, now that Adele had had her asylum interview and a decision would be forthcoming in two weeks. He also hoped that seeing Philippe with his wife and their newborn son would move the deportation officer to reconsider her decision to put Philippe in jail.

Joe's strategy was not successful. Philippe was taken to the Salisbury County Jail on the eastern shore of Maryland, a three-hour drive from Washington. He was imprisoned in a county jail, with American criminals, despite the fact that he had committed no crime. Philippe found the experience terrifying. He had been in jail before, in Cameroon, where he was beaten and tortured, and his new imprisonment brought back traumatic memories. He spoke only a little English and could not communicate well with the guards or the other prisoners. His second week there, one of the other prisoners told him to be careful, because his cellmate was in prison for having killed a man. He began to fear all the other prisoners, not knowing what violent crimes they might have committed.

Philippe felt afraid, but more than anything he was depressed. "In Cameroon, I knew why I was in jail. In the United States, I didn't know why. It didn't make sense—just thirty minutes late. If you are in good faith, if you try to get there on time, they should listen to you." Philippe was also depressed about his family. As a new father, he wanted to be a support for his wife and son, but instead he found himself a burden upon them.

In some parts of the United States, the INS operates its own detention facilities or pays private contractors to operate prisons that hold only immigration detainees. These facilities are not pleasant places, but at least asylum seekers are housed with other immigration detainees, not with criminals. The immigration jails are also held to certain federal standards for the quality of facilities, the availability of legal information, and access to medical care. In the Washington area, however, there are no INS prisons, so immigration detainees are held in county jails, where they are imprisoned with criminals and treated as criminals. Recently the INS has decided that county jails that hold INS detainees will be held to minimum standards, and these standards will be fully in place by the year 2003. At the time of Philippe's detention, however, there were no standards in existence for county jails' treatment of INS prisoners.

Adele could not call into the prison, and Philippe could only call out by placing a collect call. In-state collect calls cost eighty-nine cents per minute, so Adele soon ran up a large phone bill. She could not afford to pay it, and their phone service was disconnected.

Adele suffered also from Philippe's detention. "I had to be strong all the time—I had to work, I had to be there for the baby, I had to be there for Philippe. A new mother, she shouldn't have to work, the husband should do that while she stays home. I had to work, and I had to be strong for my husband. It was too much. I couldn't cry, I couldn't fall down, I couldn't give up. I had to be strong for the baby, too. If the mother is sad, the baby feels that, it's bad for the child." When I asked Adele how she stayed strong, she replied that "I prayed, all the time. I am not a religious person—I don't go to church much. But through this whole thing, I just prayed and prayed. It was my way of keeping myself going."

Meanwhile, Joe was working on Philippe's release from jail. Philippe did not have a passport, so the INS had asked the Cameroon embassy for travel documents for Philippe. It would take the Cameroon embassy a few weeks to provide them, but then Philippe would be deported. Joe applied for a stay of removal, which, if granted, would prevent the INS from deporting him. Adele paid the $150 fee for the stay of removal application, and she and Joe waited for the result.

An INS official adjudicates requests for a stay of removal, and there is no appeal of a negative decision to an immigration judge. Fearing that the INS would deny the request for a stay, or that the INS official would first approve the request but later change her mind, Joe decided also to file an application for protection under the newly ratified U.N. Convention Against Torture. Philippe qualified for protection under the treaty, and the application for Torture Convention protection formed a backup plan in case Adele's asylee relative petition did not succeed. More important, the INS had a policy at that time of granting an automatic stay of removal to any alien with a pending application for Torture Convention protection. As long as Philippe's application was still being considered, he could not be removed from the United States.

For Adele's part, it was not clear if she would be granted asylum; it was not even clear when a decision would be made. Philippe was arrested on the day of Adele's interview, and two weeks later when she went to pick up the decision, she was informed that a decision was not ready and that she would have to return for a second interview. The next week, Philippe's third week in detention, she came back for her second interview, where the asylum officer questioned her about the other person in the INS computer named Adele Fontem. Even after this interview, the INS did not issue a decision for several weeks. Finally, after I called and wrote them several times requesting a decision, Adele was sent her recommended approval notice in the mail.

Eventually Adele would have to file an asylee relative petition for Philippe, which, when approved, would give Philippe status and allow him to leave the jail. Normally, asylees file these kinds of petitions only for spouses and children who are outside the United States; spouses and children within the United States are usually included on the principal applicant's case and are granted asylum at the same time as the principal applicant. Even in situations where an asylum applicant marries while her case is pending, or where children are born after the application is filed, it is usually an easy administrative matter to add the new dependent to the case.

Philippe's situation was different. His immigration case was already under the jurisdiction of the immigration court, and the immigration court is considered a higher judicial authority than the INS. Since the court had ordered him deported, the asylum office could not, by itself, overrule the judge's decision by granting him derivative status as the spouse of an asylee. Adele would have to file an asylee relative petition with the INS. After it was granted, Philippe would have to file a motion to reopen his case with the judge, based on the new information—not available at the time of his first court hearing—that he had been granted derivative asylum status. The judge could then reopen Philippe's case and withdraw the order of deportation.

Even further procedural hurdles had to be cleared before this could happen. Adele had been granted only a "recommended approval" for asylum. This allowed her to apply for a work permit but did not allow her to file an asylee relative petition for Philippe. She would have to wait for her "final approval" for asylum, which would come only after the INS had sent her fingerprints to the FBI, and the FBI confirmed that she did not have a criminal record. It usually took several months for the FBI to run the fingerprint checks, and six months more for the INS to approve an asylee relative petition. Unless something was done, Philippe would languish in jail nine months or more before all the paperwork was finished—if he was not deported first.

After Adele's recommended approval letter arrived, Joe asked the INS to release Philippe from jail during the time it would take to complete processing the final approval and the asylee relative petition. Almost all applicants with recommended approvals passed the fingerprint check, and the approval of the asylee relative petition was almost certain. Despite this, the detention officer refused to let Philippe out of jail.

While Joe and I were confident that Philippe would succeed eventually, Adele and Philippe were not so sure. Joe and I had explained the law to them and had reassured them, but after what they had been through they did not feel confident about anything. They also depended on our help to a degree that I did not realize at the time. As Adele told me later, "When we first had these problems, a lot of people offered to help. None of them did anything—they would promise to help, then they would never call us. When we met you, you actually helped us—we had one person. Then we met Joe, and he helped us a lot—we had two people. But we always thought, what if they call us, and say, 'I'm sorry, I'm too busy, I can't continue with your case?' We would be lost."

It seemed certain that Philippe would be granted status through Adele's asylee relative petition. But he did have an order of deportation in force against him, and the INS could send him to Cameroon at any time. To prevent this, Joe had to continue to pursue Philippe's Torture Convention application, which brought with it an automatic stay of deportation.

Torture Convention cases were handled differently in 1998, when Philippe applied for protection, than in 1999, when Aster applied. Congress had still not passed implementing legislation, so the INS was adjudicating Torture Convention applications using an informal administrative procedure. The INS would consider applications only after an alien had exhausted all other remedies and appeals. Not many applications for Convention Against Torture protection were made during this period, since most of the people who would be eligible for this protection were also eligible for asylum. Only people like Philippe, who had been ordered deported during a hearing held in their absence, or Aster, who had a criminal conviction that rendered them ineligible for asylum, asked for protection under the convention. The INS rendered decisions on only a few of these applications and held most of them under consideration while they waited for Congress to pass implementing legislation.

A month after applying for Convention Against Torture protection, Philippe was given an interview. There was no set form or format for these interviews. Asylum officers asked questions similar to those that would be asked in an asylum interview, but they took more time, trying to ensure that the interview would address all possible concerns. After the interview, they typed up their notes and wrote an analysis, then passed the information to headquarters for a final decision.

The asylum office interview for Philippe's Torture Convention application took nearly eight hours. The interview covered most of the territory covered in an asylum interview but took much longer because the interview was more thorough. At each point the interviewer stopped and asked follow-up questions to make certain he understood Philippe's testimony. The interview was further delayed by the use of a telephone translator. The acoustics in the jail were bad, and the interview took place over a speakerphone, so the INS officer, the translator, and Philippe all had to speak slowly and ask each other to repeat their words often. It took a long time to set up the speakerphone equipment and the computer before the interview, and there was a break for lunch in the middle of the day.

The asylum officer sent his notes and analysis to INS headquarters but could not tell Joe and Philippe what the decision might be. Meanwhile, Joe had continued to push the INS to move quickly to process Adele's fingerprints and issue a final grant of asylum for her. The district office worked quickly on the fingerprints, and Adele was given a final grant of asylum two months after her recommended approval. Joe then helped her file an asylee relative petition for Philippe. He also asked the INS office in charge of asylee relative petitions to expedite processing. It normally takes the INS six months to process a petition, but they can approve a petition within two months if they expedite the application.

When Adele's final approval was granted, Joe asked the detention officer to release Philippe from prison. The detention officer refused and insisted upon waiting for the approval of Adele's asylee relative petition. Philippe had already been incarcerated two months when Adele's final approval came through, and he faced another wait of at least two months, perhaps as many as six months, before he would be released. Philippe was depressed, was losing weight, and was having nightmares in jail recalling his experience in prison in Cameroon. Joe tried to get a psychologist to visit him in jail, both to counsel him and to write a report on Philippe's psychological state which Joe could use in his parole request, but the psychologist wanted to charge a fee of $750, and Adele could not pay this. She had already run up over $1000 in telephone bills, talking to Philippe from the jail.

Joe lost patience with the INS and turned from polite requests to threats. He called the detention officer, her supervisor, and the district director, and threatened to report on Philippe and Adele's situation to the press. Within days, he threatened, the *Washington Post* would run a story on a mother and father separated by the INS's arbitrary detention policies, complete with photographs of the weeping mother holding her infant son. The INS decided to release Philippe from jail.

The INS called the jail to arrange for Philippe's release, and he was let out of jail early in the evening. The INS did not, however, tell Joe or Adele about Philippe's release until the next morning. Philippe found himself stranded in Salisbury, Maryland, two hundred miles from home, with no money. He could not call his wife because their phone service had been cut off, and he could not call Joe at work because it was after 5:00 and the office was closed.

Philippe walked from the jail to the town and wandered around, wondering what to do. He found a Salvation Army office that was still open, and managed, in his limited English, to explain his problem to the person working there. He was allowed to spend the night in a back room of the office. The next day he called Joe, who arranged to have someone pick him up in Salisbury. After two months of detention, he was finally reunited with his wife and son.

He was free from prison but had certain conditions placed upon his release. He had to come to the INS District Office once a month to sign a log, assuring them that he still lived in the area. He had to inform the district office of any change of address, and he could not travel outside the Washington/Baltimore area without permission. The district office did give him a work permit, which he could use until he had permanent legal status as a derivative asylee. He continued to sign in once a month for the next three months, until the asylee relative petition that Adele had filed for him was finally approved.

What is striking in Philippe's case is not just the extent of his suffering but the uselessness of it. Why did the judge order Philippe deported when he was an hour late to his hearing? Why are judges, and the BIA, so unforgivingly strict in their application of the rules on attending hearings? Why did the INS insist on putting him in prison and not release him until threatened with adverse media attention?

Many of the procedural rules in immigration hearings, including the rules about nonattendance at hearings, are strict because of past abuses of more lenient rules. In immigration law, when an alien is fighting deportation, any delay in being deported is itself a victory. If aliens could skip hearings and then reopen their cases without penalty, some would do so, gaining time and postponing their deportation. The stiff penalty for not being present at a hearing, and the limited circumstances that justify nonattendance, are meant to discourage this kind of delay tactic.

But these strict rules do not take into account the difficulties that asylum applicants have in finding transportation to their immigration hearings. Asylum applicants, who are not legally allowed to work, depend on others for food, shelter, and transportation. Some of them must travel miles to get to immigration court for their jurisdiction. Asylum applicants who live in North Carolina, for example, must go to Atlanta, Georgia, for their hearings. They depend on relatives, friends, or even strangers to transport them to court, and these people may not take the asylum proceedings as seriously as the applicants do.

Given this situation, judges should be flexible in accounting for the fact that some applicants arrive late to their hearings. During a master calendar hearing, a judge might see as many as twenty aliens in the course of a three-hour court session. Some judges allow for lateness, first seeing the aliens who are present and holding time at the end of the session for latecomers.

In Philippe's case, the judge conducted Philippe's hearing even though Philippe was not there yet, without waiting to see if he would arrive late. He did this even though there were other aliens who had already arrived, whose cases he could have heard first. Why did he do this? Judges have large caseloads, and some judges look for any excuse to reduce their docket. Since an alien who is late for his hearing is technically absent when called, a judge can complete his case in five minutes, take the case off his docket, and not have to think about it again.

Also, many of the immigration judges were INS trial attorneys before they were immigration judges. As trial attorneys, their job was to see to it that aliens were successfully deported, and many of the judges still have an "enforcement" mentality. Judges with INS experience are skeptical of and unsympathetic to the claims of undocumented aliens to asylum status. A judge who is already skeptical of asylum seekers is particularly likely to order an alien deported *in absentia*.

While this may explain the judge's ruling against Philippe, it does not explain why the INS kept Philippe in jail even after it was obvious that he would be granted legal status through his wife. I attempted to interview the Baltimore district office for this book, but they could not consent to be interviewed, so I could not find out about their policy on detention and parole decisions.

It is difficult to discuss the INS's general decision-making practice for detaining aliens, because this practice varies widely among INS districts.[3] Whether an alien is released on parole depends more on the personality of the district's director and detention officers than on an alien's individual case. In the Washington district, which includes Virginia and the District of Columbia, most asylum applicants are released while they await a final decision, provided they have a place to go to. If Philippe and Adele had lived in Virginia, Philippe would almost certainly never have been arrested in the first place, and he almost certainly would have been released as soon as Adele's recommended approval was issued. In the Maryland district, the district director seems to leave decisions to the discretion of individual detention officers, so that some aliens are released, others are not. Other districts vary—the New York district director, for example, almost never grants pa-

---

3. See "Refugees Behind Bars: The Imprisonment of Asylum Seekers in the Wake of the 1996 Immigration Act," Lawyers Committee for Human Rights, August 1999.

role to asylum applicants and many advocates suspect he uses detention as a tool to discourage aliens from applying for asylum.

Adele and Philippe suspect that the INS was so strict in their case for several reasons particular to their situation. Adele told me that the INS always had doubts about the authenticity of their marriage, given that they did not marry until after Philippe had received a final order of deportation. Furthermore, at the time of Philippe's incarceration, her asylum application had not been approved, so it was not clear whether she would be able to file an asylee relative petition for him. After he had been arrested, the INS officials were afraid to take responsibility for his release. If they released Philippe, and then Adele was not given a final approval or the asylee relative petition was not granted, Philippe would almost certainly run away. The possibility of either of these events occurring was small, but it was a risk that no INS officer was willing to assume. Only when not releasing him also became risky, because of Joe's threat to call the media, did the Baltimore district office let Philippe out of jail.

Of course, the arbitrary nature of parole decisions is not only the fault of individual INS officers. The real problem is the fact that there is no coherent system and no appeals process for parole decisions. Before 1996, many parole decisions were made by immigration judges and could be appealed, but the 1996 law took the power to make parole decisions in most cases away from judges. Individual detention officers are reluctant to parole asylum seekers, fearing they will be blamed if the asylum applicant does not appear for his or her hearing.

INS headquarters has issued general guidelines on how INS district offices should make parole decisions, but it does not intervene when district directors do not follow these guidelines. There is no way a detainee can appeal a parole decision, either to INS headquarters or to the immigration court. Even in New York, where the district director defies INS policy by almost never granting parole, INS headquarters has done little to make him change his behavior. Until Congress allows aliens' parole requests to be heard by judges, and for adverse decisions to be appealed, asylum seekers will continue to suffer from the INS's arbitrary and inhuman policy of detention.

Aster Cheru

Aster passed her "reasonable fear" screening interview in July 1999 and was released from jail in August. Her first court hearing did not take place until November. The judge reviewed her file, asked her if she still wished to apply for restriction on removal and protection under the Convention Against Torture, and then set another master calendar hearing for January. Apparently either the court or the INS had not had time to get all her documents ready to process her case.

In January the court held the second master calendar hearing and gave Aster an individual hearing date in May 2000. We asked for an earlier date, but the judge could not give us one. By law, the court must give priority on its calendar to newly filed cases, those which the court is supposed to adjudicate within 180 days. The first hearing time that the judge had on his calendar for a nonpriority case was May.

We asked for an earlier date because Aster's uncertain immigration status was preventing her from regaining custody of her children. Aster had two custody cases in court—one for her daughter, Beth, who was in foster care, and one for her sons, Joseph and John, who were living with their father. When Aster was released from jail in August, I had told the lawyers and social workers responsible for Aster's children that the judge would probably rule on Aster's immigration status before the end of 1999. Accordingly, both family court judges decided to wait on making a final decision on custody until November. When Aster's master calendar hearing was rescheduled to January, the family court judges decided to wait again, and then they decided to continue to wait until Aster's individual hearing in May.

Aster and I were disappointed that we would have to wait so long for her individual hearing, but it gave us plenty of time to prepare and there was much to do. Her original asylum application was full of errors, so we wrote a new one, with a complete account of her political activities in Ethiopia and the persecution she and her relatives had suffered. We then compared this version of her story with that contained in the asylum officer's notes from the "reasonable fear" interview, in order to be ready to explain any inconsistencies between them. We prepared to explain to the court why her original asylum application was not correct. Finally, we practiced for Aster's oral testimony in court, guarding against the possibility that she would become nervous on the witness stand and forget or misstate the facts of her story.

We also needed to address Aster's eligibility for "restriction of removal" status after having been convicted of a crime considered an "aggravated felony." The law states that any person convicted of an aggravated felony is not eligible for asylum and that any person convicted of a "particularly serious crime" is not eligible for restriction of removal. The law defines the term "aggravated felony" but does not define the term "particularly serious crime."

By not defining "particularly serious crime," the law left this definition up to the courts. Since 1996 the Board of Immigration Appeals has issued a number of precedent decisions that have defined this term. In *Matter of Q-T-M-T-*[4] and *Matter of S-S-,*[5] the board ruled that not all aggravated felonies are to be considered "particularly serious crimes." In cases where an alien had been convicted of an aggravated felony or felonies where the combined sentence was five years or more, the alien would be considered to have been convicted of a particularly serious crime and would not be eligible for restriction on removal. If the sentences imposed totaled less than five years, judges would have to decide on a case-by-case basis whether the crime was "particularly serious." In making this decision, the BIA stated, judges should consider whether the alien had rehabilitated and was still a danger to the community.

Other BIA precedents decided whether certain criminal convictions were "particularly serious" ones that would prevent an alien from being granted restriction of removal. The BIA ruled that crimes such as robbery with a deadly weapon,[6] aggravated battery,[7] drug trafficking,[8] and possession of heroin with intent to

4. Int. Dec. 3100 (BIA 1996).
5. Int. Dec. 3374 (BIA 1999).
6. *Matter of L-S-J-*, Int. Dec. 3322 (BIA 1997).
7. *Matter of K-*, 20 I&N Dec. 427 (BIA 1991).
8. *Matter of U-M-*, 20 I&N Dec. 327 (BIA 1991).

deliver[9] were all "particularly serious" crimes. Crimes such as helping a single undocumented alien enter the United States illegally,[1] simple possession of cocaine,[2] and most single convictions for a misdemeanor offense[3] were not "particularly serious."

I was able to use these arguments to support Aster's claim that her crime was not so serious that it would disqualify her from receiving restriction on removal. Since the BIA cited that some of the factors involved in making this decision would include whether the alien had rehabilitated or whether the alien was still a danger to the community, I included many details about the circumstances that caused Aster to shoplift, her interactions with social workers afterward, and how she had reformed since that time. I even asked her family counselor to write an affidavit or to testify at the hearing.

I included all this evidence to show that Aster was not a "danger to the community," but I also wanted to play on the judge's sympathies. In theory, once a determination was made as to whether shoplifting was a particularly serious crime, the judge would turn to the question of Aster's fear of persecution in her home country. The only determining issue should have been the probability that Aster would be persecuted if she were to return to Ethiopia. But judges are human beings, and hearing details about Aster's husband's physical abuse of her and attempted sexual abuse of her daughter might encourage the judge to give Aster's case a more sympathetic hearing.

Even if the judge ruled that Aster had committed a particularly serious crime that prevented her from being granted restriction on removal, she would still be eligible for protection under the U.N. Convention Against Torture. The INS had formulated regulations implementing the Torture Convention, and these regulations created a new status called "deferral of removal," which was available to aliens convicted of particularly serious crimes. Under "deferral of removal," an alien who proved there was a

9. *Matter of Gonzalez,* 19 I&N Dec. 682 (BIA 1991).
1. *Matter of L-S-,* Int. Dec. 3386 (BIA 1999).
2. *Matter of Toboso-Alfonso,* 20 I&N Dec. 819 (BIA 1990).
3. *Matter of Juarez,* 19 I&N Dec. 664 (BIA 1988).

probability that she would be tortured in her home country would not be deported and would be eligible, at the discretion of the INS, for parole from detention and a work permit. Since the INS could still choose to detain an alien with deferral of removal status, this status was not as favorable as restriction on removal.

After writing a brief arguing that Aster's crime was not a particularly serious one, I turned to the second issue in her case: proving the probability that Aster would be persecuted or tortured if she were forced to return to Ethiopia. The standard for restriction on removal and deferral of removal is higher than the standard for asylum cases—under restriction and deferral, aliens must show there is a probability, or more than a 50 percent chance, they would be persecuted or tortured if returned to their home country. For asylum, applicants must show only that there is a "reasonable possibility" of persecution, which the Supreme Court has stated can be as little as a 10 percent chance of persecution.[4]

While it is difficult to prove that an applicant would probably be persecuted upon return to his or her country, it is quite possible to prove this if the applicant has been persecuted in the past. The BIA has ruled that where an applicant can prove past persecution, judges should presume that there will be persecution in the future. At the time of Aster's hearing, the law stated that this presumption could be rebutted only by evidence that country conditions had changed.[5]

Because the regime whose agents had imprisoned and tortured Aster was still in power in Ethiopia, the court would almost certainly agree with our assertion that country conditions had not changed and that Aster would still be persecuted if she were to return. I submitted evidence—reports from Amnesty International, Human Rights Watch, and other sources—to show that the Ethiopian government had not changed its ways since 1991, when Aster had been imprisoned. The same party still ruled the country, and its leadership continued to torture and murder political oppo-

4. *INS v. Cardoza-Fonseca*, 480 U.S. 421 (1987).
5. *Matter of Chen*, 20 I&N Dec. 16 (BIA 1989), and 8 CFR 208.13(b)(1). On December 6, 2000, the INS changed the law by issuing regulations stating that the presumption could be rebutted by evidence of a "fundamental change in circumstances." This issue is discussed in more detail in Chapter Ten.

nents. The government had held elections in 1994, but these were widely considered to be fraudulent; the government had outlawed the most prominent opposition party before the elections and harassed the others to the point where they could not effectively function.

The last element we had to prove in Aster's case was past persecution. Unfortunately we had no documentary evidence of Aster's arrest and imprisonment, and there were no witnesses to her torture who would be willing to testify on her behalf. Most of her family were dead. The few surviving members of her family were still in Ethiopia, so they could not testify. As in most asylum cases, Aster's own testimony would be the most important evidence in her case. Aster would have to tell her story to the judge at the hearing, and she would have to convince the judge that her story was true.

Judges evaluate the credibility of asylum applicants' stories in the same way that asylum officers do. They assess whether the testimony is detailed, plausible, internally consistent, and consistent with the documentary evidence about the applicant's home country. With victims of severe trauma, the requirement that testimony be detailed creates some problems. For example, before telling me about it, Aster had never told anyone about her rape in prison. If she were to testify about the rape at her hearing without having talked about it before the hearing itself, it was possible that she would break down on the witness stand and be unable to talk about the rape in detail. She might even refuse to mention the rape at all. To prevent this from happening, we had to practice her testimony about the rape and torture before the hearing itself.

We also had to watch to make sure that her oral testimony on the day of the hearing was consistent with the written versions of her story. By the time of her hearing, the judge would have three versions of her story already in the file—the story that was written in her original asylum application, filed in 1992, the story that was presented in the INS officer's notes from the "reasonable fear" hearing, and the story that she presented in the written statement that we had filed shortly before the hearing. The judge would compare these three stories with her oral testimony to see if the versions were consistent.

There was nothing we could do about the fact that her original application for asylum did not contain her true story. We could only explain the circumstances under which she had signed the form—that her husband had filled it out and told her to sign it, and that she did not speak or read English well enough at that time to know what she was signing. Since this happened often with asylum claims, we could hope that the judge would be sympathetic, provided that the testimony she gave later was detailed and consistent. It was much more important to ensure that the three later versions of her story all agreed.

While Aster's own testimony was the most important evidence, we looked for other forms of evidence that could corroborate her claim. I included a number of human rights reports in her case, to show the judge that it was not unusual for a person of her political background and activities to be arrested and tortured for her political opinion. I sent an intern to look for information about her brothers' death in any of the English-language publications in the Africa Reading Room of the Library of Congress, but she could not find anything. She did, however, find an article that mentioned Aster's brother's name and official title in connection with an economic report on Ethiopia. At least we could show the judge that Aster's brother did in fact hold a high position within the Ethiopian civil service at one time.

I also sent Aster to a doctor, so she could get a report describing her scars from torture. She had a large scar on her groin where she had been stabbed by one of the government soldiers who had raped her; she had scars on her wrists from being tied tightly; and she had scars on her legs from being beaten. Scars can be ambiguous evidence in that they can be caused by torture or by ordinary accidents or criminal assaults. In Aster's case, however, the type and location of the scars were particularly indicative of torture. It is unusual to have scars on one's calves and feet, and scars around the wrists indicate cuts or abrasions from ropes or handcuffs. The scars on her groin corroborated her story of being raped and stabbed. The doctor's report described the size and location of the scars and also stated that, in the doctor's expert medical opinion, the appearance of the scars was consistent with Aster's statements about how and when her wounds were inflicted.

Finally, I asked two of the social workers and counselors who worked with Aster to write letters to the court, describing what she had told them about her life in Ethiopia during their counseling sessions. While Aster could have been fabricating a story about persecution to the judge simply to win her immigration case, it would be quite surprising if Aster had fabricated a story to a social worker over the course of counseling sessions for a period of six years. The counselors' testimony about Aster's previous statements to them acted as strong corroborative evidence to her story.

After assembling all this information, I submitted it to the court ten days before the hearing, as the rules require. I contacted the INS attorney the week before the hearing to discuss the case informally and to see if she would be willing to concede all or part of the case, given the strong evidence in the record in Aster's favor. The INS attorney did not call me back, and I later learned that she had been out of the office all that week. Aster and I went to court prepared to argue every aspect of her case.

Immigration court hearings are nerve-wracking experiences, both for asylum applicants and for their representatives. To some extent I enjoy the pressure, the adrenaline rush, and the on-stage feeling that goes with them, but the experience is stressful and the stakes are high. Losing a case at the asylum office just leads to a referral to court, but losing a case in court leads to a deportation order being issued.

Representing a case in court is very different from representing a case at the asylum office. At asylum office interviews, the applicant's representative can do little and is usually restricted to observing, taking notes, and then offering a short statement at the end. By contrast, in court the representative is actively involved almost the entire time, asking questions to witnesses and making arguments to the judge. Even when the government attorney is asking questions, the applicant's attorney must listen closely, making notes of problems that arise and objecting to inappropriate questions. The stakes are higher, and the chances of winning are smaller. Many immigration judges in the Washington and Baltimore area are unsympathetic to asylum seekers and often deny even strong asylum cases. A judge's denial of an asylum case may be appealed, but because of the large number of cases pending at the Board of Immigration Appeals, it usually takes three years for the BIA to issue a decision on an appeal.

The pressure to win in court is particularly high where an asylum applicant's individual hearing is scheduled within 180 days of the filing date of the application for asylum. If the judge denies the case within that 180-day period, the asylum applicant cannot get a work permit even while the case is on appeal. The applicant can stay in the United States during the three years the case is on appeal, but cannot work legally. The asylum seeker must find some way to survive, either by depending on friends and relatives or by working illegally while the appeal is pending.

In Aster's case, at least she had a work permit, which she could continue to use while her case was on appeal. In theory the INS could choose to put her back in jail during the time of her appeal, but in practice this was very unlikely. The INS would have had to pay for her to be detained, and, given that her story had already been featured in one newspaper article, they would fear further bad publicity. Still, detention was always a risk for Aster. After all, it had made no sense for the INS to detain Philippe, but they had done so; there was no way to be certain that the INS would not make the same irrational and cruel decision in Aster's case.

Aster's hearing was scheduled for 2:00 p.m., and I arrived at the court thirty minutes before the hearing. Aster was already there; she was so nervous that she had arrived two and a half hours early. The guard unlocked the courtroom at 1:50, and we went in. The court interpreter arrived a few minutes later. The court employs its own full-time Spanish interpreter but hires interpreters from the Berlitz translation service on a part-time basis for other languages. This interpreter was an older man, very polite, who had lived in the United States for almost twenty years. Aster was suspicious of him because he was from the Tigrean ethnic group, the same group that now controls the Ethiopian government. Aster told me that some of these translators worked as informers for the Ethiopian government, and she was afraid to speak freely in front of him. I could not reassure her because I knew that the courts do not screen the interpreters they hire from Berlitz. It was unlikely that he was an informer, but it was possible. I could only tell her that she had no choice but to continue with this interpreter, because the rules of the court did not allow her to choose the ethnic background of her interpreter or to provide an interpreter herself.

The INS lawyer arrived a few minutes later, and I talked to her briefly before the hearing began. She had not looked at the case closely, and she would not agree to concede any part of the case. I tried at least to get her to agree that Aster had not committed a "particularly serious crime" and was thus eligible for restriction on removal. She declined to do this. She said that the case law established a presumption that an aggravated felony was a particularly serious crime, and we would have to rebut that presumption; she thought it would be difficult for us to win on that point. She did say that if the judge decided on his own that Aster's crime was not a "particularly serious" one, that she would not contest the judge's decision.

The judge, Christopher M. Grant, opened the proceedings by starting the courtroom tape recorder and speaking into it, giving Aster's name, alien number, and the date and location of the hearing. There are no stenographers at immigration court, so a tape recorder is used to make a record of the proceedings. After the judge makes his decision, both parties have thirty days to appeal. If neither party appeals, a transcript is not necessary and the judge's written order becomes the only record of what occurred during the hearing. If either party appeals, the tape is sent to a transcriber and the testimony recorded during the hearing is turned into a written transcript. Since many immigration court decisions are not appealed, this procedure saves money in many cases.

The judge asked me to "enter my appearance" for the respondent on tape, and I stated my name. The INS attorney stated her name as well. The judge reviewed the documents that were on the record, labeling them on the tape as "Exhibit One," "Exhibit Two," and so on. He then turned off the tape and talked to us briefly off the record.

The judge said that he had read my brief and studied the evidence relating to Aster's criminal conviction. He stated that the brief and the evidence were extensive and persuasive, and he was very likely to find that her crime was not a "particularly serious" one, making her eligible for restriction on removal. He asked the INS lawyer if she had any objections, and she said that she had not seen the brief that he was referring to. He described the packet of materials that I had submitted ten days before, and she rummaged around in her case file, looking for them. Her file for Aster was several inches thick, so she had to spend a minute looking through it; still, she could not find the document packet.

The judge concluded that since I had submitted the documents exactly ten days before the hearing, it was possible that the clerical staff at the INS District Office had not placed the document packet in the file. While this was the INS's error, in the interest of fairness he called a ten-minute recess so that the government's lawyer could look through the evidence I had submitted. I loaned her my own copy of the brief and documents packet to look through, and I left the room with Aster to explain to her what was going on.

We had just left the courtroom and closed the door when Aster grabbed me and hugged me. While the judge had spoken in technical language, she had understood that the judge was inclined to treat her criminal offense as not serious. She had been worried about this, much more worried than I had realized; since her criminal offense had caused her to be detained, and almost deported, the year before, she still saw her criminal offense as the most difficult element in her case. I knew that the most important issue was whether the judge believed her to be a victim of past persecution. If he did not believe that part of the case, his opinion on her criminal offense would not matter.

Still, the judge's statement represented a victory and boosted our morale at the start of the hearing. It helped us in another way too, because not having to argue this part of the case freed up time for us to go through her testimony about persecution in Ethiopia in greater detail. The best news of all was that the INS attorney had not seen any of the documentation in her case. She had obviously not seen the case before today, and had not had time to read any of the documents thoroughly. Being unprepared, it would be difficult for her even to follow the proceeding, and unlikely that she would be able to catch Aster on inconsistencies or make an effective argument against her claim.[6]

When we returned to the courtroom, the judge asked me if I had an opening statement to make, and I responded that I would rather give as much time as I could to Aster's testimony. The judge then stated that he would find in his decision that Aster's crime was not "particularly serious," and that she was therefore eligible for restriction on removal. He again asked the INS lawyer if she opposed this decision, and she stated that INS was willing to follow his decision in the matter. The judge said he would take her statement to mean that INS would not appeal this part of his decision, and that he would not, therefore, need to elaborate on his reasons for finding in Aster's favor.

The judge swore Aster in and then explained to her in detail what he expected of her. He advised her to tell the truth, to ask for clarification when she did not understand a question, and not to guess when she did not know the answer to a question. He told her that she might not remember some facts or know why things occurred, particularly in regards to things that had happened to her family while she was still a child. Aster began to cry when he mentioned this, before she had even begun to testify. The judge told her that he understood that some of her testimony might be painful to recount, and he realized that because the interpreter, her representative, and the judge himself were all men, it might be difficult for her to talk about some of the things that had happened to her.

I began by asking Aster about her date of birth, her family background, her father's occupation, and the current location of her parents and siblings. I questioned her about each family mem-

6. This is a fairly common occurrence. The INS district counsel's office is underfunded and understaffed, and trial attorneys often have no time to read case files before going to court. This often works to asylum applicants' advantage, but it can be harmful as well. It is common practice, in most court settings, for the attorneys for both sides to meet before the hearing and discuss the case, looking for points of agreement and settling them out of court. As it is usually not possible to do this with the INS attorneys, it is necessary to contest every aspect of the case in court.

ber, individually, and their manner of death. Of all of Aster's family, only her sister was still alive and in contact with Aster—one of her brothers had fled Ethiopia in the 1970s, but Aster no longer knew where he was. The judge interrupted occasionally to ask his own questions. The judge has the right to speak at any point in the proceedings, and his interruptions were a welcome development—they indicated that he was paying attention and was interested in her testimony.

Aster testified about her brothers, whom the Ethiopian government sought to arrest on the grounds that they were members of the Ethiopian People's Revolutionary Party (EPRP). The judge interrupted to ask why, if Aster's father had been a wealthy landowner, her brothers would join a Communist party whose main platform was the redistribution of wealth and land. Aster explained that the EPRP was very popular with young people at the time, and that young people, rich or poor, had opposed Emperor Haile Selassie. The EPRP was also the only viable opposition to the ruling Dergue party, and they may have sided with the EPRP because of their opposition to the government, which had killed their father.

Aster recounted the story of her life through her arrival in Addis Ababa and her appointment to the position of vice president of the local Women's Association. While we had emphasized, in the written statement, the Women's Association's role in distributing government propaganda, Aster stated in her testimony that the Women's Association's activities consisted of advocating for women's needs and helping women resolve problems with each other and with their families. Aster either forgot about this part of her job or did not wish to talk about it, possibly because she wanted to show the judge that she did not like the Dergue and did not support their policies.

I did not want Aster's testimony to seem inconsistent, so I asked some follow-up questions. I asked Aster to list her duties with the Women's Association, and she did, but still she did not mention her political duties. I asked her if there was anything else that she did, but she replied that that was everything. Since one cannot ask leading questions during direct examination, I could not ask her a question such as, "Did you distribute government propaganda?" I left the subject for the time being and wrote a note to myself to return to it later, if necessary.

I then asked Aster about her political activity after the Ethiopian People's Revolutionary Democratic Front (EPRDF) took over the government in 1991. She had participated in two demonstrations, one to protest the government's changing the Ethiopian flag, and the other to protest the government's allowing a referendum on the secession of Eritrea. Again the judge broke in to ask her some questions, because he did not understand her motivations for her political activities. He thought it was strange that she was so attached to the Ethiopian flag when the government represented by that flag had killed her father and brother. It took some time for her to explain herself, but Aster finally made it clear that she saw the flag as representing the Ethiopian nation, or people, not the Ethiopian government. While she had always opposed the Dergue government, she saw the flag as a symbol of the Ethiopian nation and heritage. Similarly, she saw the new government's decision to allow Eritrea to secede as unpatriotic, as it diminished the territory and population of the country. For her, the flag issue and the Eritrean issue were connected—the new rulers' lack of respect for the flag mirrored their lack of respect for Ethiopia's territorial integrity.

Aster then talked about how she had encouraged women from her neighborhood to participate in political activities. She wanted to help start a political party that would transcend ethnic divisions, and she thought the best way to do this was to bring back the EPRP. She described the new government's policy of allowing only ethnically based political parties to form as "undemocratic." The judge interrupted again to question her on this point. He stated that the new government was allowing ethnically based organizations to form whereas the Dergue government had allowed no independent organizations. Wasn't the new government therefore more democratic than its predecessor? It took some time for Aster to understand his point, but once she did, she could explain herself. The new government was "undemocratic" because it limited the kinds of parties that could form, instead of allowing citizens to associate and express themselves freely. The ethnically based parties would encourage division among the government's opponents, and only a multi-ethnic party, like the EPRP, would be able to mount an effect challenge to the new government. The government's policy of allowing ethnically based parties was only an attempt to divide the opposition and render it ineffective.

The judge also asked her about the EPRP. "Do you know that the EPRP is a Communist organization? Were you trying to bring a Communist government to Ethiopia?" Aster answered that she knew the EPRP had been Communist, but she thought it had changed. She had been working only in the neighborhood and had no contact with the EPRP's leadership, most of whom were living outside Ethiopia at the time. She wanted to start the EPRP again because she remembered it from her childhood as being a powerful opposition party. It had been outlawed for almost fifteen years, and she had only a vague idea of what it stood for. The main political issues of interest to her were the Ethiopian flag, Ethiopia's territorial integrity, and the importance of making a transition to a truly democratic system of government.

The judge also asked her about the use of force. He told her that the EPRP had taken up arms against the new government in July 1991 and was still fighting an armed insurrection. "Did you know about the EPRP's insurrection? Did you support it?" Aster answered that she had had little to do with politics after coming to the United States, and did not know much about what the EPRP had done since 1991. He asked her if she had engaged in violence during any of the demonstrations she attended, and she answered that she had not.

Aster then talked about her arrest, detention, and torture. The judge had fewer questions here and allowed her to tell her story in her own words and her own time. He did ask why she was arrested and whether the security people knew about her political activities and background with the neighborhood Women's Association. The judge seemed surprised that she had talked back to her interrogators, since by doing so she had brought severe torture upon herself.

Aster replied that when she was arrested, the EPRDF soldiers did not accuse her of anything specific but simply told her to tell them her life story and the history of her political activity. When she refused, they did not ask more specific questions or accuse her of specific activities, they just insisted that she tell them what she had done. Later, in prison, her interrogators threatened her, beat her, tortured her, and raped her, but they did not accuse her of anything specific. She did not tell them anything, except for the one time when she lost her temper and accused the EPRDF of being worse than the Dergue. It was clear that the security agents suspected her of being a political enemy, but she did not know what exactly they suspected she had done.

As Aster spoke, I compared her oral testimony with the written version of her story. Her oral testimony matched her written statements on most points, but there were a few exceptions. In her written statement she talked about the political nature of her work with the Women's Association; at the hearing she seemed to want to avoid talking about this and talked only about the nonpolitical aspects of her work as vice-president. In her oral testimony she said that while in prison she had been kept in a small cell with forty other women. This contradicted her written statement, which said there were only ten other women in her cell. In her oral testimony during her second interrogation session, the interrogator had told the guards that Aster was a relative of former dictator Mengistu. In her written statement, Aster had said that the interrogator had said this during the first interrogation.

Other than these minor points, there were no inconsistencies between her written statement and her oral testimony. I noted these inconsistencies in her file so that I would remember to ask her about them during redirect, if the INS lawyer did not do so herself. I could tell from the judge's facial expression and reactions while Aster was speaking that he had noticed the inconsistencies, so it would not be a good idea just to ignore them.

It seemed, however, that the INS lawyer had not noticed these inconsistencies. During the ten-minute recess she had looked at a copy of the legal brief and supporting documents, but I had not given her a copy of Aster's written statement. About one and a half hours into Aster's testimony, she realized that the judge and I were referring to a written statement that she did not have, and she asked the judge for a copy. He gave her a five-minute recess so that she could make a copy of the statement herself.

When we returned from the recess, it was 4:40, and the INS attorney told the judge that she could not stay later than 5:00 because of a doctor's appointment. The judge gave us an appointment to return in three weeks, the earliest time he could find on his calendar, when I would finish my direct questioning and the INS attorney would have time to cross-examine Aster. I continued to question Aster until 5:00. She explained the circumstances surrounding the death of her brother, Dawit, and the judge asked us to provide some independent evidence of the event. He either wanted to speak to a witness, someone who had been in Ethiopia at the time of Dawit's death and had knowledge of it, or he wanted to see a newspaper record of the event. We had three weeks to find this information and could submit the new evidence at the rescheduled hearing.

In the time between the first and the second hearings I sent a student volunteer, who spoke and read Amharic, to the Library of Congress to look for newspaper articles that mentioned Dawit's death. The volunteer spent two afternoons at the library but found nothing. The Library of Congress carries English-language journals that report on African politics, but the death of a civil servant was not important enough news for one of these journals to report. The library also had Ethiopian newspapers, but these were not indexed, so to find an article about Aster's brother would involve searching through all the newspapers from 1993, one by one. We had to give up the possibility of finding documentary evidence to confirm the fact of Dawit's death.

We were ready for the second hearing when, three days before it, the INS attorney filed an "emergency" motion to reschedule the hearing again. She had another doctor's appointment on the day of the hearing. I opposed her motion, arguing that Aster had waited long enough and that the INS could send another lawyer. The judge accommodated both sides by granting the motion but setting a new hearing date only three days later.

Aster and I went to court on the rescheduled date and found that the INS lawyer who had originally been assigned to the case was not there; the district office had sent another attorney in her place. This attorney not only did not know anything about the case, she did not even have a copy of the case with her. She asked me if she could look at my copy, or if I could tell her about the case, but I refused. Since the INS did not cooperate with me earlier, when I asked them to stipulate that shoplifting was not a "particularly serious crime," I saw no reason to cooperate with them now. Their lack of preparation would work to our advantage.

I finished my last few questions to Aster, and then it was the INS's turn to cross-examine her. Since the new attorney had not read the first attorney's notes and knew nothing about the case, she could not ask effective questions. The judge intervened and began to ask Aster the same questions that I had asked her earlier, so that the INS attorney would be able to follow the general outline of Aster's story. He questioned her for almost thirty minutes, going through most of her story. This enhanced Aster's credibility with the judge, since her answers were consistent with the testimony she had given before.

The INS attorney then went through her cross-examination. She followed the standard practice for cross-examination at asylum hearings, looking for inconsistencies between the applicant's oral testimony and written statement, and between written statements made at different times. This was difficult to do without the written file, but she did know that Aster had two asylum applications, one from 1992 and another made from jail in 1999, and she guessed that they did not agree. She asked Aster who had written her first application for asylum, and if she had understood what was written on it. Aster explained that the lawyer who prepared the first application did not speak Amharic, and that she did not speak much English at the time. She had relied on her husband to translate for her, and he had not read the application back to her in Amharic. She did not know what it said until she looked at it again years later, after she had learned how to speak and read English.

The INS attorney then asked her questions about her problems in Ethiopia, particularly how she learned of her brother's death given that she was not in the country when it happened. Aster explained how her sister had told her about their brother's death, and how her sister said that it was widely rumored in Ethiopia that their brother had been murdered. Since the television news and newspapers never showed the wrecked car, and since their brother's body was never returned to the family, the rumors seemed to have some basis.

The INS attorney asked how Aster managed to hide in Ethiopia after she escaped from jail, and if the Ethiopian government had looked for her. Aster answered that since she was staying in a distant city where she had no relatives, the government did not think to look for her there. She did not know if the security forces had looked for her at her house. The INS attorney also asked how Aster managed to get a passport and exit visa to leave Ethiopia, given that she was a political suspect who had escaped from jail. Aster explained that her brother had used government connections and bribes to get her permission to leave the country. The INS attorney asked, "Did you have any problems at the airport when leaving Ethiopia?" "No, my brother arranged everything. I was very scared, but nothing happened."

"Did you renew your Ethiopian passport after coming to the U.S.?" "No." "Have you continued your political activity in the United States." "No." "Why not?" Aster answered that at first she did not know much about Ethiopian political groups in the United States and didn't know how to find them. Later she became busy with work and her children and no longer had time to be involved in politics. The INS attorney asked, "Nine years have passed since you left Ethiopia. This is a long time, and you haven't been involved in politics here. What makes you think the government is still looking for you?" Aster answered that she was still afraid— because of her connection to her brother, because of her brother-in-law's recent arrest, and because she had escaped from jail before, meaning that the Ethiopian government would consider her particularly deserving of punishment if they caught her again.

Aster stepped down from the witness stand, and the judge gave both sides the opportunity to make a closing statement. I usually keep my closing statements short, addressing specific issues that I have not already addressed in writing. In this instance I tried to address the concerns that the judge had raised during the course of the hearing about the plausibility of Aster's story, particularly in regard to Aster's political opinions. I explained how her opposition to the change in the flag, to Eritrea's secession, and to the new government's policy of allowing only ethnically based political groups, made sense in the context of the politics and history of Ethiopia.

I then addressed the credibility of her story. While there were a few inconsistencies between her oral testimony and her most recent written statement, these inconsistencies were minor and not material to her claim. Her original asylum application and statement, filed in 1992, should be disregarded, I said, because of the way it was prepared. In addition to Aster's credible testimony, the judge should consider the doctor's report and the letters we had submitted from Aster's family counselor and the counselor at the prison. The judge should find that this evidence, taken together, was more than enough to prove that Aster had suffered past persecution. Once this was found, the burden lay with the INS to rebut the presumption that Aster would be persecuted in the future. Since there was no information in the record to indicate that country conditions in Ethiopia had changed, the judge should grant Aster restriction on removal.

The INS attorney stated that since she was not familiar with the case, she had no closing statement to make. She would reserve any arguments for a possible appeal, after she had time to review the case.

The judge announced that he would render his decision that day. Unfortunately, judges rarely simply tell applicants whether they have won or lost. Instead they recite a long legal opinion, starting with a summary of the law, going on to a summary of the facts, then to their decision about each aspect of the case, and only at the end stating whether they will grant the immigration status requested. Applicants and their representatives are on an emotional roller coaster, as they try to guess from the judge's preliminary statements what the final result will be.

The judge began his opinion by reciting the relevant law of asylum and restriction on removal, then summarized the facts of the case. This process took about ten minutes while Aster waited nervously to know if she had won. He then stated his opinion about the different elements of the case. First, he found that Aster was eligible for restriction on removal, because her shoplifting offense was not a "particularly serious crime" that would prevent her from being granted this status. He found that her testimony was credible, both because of her demeanor, which was emotional, "fervent," and convincing, and because her testimony was consistent in almost all its details. Her original asylum application was not consistent with her later statements in some areas, but she had given enough information about the circumstances under which that first application was prepared to explain why the first application was not accurate.

The judge stated that Aster had suffered harm severe enough to be considered persecution, and that she had demonstrated that the harm she had suffered was on account of her political opinion. Since she was a victim of past persecution, the burden shifted to the government to prove that country conditions had changed, but nothing in the record indicated that conditions had improved.

Finally, the judge stated that, if she were statutorily eligible for asylum, the discretionary factors in her favor were "immense." A mother of three children, two of whom were U.S. citizens, and a victim of severe torture, she would normally deserve a favorable exercise of discretion. Her minor criminal offense, which was committed under the stress of domestic abuse, did not outweigh the discretionary factors in her favor. However, the current law did not allow him to consider an asylum claim from her, so he could only grant her restriction on removal. Having granted this status, it was not necessary to consider her claim for Convention Against Torture protection, so he would not rule on this application. Accordingly, he ordered that her application for restriction on removal be granted.

Aster's reaction to the favorable ruling was one of relief, not joy. She cried as the judge read his decision, overcome by the emotion caused by recalling the traumatic events of her life and by her relief that she would not be deported. I also felt more relieved than happy. At least Aster would not be deported. But before she got her life back, she had to fight for custody of her two youngest children and reestablish a relationship with her teenage daughter, who was still living in foster care.

After I left the court building, I saw the interpreter outside. He said hello to me and commented that Aster's case was the saddest story he had ever heard in immigration court. He said he had heard about her brother's death, and he knew about the story that it was a murder. "She was from a very powerful family," he said, "before the Dergue." I wondered about Aster's comment that the interpreters in immigration court were all Tigreans, and that some of them were informers for the Ethiopian government. This interpreter certainly knew who she was. He seemed a nice enough person, but there was nothing to prevent him from telling Aster's story to a government official at the Ethiopian embassy, who might then take reprisals against Aster's sister, still living in Ethiopia.

•

7

ⅉⅉⅉⅉⅉⅉⅉ

Safety

Adele and Philippe Fontem

When Philippe was put in jail, Adele was forced to go back to work, despite the fact that her son Richard was only three months old. The owner of the store where she had worked in the past gave her a job and let her keep Richard in a crib in the store's back room.

When Philippe was released from jail, he took on several jobs—at a store during regular working hours, on the staff of a catering company in the evenings, and in a restaurant on weekends. Because they had many debts, Adele kept her job, but scaled back her hours. Their phone bill, still owing from the time Philippe was in detention, amounted to over $1,500, and they were behind in their rent and utilities bills.

When they finally climbed out of debt, Adele stopped working to spend more time with Richard and began to explore educational opportunities. She looked into taking classes in computer skills or continuing her university education. She took an unpaid internship at the Library of Congress, working in the Africa Research Room. "We needed money," she said, "but I took an unpaid job anyway. I had been staying home with Richard, and working at a shop, and never doing anything with my mind. I was so bored, I was going crazy! I wanted to do something where I would be using my mind."

Adele worked with the researcher responsible for cataloguing new information on Liberia. The Library of Congress holds many materials, not only books, and Adele helped the Liberia researcher classify incoming materials—pamphlets, government documents, reports, journals. After they recorded each new item, it was sent to a bindery. Adele had to read through the materials to determine what they were, and she had to learn enough about Liberia to understand how each of the new acquisitions should be classified. Adele enjoyed the work, but she had to quit after a few months. She and Philippe needed more money, and she had known from the beginning that the internship would not lead to a paying job. The person who had originally hired her had warned her that there were few paying jobs at the library, and, in fact, one needed an advanced degree to get even an entry-level job as a researcher.

Meanwhile Adele and Philippe had discovered another project that interested them—starting their own business in trading African art. Earlier, Adele had enrolled in a job-search program for refugees and asylees. The employment advocate assigned to her case had found several jobs for her, but she had turned down each one—largely because they were low-paying jobs, no better than the illegal employment she had found at the retail store. In frustration, her caseworker confronted her with her refusals and asked her if she were really interested in finding work. Adele answered that she was more interested in going into business for herself. She even knew what kind of business she wanted to start. She wanted to ship Cameroonian art to the United States and sell it to stores and dealers here, but she could not start her business until she had saved enough money to do so. Her caseworker told her that there was actually a program in the area that helped refugees and asylees start their own businesses. The program was funded by the U.S. government and was administered by a local nonprofit organization. Adele made an appointment with one of the loan officers there and went to explain her business plan.

The loan officer asked her about her experience in business, her contacts with art suppliers in Cameroon, and her plans to market the art in the United States. He was impressed with the knowledge of business and accounting that she had gained from working in the pharmacy in Cameroon and thought she had good ideas about how to transport the art to the United States. If she would work with him to develop an effective plan for marketing and to change a few other aspects of her business plan, she would be approved for a loan.

The business loan program offered loans of up to $10,000. Adele and Philippe took out a loan for $6,000 and chose a repayment plan that would require them to begin paying back the loan immediately, with the full amount repaid in one year. With the $6,000 they bought a computer and printer and used them to make up a catalog and keep records. They already had a car, an old station wagon, that they could use to transport the art to dealers in the Washington area.

They sent the rest of the money to Adele's mother in Cameroon, and she arranged for other relatives to travel to rural areas and buy masks and sculptures from local artisans. Adele's mother collected the art and shipped it via air cargo to the United States.

By speaking with her friends in the African community, Adele found some stores that sold African art. The quality of the art that she had available from Cameroon was impressive, and stores started buying pieces for retail sale. Adele and Philippe went to flea markets and art fairs with her stock and sold pieces directly to clients. As their business became better known, individual collectors began to call them and came to their apartment to look over their stock. They also took special orders from collectors and dealers and then called Adele's mother in Cameroon to find and ship the pieces that people wanted.

Their biggest success was becoming a supplier to the gift shop at the Smithsonian's Natural History museum. Adele went there in person with their catalog, which contained photos of the art and the prices. The gift shop of the Natural History museum sells African art in connection with its exhibit on African culture. The shop's buyer was impressed with what she had to offer and Adele ordered some pieces for the shop. Soon she had a standing contract with the museum that brought in a steady monthly income.

Within a couple of months of starting their business, Adele and Philippe were doing $2,000 to $3,000 a month in sales, of which $1,500 to $2,000 was profit. Adele became pregnant again, which made it necessary to cut back on their business activities, but they nevertheless made a good profit from sales to the Smithsonian and to private collectors who contacted them personally.

While Adele was building their art business, Philippe continued to work at several jobs. In the evenings and on weekends he worked as a waiter at a country club, and during weekdays he was a teller at a bank. He also picked up shifts as a parking attendant or a taxi driver on weekday nights. He has now scaled back on this work since their second baby was born.

Philippe and Adele are now focused on finding jobs that pay well enough to support them and their children while leaving them enough time to spend with each other and their sons. Philippe has almost completed training on Oracle, a computer database program, and Adele will begin taking classes when Philippe stops. "We decided that computers were the best way to make money here. We wanted to find jobs that we could start soon, without going back to school for years and years." They would like to buy a house and are trying to save money toward a down payment. "Everybody in America has a car, a computer, and a house," Adele jokes. "We have the first two, so now we need the third one and we're finished."

I asked Adele about their long-term career goals, and she laughed. "We don't have the big American dream, of having a big career. Maybe we used to, but with two children now, we just want to get by. To work, to go to school, these things take too much time—the important thing is to spend time with each other."

Adele has stopped having anything to do with politics; with two babies to take care of, she has enough to worry about. But she and Philippe help other refugees and immigrants from Cameroon, just as they were helped, and they often have long-term guests staying at their apartment. Philippe, however, continues to be active in Cameroon's pro-democracy movement. He has maintained his social connections with political activists and makes a point of helping other SDF members who have fled Cameroon for the United States. He lets asylum seekers stay at his house or helps them find other places to stay. He contributes money to the SDF party and sometimes attends meetings of the party, which has a branch office in the United States. He met the chairman of the party during one of his visits to Washington, and made a point of thanking him for the party's actions in helping him and Adele escape Cameroon.

Therese Kabongelo

For Therese, winning her asylum case was only the first step in starting a life in the United States. INS's regulations state that asylum applicants should receive a work permit thirty days after getting a recommended approval for asylum. In fact, it normally takes the INS two months to issue a work permit, and in Therese's case it took the INS almost three months to grant her employment authorization. During this time Therese continued to survive on almost no income: eating donated food, wearing donated clothing, and paying rent with money given to her by Lutheran Social Services.

She had previously tried to find illegal employment, as a babysitter or a housekeeper, but her lack of English had limited her ability to find even this kind of work. She enrolled in Lutheran Social Services' employment program, which specializes in finding jobs for refugees and asylees who do not speak English. The first two jobs they found for her were not suitable, however. One was at an all-night photomat, but it was so far from her house that it would have taken her hours to get there on public transportation. Another job was at a meat-processing plant. It would have required her to stand for hours at a time and work on a refrigerated assembly line, neither of which her health would permit. Finally, Therese found a regular babysitting job for a family with two infant children. She worked there for two months and then moved to another babysitting job that paid more. At both these jobs she lived in the house five days a week. She spent her weekends at the house of a friend from church, so she was able to save money by not having to pay rent.

At last it looked as if Therese had found some safety and stability in the United States. She had permanent legal status, a place to live, and a salary adequate for her needs. The only thing that remained for her to do was to bring her children from Congo to the

United States. Her two oldest sons were already over twenty-one and would not be eligible to come to the United States as derivative asylees. She could ask the U.S. State Department to resettle them as refugees, or she could wait until she had a green card and file for immigrant visas for them, but she could not bring them to the United States quickly.

Therese could bring her other six children to join her. Immigration law and regulations state that asylees can bring their spouse and minor children to the United States almost immediately, using an asylee relative petition. In practice, the process takes at least nine months from the date of final approval, because of processing delays at the INS, the State Department, and the embassies. It usually takes even longer than that, because asylees cannot file for their family members until their criminal background checks clear and they receive their final approval.

At the time Therese applied for asylum, the INS was in the process of changing the way it did fingerprint checks for criminal record screenings. The INS had been using "designated fingerprint services," which were private companies and nonprofit agencies that had permission from the INS to take applicants' fingerprints. Under the old system, designated fingerprint services took applicants' fingerprints on special cards provided by the INS, and the applicants sent the cards in with their applications for asylum. These cards were then forwarded to the FBI, which compared the applicants' fingerprints with those in its national criminal database.

Unfortunately, many of the designated fingerprint services agencies did a poor job, and as many as one-third of all fingerprint cards were rejected by the FBI as being incomplete or unreadable. The FBI was slow in doing the fingerprint checks, since they gave priority to fingerprint checks needed for actual criminal investigations, and the INS sometimes misfiled or lost the cards and the FBI results. As a result, many asylum applicants waited months after their cases were approved by the asylum office before receiving a final approval and being allowed to send for their relatives.

Therese sent in her fingerprints with her asylum application in December 1997, was interviewed in January 1998, and received her recommended approval letter the same month. Her final approval took much longer to arrive. After waiting for eight months, I wrote the asylum office in September, asking them to speed up approval of her case. I sent a fax and called them to follow up. They replied that they had not sent her fingerprints to the FBI until April, and that it normally takes six months for the FBI to respond, so we should expect the final approval in October or November. The asylum office offered no explanation why they had waited so long after Therese's recommended approval to send her fingerprints to the FBI, but at least it looked as if the approval would be coming soon.

November came around and the final approval still had not arrived, so I inquired again. The asylum office still had not received the fingerprint results from the FBI. In December I called again and found that the office had the fingerprint results. Therese had no criminal record, of course, so all they had to do was issue the final approval letter. By January they still had not done so, so I called and complained again. Finally, on February 2, 1999, more than a year after her recommended approval, Therese received her final approval letter and could begin the nine-month process of sending for her children.

Therese's experience was unusually unlucky, and the INS has improved the fingerprint process since that time. On March 29, 1998, the INS stopped using the designated fingerprint service system and opened its own fingerprint centers, which are operated by a single private contractor. It uses computers to take fingerprints and search the FBI records, and the process now works much more efficiently. Most applicants receive their final approval letters within two months of their recommended approval, and only rarely must applicants redo fingerprints because of errors. Unfortunately, the delay in processing asylee relative petitions has not changed, and they still take nine months to complete. Advocates for asylum seekers have complained often to the INS about this delay and have asked the INS leadership to reallocate staffing resources so that asylee relative petitions may be processed more quickly. So far, however, nothing has been done.

By the time Therese received her final approval, she had been in the United States for a year and a half. She would not see her children again for another nine months, by which time she would have been separated from them for more than two years. She still had not saved enough money to pay for all their air fares to the United States, but she did have enough to bring over three of her children. Her two oldest children were not eligible for asylee relative petitions, so she decided to bring over her three next-oldest children—aged sixteen, seventeen, and twenty—who were at highest risk of being targeted by the people who had attacked her and her husband, and of being forcibly recruited into the government's army or one of the rebel groups. Her three youngest children were staying with her sister and were in less danger.

Before filing the petition for three of her children, Therese decided to go back to Africa to visit all of them. She had always been worried about her children, and she finally decided that, despite the expense, she could not bear to be separated from them any longer. She decided to travel to Kenya and ask her sister to send her children there to meet her. After a visit she would return to the United States, and the three older children would come soon after.

I advised Therese not to go, since it seemed like a lot of money to spend on just a visit, when Therese should save her money to bring her children to the United States permanently. Kenya is also a dangerous place, where violent crime is common, and I was afraid that she would go to Uganda, Rwanda, or even Congo if she could not arrange for her children to come to Kenya. While I did not want her to go, I could not stop her—after all, Therese was a grown woman and could make her own decisions. I helped her get a refugee travel document, a passport-like document which refugees and asylees can use to travel outside the United States and she left the country in May 1999. She said she would come back after a few months.

A few months passed and Therese still had not returned. I was not worried, as I thought she had simply decided to stay longer, being unable to leave her children so soon. I thought she would certainly come back before the fall. Therese had become more than just a client, she was a friend of mine and my fiancée's. We had invited her to our wedding in September, and she had promised us she would return in time to attend.

September came and went. I checked with her Congolese friends in the United States, and they had heard no news from her either. She had not sent us a letter or called us since she had left the country. We were puzzled. If she had been robbed, had run out of money, or had gotten in some other kind of trouble, we thought she would call or write us to ask for help.

More time went by and still we heard nothing from her. In May 2000 we finally gave up on hearing from her again. Her refugee travel document was good only for one year and had expired, so she would not be able to return to the United States now even if she wanted to, without getting advance. permission from a U.S. embassy or from the INS. If she were going to come back at all, she would have come back by now. If she had decided to stay in Africa, she would have written us so we would know where to contact her.

I can guess what happened to Therese, but I will never know for certain. Therese had seemed depressed before her trip, and my wife suspects that Therese may have decided to commit suicide and invented the story about going to Africa to cover her disappearance. I think it is unlikely that she would commit suicide when she had her children to take care of, especially after she had found safety and an income in the United States. I think she went to Africa and was imprisoned or killed there. She may have been robbed and killed in Kenya, or she may have caught a serious illness and died for lack of someone to take care of her. The most likely possibility is that she went to Congo, despite the danger, to try to find her children, and was caught and killed there by Kabila's soldiers.

Therese was not a family member, but she was a good friend, and my wife and I cared about her very much. I now understand, in a limited way, how people feel when their friends and family members are "disappeared" by persecuting governments, or when relatives are arrested and never heard from again. You assume that the person involved is dead, but you never know for sure if you will hear from them again. You also wonder about the circumstances of their death. You wish you had done something to help them or had stopped them from taking the risks that led to their disappearance.

Thinking about Therese, and writing about her, makes me sad, but on the whole I am grateful to have known her. She was a strong and beautiful person. It is sad that she got so far only to have lost everything at the last. I can only hope that in this book I have been able to convey some of her strength and beauty, and that her strength may inspire readers as it has inspired me.

Aster Cheru

Aster won her court case in June 2000, and as this book went to press she had only just begun to rebuild her life. She has continued with her job and taken a second one, at a coffee shop, to have enough money to replace the clothing, furniture, and possessions she lost when she was taken to jail—things she needs to convince the custody court that she can provide a suitable home environment for her children.

Her relationship with all her children had been strained by her detention. Her daughter, Beth, continued to live with a foster family even after Aster was released from jail. Like many fourteen-year-old girls, Beth wanted a measure of independence from her mother. Her foster parent was less strict than Aster and let her go out more often, and her foster parent had a nicer house and more possessions. Beth was finishing her freshman year in high school, and her mother lived in a different school district; Beth did not want to change school districts and lose her new friends.

I also suspect that Beth wanted some distance from her mother because her mother was not completely stable emotionally. Her experiences in Ethiopia, along with her experience of being in-carcerated in the United States, had made her anxious and fearful. She distrusted the world and wanted to keep Beth away from it, which made her a particularly strict parent. She felt vulnerable and unstable herself and looked to Beth for friendship and emotional support.

I found it strange that the court did not give Aster immediate custody of Beth after she got out of jail and found her own apartment. When Aster first left the jail, she stayed at a shelter for bat-tered women, and I can understand that the court did not want Beth to stay there. Once Aster got her own apartment, I do not see why they did not return Beth to her, regardless of Beth's wishes.

Aster won visitation rights for John and Joseph soon after she was released from jail, and they came to stay with her every other weekend. Her ex-husband opposed even this limited contact and attempted to use her immigration problems as a reason that she should not be granted visitation. Fortunately the judge did not agree with this argument. Aster wanted full custody, but her family court lawyer did not think it advisable to file for full custody until Aster's immigration status was finally resolved.

By the time Aster was finally granted withholding of deportation, it had been nearly a year and a half since her children had gone to live with their father. The court had to consider that they had become used to living there, and their primary bond might have been transferred from their mother to their father. To transfer custody back to Aster might cause even more trauma. This would not be fair to Aster but might be better for the children.

Aster would also have a hard time providing for the children. She had returned to her former job at a hotel and worked long hours, but she had a hard time making enough money to pay the rent on her apartment and to provide for necessities for herself and Beth. It would be even harder for her to provide for two more children, and she would have to work fewer hours and be home more often if she did have primary custody of them.

As of this writing, it is doubtful that Aster will ever regain primary custody of her sons. She cannot afford to pay an attorney to represent her in family court, and she has been working so many hours that she had not even had time to pursue the matter. Her victory in immigration court was only a partial one. She succeeded in getting out of prison and avoiding deportation to Ethiopia, but she will probably never completely get back the life that she had before she was imprisoned.

8

⊓⊔⊓⊔⊓⊔⊓

The Mercy Factory

SO FAR I have examined the asylum system only from the perspective of the applicants and their representatives. What does the system look like from the perspective of the adjudicators—the asylum
officers and the immigration judges?

In researching this book I contacted the INS asylum office in
Arlington, Virginia, and the Arlington and Baltimore immigration
courts, the venues where the people profiled in this book pursued
their asylum claims. The staff of the asylum office were glad to
participate, and after receiving permission from INS headquarters,
I interviewed the director of the Arlington asylum office and seven
members of the office's staff. I contacted the immigration judges in
Baltimore and Arlington, the venues where I normally practice,
but only one judge was willing to be interviewed for the book.[1]

Asylum officers and immigration judges view asylum seekers
differently. Most asylum officers worked with refugee assistance
organizations before becoming asylum officers, whereas most immigration judges have previous work experience as attorneys for
the INS. Asylum officers receive extensive training in country con-

---

1. There are four judges in each of the two jurisdictions, and I wrote to all eight
of them to request an interview. Four of the judges replied to my request with polite letters, explaining that they did not think it appropriate to comment about immigration
law or policy to the media. Three of the judges did not respond to my request at all.

ditions, interviewing skills, issues in cross-cultural communication, and sensitivity to applicants' suffering from post-traumatic stress. Immigration judges receive minimal training in these areas. Asylum officers only interview asylum applicants, whereas immigration judges hear a wide variety of cases, including many cases of removal for criminal offenses and immigration fraud. Judges are more likely to be skeptical about an asylum seeker's credibility. Asylum officers, while usually less informed about immigration law, are more cognizant of country conditions and cultural factors, and are more likely to give asylum seekers' testimony "the benefit of the doubt," as international refugee law requires.[2]

Asylum Officers

Most asylum officers come from work backgrounds in refugee assistance. For example, the director of the Arlington asylum office, Marla Belvedere, worked with refugees as an advocate before joining the Asylum Corps. She began her career as an intern with the U.S. embassy in India, where she worked with Afghan and Iranian refugees who were seeking resettlement in the United States. When her internship ended, she found a job working with the Hebrew Immigrant Aid Society in New York City, where she assisted newly arrived refugees, most of them Jews from Iran and the Soviet Union. She worked there for five years, then applied for a position in the Asylum Corps when it was founded in 1991. She started as an interviewer, was promoted to supervisor, and then worked as a training coordinator at INS headquarters for a while. In 1998 she was made the director of the Arlington asylum office.

Ms. Belvedere looks for a background in refugee work, particularly overseas experience, when hiring new asylum officers. Having worked with refugees before helps asylum officers understand refugees' situation and needs. This helps them ensure that their interviews are nonadversarial and their decisions are fair. But they must also evaluate carefully the validity of asylum seekers' claims. Before approving a case, they must decide whether the ap-

2. *UNHCR Handbook*, paragraph 196.

plicant meets the legal requirements of asylum, and they must evaluate the credibility of the applicant's testimony.

A number of important issues must be examined in deciding whether an applicant meets the legal requirements to be granted asylum. For example, asylum officers must determine the level of harm that the applicant suffered and decide if it was severe enough to be termed "persecution" rather than discrimination or harassment. They must examine whether the harm suffered was due to political opinion, religion, race, nationality, or membership in a particular social group. If the persecution suffered happened some time ago, they must learn about current conditions in the country of origin to see if there has been a fundamental change since the applicant left the country.

Asylum officers are trained to assess credibility in several ways. First they must look at the applicant's statements for consistency—whether the testimony given in the interview matches what the applicant wrote on the asylum application. They also look to see if the applicant's story is consistent with information about conditions in the applicant's country of origin. They check documentary evidence presented by the applicant, such as passports, identity documents, letters, and affidavits, and compare this evidence with the applicant's statement and other information.

I spoke with asylum officers about how they determined credibility. One officer, Richard Jungkuntz, talked about the importance of detail in evaluating testimony. He tries to get a general sense that applicants "are taking me where they've actually been." Another officer, Elizabeth Heyward, talked about how it is helpful when she hears "off the wall" details—small facts, not material to the claim of persecution, which indicate that an applicant is remembering real events. For example, she said, if the applicant is describing a soldiers' raid on her house, then says something like "and then, my aunt came in, who had just returned from visiting my uncle in the next village," you get the impression that the events really happened.

Another officer, who asked that I not use his name in the book, described his strategy for interviews. He uses the same pattern of questioning for each person, though the actual questions vary with the fact pattern of the case. "I ask the applicant to put the frame around the picture first, then to paint the portrait." By this he means that he starts by asking basic questions about the applicant's life—information about his parents, his siblings, his education, and work history—and then focuses on the applicant's story of persecution. This helps with credibility, as he can compare key details and dates from the "frame" of the picture with the testimony about the story of persecution—the "portrait."

Another asylum officer, Ellen Whalen, focuses on detailed testimony, particularly facts she can verify through external sources. Asylum officers use a variety of external sources, including human rights reports, Internet news sites, and information collected by the research branch of the Asylum Corps, the Refugee Information Center. "For example," she said, "if the person is talking about their political activism and their membership in a political party as the basis of their claim, and they have no proof that they were members of that party, I want to get into how they joined, how much the membership card cost, who the leaders are, what the party platform is, and so on. All of these things I might be able to corroborate, either from the information we get from the asylum office or from the Internet."

In some cases, evaluating the credibility of testimony is particularly difficult. For example, poorly educated persons may have a genuine claim but may nonetheless give inconsistent and vague testimony because they lack the intellectual ability to remember and articulate their stories well. Victims of rape, torture, or other severe trauma may have difficulty telling their stories because of the psychological damage caused by the trauma.

Kathie McCleskey, who started her career with the Asylum Corps as an interviewer and is now responsible for training and quality assurance, talked about her experience interviewing poorly educated Haitian applicants at the Miami asylum office in the early 1990s. "I'd make sure I really understood the country. And I would understand what somebody with their education level would reasonably be expected to know." Ms. McCleskey asked applicants about concrete details, things they should be able to remember: the size and shape of their prison cell, what they were given to eat, whether others were detained with them, and so on. She became frustrated, however, with the lack of independent information about country conditions within Haiti.

She asked other departments of the INS and the U.S. embassy in Haiti to assist her by providing information about prisons and other verifiable facts. When this information was not forthcoming, she put together packets of information about country conditions in Haiti and other common countries, based on what she could learn from independent human rights reports. She also relied on the Refugee Information Center, which takes questions from the field and researches answers. It also operates an e-mail forum on the secure, internal INS server which allows asylum officers to ask questions about particular countries and situations and to receive answers from other asylum officers who may have encountered the same situation in their own work.

The INS trains its officers to help traumatized asylum seekers speak clearly about what happened to them. "The training for asylum is excellent," Elizabeth Heyward said. "They have a four- to five-week training course in Georgia, where you go to class eight hours a day, and one of the things they teach you is that people who are severely traumatized might not be able to give you any detail—at all. They either can't remember, or their mind just won't let them recall it." I asked her how she determined credibility in these cases. "I asked them the same question," she said. The trainer, who was a psychologist, not an asylum officer, told her, "Well, that's not my job. My job is to tell you what the medical symptoms are."

She came up with her own strategies for these difficult cases. "You have to look for ways to get them to talk, because if you can't get them to talk, it's really hard to find their story. Sometimes they can talk about everything but the trauma, so you talk around it—they train us to do that, too. Get everything you can around it, you know: what happened when you went in, what happened when they let you out, but not what happened when you were there."

Sometimes, Dave Lewis said, the applicant is already seeing a psychologist or trauma counselor. In these cases the applicant can bring a report from a psychologist or trauma counselor, attesting to the truth of their story. In other cases he has to use skillful interviewing techniques. Usually he can get the information he needs to evaluate credibility by asking questions about other things, without asking too many questions about the traumatic experience itself. "I very seldom ask them to go through that, unless it is something that perhaps you suspect didn't happen. And then you might touch on it, just to test the water, so to speak. But very seldom do I force a person who's been through a traumatic experience to go back through that." Another officer follows a similar procedure. "If it's really horrific, I'll just read to them from the affidavit and ask them to answer yes or no to whether the affidavit is correct. I'll look for credibility on other things."

Another problem arises where an asylum seeker is not represented by counsel or has a dishonest or incompetent lawyer. In these cases the asylum officer's job becomes more difficult and more important. We have seen, in Philippe's case, how a person with a genuine fear of persecution was unable to win asylum at the first interview because bad representation prevented him from effectively articulating his claim. Many of the asylum officers spoke with pride about the strategies they used to overcome these difficulties and find the applicant's true claim.

Elizabeth Heyward, who formerly practiced immigration law as an advocate, said that she always likes to see well-written, detailed asylum applications, but she tries not to make any decisions until she actually speaks to the asylum applicant. "You're not sure until they start talking. Sometimes it's the preparer; sometimes they can't speak English. Sometimes they have a great lawyer, so it's all in legalese; sometimes they have an overworked lawyer, and it's not as detailed as it could be. So I keep an open mind—we're trained to keep an open mind."

I asked the officers about cases where they did discover that applicants were lying to them. Did this bother them? "When you first come back from training," answered Ms. Heyward, "and you start interviewing, it bothers you, because in life we don't like to be lied to. And you talk it over with the other asylum officers, and they say, you know, you just can't let that bother you. Because oth-

erwise you'll never make it. You'll end up angry with the applicant. . . . You just close that. You can't let that affect the tone of
the interview."

I asked her if it was difficult for her to cut off those emotions.
She said no, because she understood what motivated people to lie.
Another asylum officer, Kathie McCleskey, agreed. "Have I ever in
my life lied to get any kind of a benefit? Oh sure. Has everyone
lied somewhere or other? Probably. I just think, here's this person
who's sitting in front of me, they're just making their way through
life."

Another officer, Ellen Whalen, said it was not her job to
worry about whether people were lying to her. "I don't worry
about whether their testimony is true. I worry about whether their
testimony is believable, consistent, and sufficiently detailed under
the standard articulated in *Matter of Dass*.[3] That's what we were
trained to do." By following this standard, she keeps the process
of assessing credibility an objective one and keeps her own personality and feelings out of the process.

While being careful not to be adversarial, asylum officers
must also control the interview and make an effective check for
credibility. In one of my cases, which Ms. Heyward adjudicated,
my client was talking about an interrogation session he had endured. Ms. Heyward asked him to give five examples of the questions he was asked in interrogation. He gave two examples and
then began talking about something else. She interrupted him and
politely but firmly said, "I asked for five examples, and you've
given me two. Can you give me three more?" He thought for a
second, then gave her three more examples of the questions he was
asked. By insisting on specific examples, and by asking for detail
in addition to what was contained in the written statement, she
was able to see that he actually had endured an interrogation and
that he was not simply reciting to her a memorized story.

One factor that adjudicators consider in evaluating an applicant's testimony is plausibility—whether it is likely or possible that
a series of events actually happened. Dave Lewis has worked with
refugees for over fifteen years, both in the United States and over-

3. 20 I&N Dec. 120, 126 (BIA 1989).

seas. He said that "one of my strengths has been to take my past experience and delve into it, when the time comes, to remember that the situation the applicant is describing is not so unreasonable that it couldn't have happened. To have been in refugee areas, to have been in countries where refugees are coming from, to have been there and have lived under it, is a tremendous resource. And to be able to listen to someone describe something that another person would think unbelievable, but to know that you've *seen* it, is worth a lot of weight. Another person, not having had the opportunity to go down that road, would rely more on a rigid, legalistic way to deal with it."

Another officer, Joanna Brown, worked with a resettlement program for Southeast Asian refugees, based in Bangkok, Thailand, for twelve years before becoming an asylum officer. When I asked her about evaluating plausibility, she laughed and pointed to a piece of paper on the wall of her office, which held a quote from Lewis Carroll's *Through the Looking Glass*: "There is no use trying," said Alice, "one can't believe impossible things." "I dare say you haven't had much practice," said the queen. "Why, sometimes I've believed as many as six impossible things before breakfast." As Ms. Brown explained, "We rarely use plausibility as a ground for referring an asylum claim. They teach us that in the training. Implausible has to be really implausible, like 'I saw someone six miles away and recognized his face.'"

All judgments of credibility are complicated by the inconsistent quality of interpretation in asylum interviews. Asylum applicants are responsible for bringing their own translators to the interviews. Some applicants bring dishonest translators who coach the applicant in answering questions or even answer for the applicant. Others bring honest but incompetent translators who mistranslate the applicant's answers and can cause the case to be denied for inconsistencies or lack of detail.

Asylum officers differ in their assessment of the seriousness of this problem. Some felt that incompetent or dishonest translators were a problem, but one that could be overcome by skillful interviewing techniques. Other asylum officers felt that translation problems were the most serious difficulty they faced in their jobs.

One asylum officer called the problem of applicant-provided

interpreters the "Achilles' heel" of the asylum office, with the problem of incompetent translation and dishonest translation about equal in scope. When I asked Ellen Whalen if there were problems with translation, she answered, "I wouldn't know. I'm not fluent in any of the languages. . . . For example, if there was a Somali translator who was completely translating everything falsely, I probably would not have any idea. I would just write into my notes whatever the interpreter was saying." In a few cases, where the error was flagrant, she was able to detect the mistake. "Sometimes it would be obvious from the answer that they had to be using the wrong word," or "the applicant would say two or three words and the interpreter would go on with the contents of the affidavit for a couple of paragraphs." Other than these rare occurrences, she said, she would not be able to tell if the translation were inaccurate or dishonest.

In many cases the translator is a friend or a family member who makes mistakes due to lack of ability or experience. A good asylum officer can help to correct this problem and compensate for the translator's lack of skill. According to Ms. Whalen, "Sometimes a translator will say something like, 'She means this,' or 'This is what happened,' and I have to correct him. I try to do it gently, because they're not professional translators. They mean well, and you don't want to scare them into silence." By taking an active role in explaining to translators what is required of them and correcting them politely when they overstep the boundaries of their role, asylum officers can encourage better translation. Many asylum officers, however, favor changing to a system of government-hired translators, similar to that used by the immigration court.

Asylum officers do difficult and stressful work. Most of them express satisfaction with their jobs and feel like they are making a difference and doing important work. According to Dave Lewis, "A good officer takes the time to be creative. And the key is to be creative in a nonadversarial sense. It takes a year to develop interviewing skills. I have to admit that I thought I was a good interviewer when I joined the asylum corps back in 1991, but I'm still learning, and I've been interviewing for over six years. And you've never learned all the angles. You have to continually stay on top of your game, and I think it's one of those skills that you're always honing—you never get to the point where you say, okay, I've got this one down pat. That's what makes this such a unique job."

While they express pride in their work and satisfaction with helping others, asylum officers talk about the psychological stress they feel from their work. Elizabeth Heyward said that she still feels strong emotions, at times, when hearing peoples' stories of persecution. "Sometimes in interviews, my eyes get watery. Sometimes I just have to cry." Now she's learned to change the subject if she starts to get teary, and asks applicants to talk about other matters until she can regain her composure. She finds it most disturbing when she feels she may be further traumatizing an applicant by making her relive her experiences of torture. "I remember one person—she was dying, crying about a rape. I was about to break up, so I moved on." Afterward she discussed the case with other officers, and they encouraged her by telling her it can be cathartic for people to talk about their experiences. "Some people are eager to talk about it. It gives them some closure, especially if, after that, they're granted asylum."

Dave Lewis deals with the emotional stress by going to the gym each day after work. "I never miss a day." The routine allows him to leave the physical and mental environment of the office, to rejuvenate his body after sitting for eight or nine hours, and to put work out of his mind until the next day. Even so, the work stays with him sometimes. "There are a lot of cases that I won't forget. I can remember probably ten or fifteen cases that are indelibly etched in my mind. Sometimes you want to be able to say things to the person after the interview . . . but you just wish them good luck, and then you cut loose."

Ellen Whalen was an advocate for a nonprofit agency for five years before becoming an asylum officer. I asked her whether being an asylum officer was more or less traumatic than being an advocate. "It's the same level of trauma," she responded, "but for different reasons. With representation you have strong emotions about what the person has suffered, and you also have the responsibility to get this person relief. Here the pressure is to make the right decision. You're thinking, 'Is this person credible?' and 'My God, what if I send back somebody who's really a refugee?'" She deals with the stress with her own routine—she goes home at the same time, every day, and walks and plays with her dog. She also relies on prayer to help her deal with the emotional trauma and the stress of making decisions that so strongly affect other people's lives.

Joanna Brown said she found being an asylum officer more stressful than working as a refugee advocate. "The power involved. Having the ability to grant or refer somebody and affect their life." Hearing the stories of trauma are also difficult. "I compartmentalize it . . . but it's the kind of thing where you're thinking about it all the time, no matter what. I try not to have a personal link . . . there's a certain distancing."

Ms. Brown also said she has had the most difficulty coping with her feelings in cases where the applicant has suffered greatly but where the harm is not connected with one of the five grounds, making it necessary to refer the case. For example, many refugees from countries in civil war, such as Sierra Leone or Liberia, have suffered terribly, been kidnapped and raped, witnessed the death of family members and the destruction of their homes, or even, in the case of Sierra Leone, had their limbs amputated with machetes as part of a terror campaign waged by the rebel armed forces. In many cases the victims of these acts were not harmed on account of their race, religion, nationality, political opinion, or membership in a particular social group. They were victimized only because they were in the wrong place at the wrong time. Where there is no connection to one of the five grounds, asylum officers have no choice but to refer the case to court. As Ms. Brown said, "I come out of some interviews thinking, 'This is horrible,' and I have to refer the case because there are no grounds. It's heartbreaking."

Dave Lewis talked about how he misses the emotional support that he got when working with a voluntary agency. As an asylum officer, he is motivated to help refugees, and he started in the field because he enjoyed interacting with people from other cultures. Now, however, his enjoyable interaction is limited because of his job. "You've got to be much more self-contained, because you have to say no when the time comes, and when you say no, that's it, your emotional involvement ends. Unlike the private voluntary sector, where you can enjoy socializing and going to refugee cultural events, that's almost precluded from my work now. I don't even go to Ethiopian restaurants as much as I used to, because I've interviewed so many Ethiopians—you tend to start shying away from interacting after work. I used to go to a lot of the cultural events by the Vietnamese, but now, being an immigration officer, you become the focus of a lot of questions—how can I do this, how can I do that. It starts following you after hours, and you just want to cut it off. Finally, you just retreat into your private life, not because you don't enjoy helping but because it becomes an oppressive, all-encompassing responsibility. We really become like islands when we're out of work. We disappear into our own homes and lives."

I spoke with Dr. Judy Okawa, a psychologist and the director of the Program for Survivors of Torture and Trauma at the Center for Multicultural Human Services, in Falls Church, Virginia, about the effects of "secondary" or "vicarious" trauma on asylum officers and judges. Dr. Okawa has led a seminar for asylum officers on how to cope with this trauma; many of the asylum officers I interviewed mentioned this training and spoke highly of it.

Dr. Okawa said that secondary trauma can interfere with good decision-making. "It is too easy to turn yourself off, to withdraw, when you hear about so much suffering." Adjudicators who are highly empathic, who can put themselves emotionally and psychologically in the place of the asylum applicant, do the best job of understanding refugees' claims and making decisions, but they are most likely to suffer secondary trauma. One of the asylum officers described the balance that must be achieved to remain effective. "You do grow emotional calluses, you do learn to distance yourself. You hear the stories, you understand the words, but you try not to picture the images." He described himself as seeking a balance between two extremes—"you can become so callous that you don't believe anyone, or you can become so caught up in the pain and anguish that you lose the objectivity you need to make a decision."

Dr. Okawa explained that one of the defense mechanisms we have against trauma is denial. This defense mechanism is effective in preserving our emotional health but dangerous to our ability to help trauma survivors. As one asylum officer declared, "Behind every 'I don't believe you' is 'I don't want to hear this.' When you look at the effects of trauma—of torture or rape or other harm—the psychological factors are more important than the physical ones. The physical pain goes away in most cases, but the psychological trauma stays. Why is that? Because trauma is the violation of core beliefs, such as 'People can be trusted' or 'The world is safe.'" When asylum officers and judges have their core beliefs threatened by secondary trauma, there is a temptation to stop believing survivors as a way of defending those core beliefs against attack.

In general, institutional factors can make working with trauma survivors either easier or more difficult, Dr. Okawa observed. "It is important to have a friendly, supportive environment and for people to have an open-door policy, so if you are upset about a case you can immediately go to a colleague and unload." She also noted that control over one's workload is important. One should have some flexibility in hours, and one should be able to alternate trauma-intensive work, such as interviewing, with less emotional work, such as writing, researching, or administrative work.

Asylum officers who I spoke with reported good relationships with co-workers and supervisors and much informal camaraderie and support. But little is done formally to support the asylum officers' emotional health. The time pressures on officers are so heavy, and their schedules so regimented, that they have little time during the day to consider their own emotional health needs. While they do alternate interviewing with research and decision writing, the time they spend apart from interviewing does not provide a good rest from the stress of interviewing. The applicant may not be there in front of them, but they are still thinking about and working with the applicant's story. The need to make a decision about the applicant's fate places even more stress on the asylum officer.

All the officers I spoke with complained of the size of their workload and the overly structured nature of their schedules. Asylum officers feel that every minute of their time is scheduled, leaving them little down time for conversing with other officers, doing serious reading about country conditions, or dealing with their feelings about what they hear in interviews. One idiosyncrasy of the officers' schedule makes Tuesdays more stressful than the other days. They are required to do nine cases a week—on Mondays, Wednesdays, and Thursdays they interview two cases, but on Tuesdays they interview three, leaving Friday open for research, writing, and administrative tasks. All the asylum officers I spoke with wanted their caseload reduced to eight cases a week, so that the third case on Tuesday would be eliminated. As an advocate, I agree with this request for other reasons. On Tuesdays the asylum officers are always rushed, trying to get through three cases in the time allotted, and their hurry makes them irritable and less effective. Both the applicants and the interviewers suffer from the hurried conditions.

One officer, while affirming that she loved her job, referred to the asylum office as "a sweatshop." "It's a quintessentially American approach to the problem," she said. "We're Americans, our country was formed by refugees, so we want to be true to our heritage. On the other hand, we like to be productive, and we don't want to spend too much money. And we don't like being duped by people."

One other problem the asylum officers mentioned was that of identifying former persecutors who are posing as victims of persecution in order to gain asylum. Asylum officers are supposed to conduct their interviews in a nonadversarial manner, but at the same time they are supposed to try to detect former persecutors in the course of their interviews. Some officers said they were uncomfortable with this role, as it required them to become a detective instead of an impartial, nonadversarial adjudicator. They suggested starting a separate office, within the Asylum Corps, that would investigate cases where the applicants might be a former persecutor or violator of human rights. This would take the responsibility away from them and would be more effective in identifying human rights abusers and bringing them to prosecution.

Immigration Judges

Immigration judges are different from asylum officers in many ways. In general, immigration judges have a much stronger knowledge of the law. All immigration judges have law degrees, and all of them have had considerable legal experience in other positions before being made a judge. Few of them, however, have any background in refugee work. As a result, they are better informed about the technicalities of immigration law than asylum officers, but they know less about the cultural and political background of asylum seekers' countries of origin.

Immigration judges are also more skeptical of asylum seekers credibility, as a general rule, than asylum officers, and more likely to deny an applicant's claim.

Most of the judges have an employment background with INS, the military, or other branches of the U.S. government. Many of them formerly worked as INS trial attorneys, which means that they have spent years arguing in favor of the deportation of immigrants. While they try to be objective decision-makers, their prior experience inevitably influences the way they view applicants for asylum. Of the fifty-two judges appointed between 1996 and 1999, twenty-six had previously worked as INS trial attorneys, and thirteen had worked in other INS positions. Twenty-four had worked as attorneys in other government agencies, and five had worked as judges in the armed forces. Only sixteen had experience with a private law firm, and only eight had worked for a nonprofit agency.[4] A study of all immigration judges has found that former government lawyers outnumber former private lawyers by a ratio of two to one.[5]

Immigration judges hear a wide variety of cases, many of them involving the deportation of noncitizens who have been convicted of crimes, who are illegally present in the United States, or who are guilty of immigration fraud. Some of these aliens have applied for asylum, even though they have little or no fear of persecution in their home countries, simply as a tactic to delay their eventual deportation. Because of their large caseload involving

4. The numbers add up to more than fifty-two because many immigration judges had worked in more than one position before becoming a judge. This information was taken from biographical press releases published on the Executive Office for Immigration Review web site: www.usdoj.gov/eoir.

5. "Chances of Safe Harbor Vary Widely," Fredric N. Tulsky, *San Jose Mercury News*, October 17, 2000.

fraud and criminal activity, immigration judges cannot help but be more skeptical of aliens' claims of asylum than asylum officers are.

Judges receive training in immigration law upon beginning their jobs. Their initial training consists of a one-week course which focuses on administrative matters as well as substantive legal issues and covers many aspects of immigration law, not just asylum. After their initial training, they are mentored by an experienced immigration judge, usually for two weeks, during which time they observe and sometimes participate in that judge's adjudications. The new judges then begin hearing cases of their own. They also receive follow-up training at the week-long immigration judges' conference that is held each year. On the whole, however, judges receive less training than asylum officers and thus are not as strongly encouraged to consider the special difficulties of asylum seekers and the importance of giving applicants the benefit of the doubt.

As a result of these factors, immigration judges are more likely, in general, to deny asylum cases than asylum officers are. They are more skeptical about the credibility of asylum seekers' statements, more likely to require documentation to prove a fact, and more likely to interpret the law and the facts of a case in a way that justifies a denial of asylum status.

The immigration judge who agreed to be interviewed for this book, Judge John F. Gossart, is a good representative of immigration judges in general. An honest, hard-working, and intelligent man with an extensive knowledge of immigration law, Judge Gossart has adopted a balanced approach in his decisions. He is independent-minded, inclined to follow his own legal reasoning in deciding cases, and in his career has made decisions that could be termed both liberal and strict on asylum issues. He takes a strict approach on asylum seekers who found temporary safety in other countries or who used false documents to enter the United States, and sometimes denies asylum to these applicants. Yet he is sensitive to the problems that asylum seekers face in presenting evidence and testifying about their claims and is particularly sensitive on gender-based asylum claims. One of his decisions, granting asylum to a woman from India who faced persecution because she was HIV-positive, constituted an unusual and liberal interpretation of "membership in a particular social group," and was featured in an article in a prominent immigration law journal.[6]

Like many immigration judges, Judge Gossart comes from a background in the INS. He worked there for eight years, first as a trial attorney, arguing against asylum applicants and other immigrants in immigration court, and then as the deputy commissioner in charge of naturalization. He became an immigration judge in 1982 and has presided over hundreds of asylum cases during his eighteen years on the bench.

Judge Gossart told me that, while he hears many kinds of immigration cases, he gives asylum cases special attention. "It's the most serious case we hear. If the person is subject to persecution, you want to be very sure of your decision, and hopefully you don't deny a claim where a person would be returned and would be subjected to persecution." Because of the serious consequences of a negative decision, asylum cases are decided differently from other immigration cases. "Traditionally, if a person doesn't meet the burden of proof, which would include ambiguity and doubt, it's resolved against the applicant. But that is not the case with asylum claims. If there's ambiguity in an asylum claim, the ambiguity is resolved to the benefit of the applicant."

Despite the importance of giving an applicant the benefit of the doubt, Judge Gossart is careful in evaluating credibility, particularly in cases where no documentary evidence is available to support a claim. "A person can be a truthful witness, or an untruthful witness who's very good at being untruthful. For example, I can tell you a story. And if I tell you a story that makes sense, and I tell you a story in a very convincing fashion, because I'm good at that, I can make a successful claim of asylum. So there's a lot of things that come into play."

One of the most important things to examine, Judge Gossart observed, is consistency. He examines both the consistency between the applicant's oral testimony and written statement, and the consistency between the applicant's testimony on direct ques-

6. "Ostracism, Lack of Medical Care Support HIV-Positive Aliens' Asylum Quest, IJ Rules," *Interpreter Releases,* January 15, 2001, pp. 233–235.

tioning and cross-examination. He listens carefully to an applicant's explanation of perceived inconsistencies in testimony. "If
the person can readily give an answer as to the inconsistency and
explain it in a plausible way, that certainly enhances someone's
credibility. But if they change their testimony, if they vacillate, if
they act unsure, or if they just avoid the question with vagaries,
well, then obviously that's going to call into question their credibility."

The adversarial nature of the proceedings, which involve both
direct and cross-examination of the applicant, helps in determining credibility. "I may listen to direct examination, and I may have
a beautiful affidavit in front of me . . . and I may say, 'Wow, that
was very consistent, everything's been very consistent, this person's
been very forthright in their testimony.' Then, during cross-examination, we begin to have hesitancy, we have vacillation, we have
delays in testimony, we have a failure to explain something in the
document that the INS believes to be an inconsistency."

Judge Gossart does not place as much weight on the applicant's demeanor. "I look at demeanor much more carefully. We're
dealing with different cultures, and we're dealing with persons
who have never been in court before, and they're just extremely
nervous. So just because someone's nervous and is frightened by
the process, that doesn't mean they're hiding something, that
they're not credible.

"I measure demeanor in conjunction with other things . . . [if
there is] a person whose testimony is consistent with the application, whose testimony is consistent under direct and cross-
examination, who could adequately explain any question of
inconsistencies raised by the INS. If the only dimension of a person perhaps not telling the truth is his demeanor, I would never
use the demeanor as a justification of a negative credibility finding."

Likewise Judge Gossart does not place much weight on the
plausibility of an applicant's story. "Somebody may tell me something that I, in my personal bias—and we all have personal biases—may say, 'I just can't believe that.' But that doesn't mean
that it didn't happen." As in the case of demeanor, he usually con-

siders plausibility as a subordinate factor in his decision; it can support a decision made on account of other factors, but it cannot by itself cause an asylum application to be denied.

Where possible Judge Gossart likes to see supporting documentation and wants an explanation for evidence that is not available. In some cases he has even denied an application without making a ruling on the credibility of the applicant's testimony, because the applicant did not provide supporting documentation that should have been readily available and had no good explanation for not submitting it. Usually, however, he gives applicants more time to provide documentation, scheduling a second hearing for a later date so that the applicant may present corroborating evidence.

I asked Judge Gossart about the stresses inherent in his job—from time pressures, vicarious trauma, and the responsibility of making decisions that so strongly affect peoples' lives. He acknowledged that being an immigration judge was "very difficult, very stressful." Each year at the immigration judges' conference, stress reduction is a subject for speakers and workshops. One advantage the judges have over asylum officers is more control over their calendar. They make their own schedules and have much less pressure from their supervisors to complete cases. In fact, Judge Gossart said he receives no pressure from his superiors to complete a quota of cases within a time limit. He does feel pressure—which he described as "self-imposed"—to give applicants a hearing within a reasonable period of time, and he is also subject to a requirement written into the immigration law that most asylum cases be heard within 150 days of filing.

Immigration judges also get more of a break from thinking about traumatic stories than asylum officers do, since part of their docket consists of nonasylum cases. But they must feel more of a sense of responsibility in their decisions. When an asylum officer decides not to approve a case, it is referred to an immigration judge for a second hearing. When a judge denies a case, he orders the applicant deported. The applicant can appeal the judge's decision, but most of these decisions are sustained by the Board of Immigration Appeals. The judge's decision generally determines the fate of an applicant for asylum.

Judge Gossart said he receives a good deal of support from his colleagues. "We have a good camaraderie here, with the judges. We talk to each other a lot, particularly about the stressful cases. That's very helpful, to talk to a colleague about the stresses of a case. Even if it's just to have somebody listen." He also tries to maintain a sense of humor. Still, "to hear the tragedies, the traumas, and the brutality that some people have endured . . . it never gets easier. Some of the stories I've heard, I shudder inside, the things that have happened to people." His experiences have also made him appreciate his own life more. "Me, my reaction is to count my blessings. I certainly, since becoming an immigration judge, have counted my blessings more than I ever have in my life."

While I have great respect for Judge Gossart, I do not agree with all his decisions. He often grants withholding of deportation but denies asylum to applicants who enter the United States using false documents or who had spent considerable time in other countries before coming to the United States. He believes that asylum is a discretionary benefit which can be denied to applicants who do not seem to deserve it.

An example of this practice is a ruling he made in the case of one of my clients. This young woman, who is now twenty-four years old, was only fifteen when the civil war began in Somalia. She is a member of a vulnerable minority clan, which was persecuted by armed clan militias on all sides in the war. At the start of the civil war, soldiers from another clan attacked her house. Her brother and uncle were killed, and she and her sister were gang-raped. Her family fled the country for Kenya, but she was separated from them on the way. She never found them again and ended up staying with some compassionate strangers who took her with them on their flight. When they reached Kenya, the family decided to live illegally in Nairobi, avoiding the refugee camps near the Somali border. She had little choice but to go with them.

She lived in Nairobi for eight years, married there, and had a child. When she was pregnant with her second child, she was arrested by the Kenyan police as an undocumented alien and sent to prison. She stayed in prison for a month, contracted malaria, and had a miscarriage; finally her friends collected enough money to bribe the Kenyan police to let her go. She considered going back to the refugee camps, where at least she would be safe from the Kenyan police, but decided not to go because the camps were dangerous and unhealthy. She decided that Kenya would never be safe for her, and her friends and relatives raised enough money to pay a smuggler to send her to the United States.

Judge Gossart heard her case and granted her withholding of deportation but denied her asylum. In his decision he stated that she has a "safe haven" in Kenya, as she could have stayed in the refugee camps there; it was her decision to break Kenyan law by leaving the refugee camps. He also explained that she did not deserve a grant of asylum because she had used fraudulent means to enter the United States. In making his decision, he cited a BIA precedent case, *Matter of Pula,*[7] which states that in certain cases asylum applications may be denied where the applicant had found a safe place to stay before coming to the United States or had engaged in serious fraud to effect an entry into the United States.

In our interview, Judge Gossart said he does not always deny asylum to applicants who have lived in other countries or used false documents, but balances these negative points with other, positive discretionary factors in making his decision. He acknowledged that conditions in Kenya were bad but justified his decision by citing the need to combat fraud and alien smuggling. He does still grant withholding of deportation, which protects applicants from being deported, but does not grant them the right to receive benefits, apply for legal permanent residency, or bring family members to join them here.

Particularly in recent years, Judge Gossart said, he has seen "a pattern and practice" of fraud that has disturbed him. "The message that we send—and I use the term 'we' in terms of the system—is that if you can get here, by hook or by crook, and you're a Somali from a certain clan and subclan—and I use Somali because you mentioned it—and you have been the victim of past persecution, you're going to get asylum. Then you can bring all the rest of your family here. I think that sends the wrong message."

For my part, I think that protecting refugees from persecution

7. 19 I&N Dec. 467 (BIA 1987).

is more important than sending a message about controlling our borders. I also think Judge Gossart has misread *Matter of Pula*. While that decision allows for discretionary denials of asylum applications, it also states that "only the most egregious" discretionary factors be cause for a denial of asylum. Furthermore, his understanding of the conditions of Somali refugee camps is incorrect. These camps are not only difficult places but unlivable ones, where refugees are not provided with even the most basic necessities of life, and violence, rape, theft, and disease are commonplace. Those refugees who leave the camps face imprisonment and extortion from the Kenyan police. These conditions are so bad that one cannot justly consider Kenya to be a "safe haven" for Somali refugees.

Judge Gossart is not alone in his opinion, however. Many judges in the Arlington and Baltimore court system, where there are many Somali applicants, deny asylum for similar reasons. In fact Judge Gossart is a fairly sympathetic judge. Other judges show an enforcement mentality, carried over from their previous work experience as INS trial attorneys.

For example, other immigration judges take a much more skeptical attitude toward the plausibility of asylum seekers' claims. Judge Gossart deserves credit for his practice of assigning plausibility a subordinate role and not denying asylum cases on the basis of plausibility alone. Other judges are not as fair; they allow their personal biases and opinions about what is possible or likely, unsupported by the evidence of country conditions, to decide cases.

One of my clients, a church volunteer and nonprofit development agency employee from eastern Congo, was denied asylum by a Baltimore judge simply because she did not believe his story. He had lived in eastern Congo during the second civil war—between Kabila's forces and the forces of Congolese Tutsis, his former allies. Both sides in this war forcibly recruited young people to serve in their armies. My client led members of his church in a protest against this practice, and he was arrested and tortured.

He broke under torture and promised to give the names of the other people who participated in the protest. His captors tied his hands behind his back and took him to his neighborhood, where they wanted him to point out to them the other participants in the protest. When he arrived, his neighbors saw he was in trouble and began to harass the soldiers who were guarding him, shouting at them and throwing rocks. One of the soldiers who was guarding him, and had previously shown some sympathy to his plight, motioned to him that he should run away, and my client did so while the attention of the other soldiers was distracted by the mob. One of his neighbors cut the bonds around his hands, and he ran to a relative's house. The next day the soldiers returned to his house and gave his wife a summons stating that he should turn himself in. He did not do so, of course, and his relatives and friends helped him escape the country and come to the United States.

I knew that his story of escape might seem difficult to believe, so I made sure that his written testimony about the escape was detailed, and we practiced for the hearing so that his oral testimony would also be consistent. He did well in the hearing and gave consistent testimony both on direct and cross-examination. We submitted the summons that his wife had received as evidence, along with some identity documents that my client had managed to bring with him from Congo. He could not submit any other corroborating evidence, however, because he had not been able to establish contact with his family. There was no phone service in the area of Congo where they lived, and though he had sent them letters, they had never responded, and he did not know if the letters had arrived.

The judge denied his case, primarily because she did not believe his escape story to be plausible. She also said that his case lacked corroborating evidence—he should have supported his testimony with letters from his family in Congo, confirming the truth of his story, and she did not find his explanation about his inability to communicate with his family through the mail to be a reasonable one. She even disallowed the summons to arrest that he provided as evidence, because she considered it a government document that was not certified as authentic by the issuing authority.

Another one of my cases, another applicant from eastern Congo, was denied by an Arlington judge for similar reasons. This applicant had spoken out against the forced recruitment practices and human rights abuses practiced by the rebel forces that controlled his area. They had come to his house to arrest him, but he had escaped out the back window, leaving his wife and his sister in the house. He hid near the house for a few minutes, trying to think of what to do next, and heard the soldiers interrogating his sister. He then heard her screaming and heard a gunshot, at which point he fled. He fled the country soon after this and never found out whether his wife and sister had survived; after arriving in the United States, he was unable to regain contact with anyone in eastern Congo.

The Arlington judge denied this case because he found my client's story implausible. He said he could not believe that any man would flee and leave his wife and sister in danger. As in the other case, my client's testimony was detailed and consistent, both on direct and cross-examination, but this did not convince the judge.

Both of these clients' cases are on appeal. Because of the large number of cases in the Board of Immigration Appeals' backlog, they must wait three years before their appeals will be heard. During this time they are not eligible for work authorization and will have a difficult time surviving while they wait for a final decision.

These are only two examples of poor decisions by immigration judges; I could give many more. While the specific reasons for each denial of asylum differ, there is a pattern of thinking on the part of the judges. Few judges have experience working with refugees or in foreign countries. They do not understand that what would be implausible in the United States is perfectly possible in other countries. They also do not understand the great difficulties that asylum applicants face in collecting evidence to corroborate their claims. Finally, their prior experience as INS trial attorneys and in other INS positions lead them to view asylum applicants' claims with skepticism.

This lack of fairness on the part of certain judges is a serious problem in the asylum system, and should be remedied. The Department of Justice should train immigration judges more rigorously so that they are more sensitive to the unique difficulties faced by applicants for asylum. The department should hire more judges who have a background in refugee work and advocacy, and fewer INS trial attorneys. The government has already begun to do this under the direction of the current chief immigration judge, Michael Creppy, but it should increase this practice. Finally, the Board of Immigration Appeals should clarify the law of asylum through its precedent decisions, making it clear that asylum seekers deserve "the benefit of the doubt" on issues of credibility, plausibility, and the availability of corroborating evidence. Unfortunately, instead of doing this the BIA has issued decisions in recent years that make it even more difficult for asylum seekers to prove their cases in court.

9

⊓⊔⊓⊔⊓⊔

Prison and
Expedited Removal

ADELE, PHILIPPE, AND THERESE all used false passports to
enter the United States. What would have happened to them if
they had been caught at the border? Would they have been allowed to apply for asylum? What would have happened to them
while their asylum applications were being considered?

The answers to these questions have changed in the last few
years. Before 1996, any person applying for permission to enter
the United States whose entry was challenged by the INS had the
right to a hearing before an immigration judge before being removed from the country. The 1996 immigration law changed this.
New, "expedited removal" procedures were prescribed for people
whom the INS suspected were not U.S. citizens, and whom the
INS suspected did not have a valid passport or entry visa. A low-
level INS official can now refuse to allow a person to enter the
United States, and applicants for entry have only limited rights of
appeal.

Under the new system, if a person arrives at a border point or
airport without a visa to enter the United States, or with a visa or
passport that the INS inspector thinks is fraudulent, he or she is

taken out of the main passport line, called "primary inspections," and sent to "secondary inspections." At secondary inspections another INS officer looks at the visa and passport more closely, interviews the person, and then decides whether the person is a U.S. citizen and whether the person's passport and visa are valid. If the official decides that the person is not a U.S. citizen and that his or her visa or passport is false, the official can order the alien to leave the country. There is no appeal to this decision, but the person applying for entry can ask that an immigration judge review the immigration officer's file. This review process is not a true appeal, because the applicant for entry cannot make argument, submit additional evidence, or appeal the decision of the immigration judge to a higher court.[1]

The "expedited removal" process provides for entrants who wish to apply for asylum. The secondary inspections officer is supposed to ask the applicants if they are afraid to go back to the country from which they came. If they say yes, the inspector is supposed to refer them to be processed under another procedure, which starts with a "credible fear" interview.

At the "credible fear" interview, an INS asylum officer interviews the applicant to find out why he or she fears return and evaluates the credibility of the applicant's testimony. If the asylum officer finds a reasonable possibility that the applicant is telling the truth, and that the applicant might have a valid reason to fear return, the applicant is referred to an immigration judge for a full hearing. Otherwise the applicant is ordered deported.

Before being sent back, the applicant may ask that a judge review the asylum officer's decision. Again, this does not constitute a true appeal, because the judge cannot speak to the applicant, and the applicant cannot make legal arguments to the judge. The judge makes his or her decision based on the asylum officer's notes. The judge may disagree with the asylum officer's assessment and give

---

1. I am using the terms "person" and "applicant for entry" because even U.S. citizens who look foreign to INS officials may be removed under this procedure. A mentally retarded U.S. citizen, Sharon McKnight, was refused entry and removed to Jamaica by an INS official in Newark, New Jersey, despite evidence presented by family members showing that she was born in the United States. *Newsday,* June 14, 2000.

the applicant a full court hearing. But if the judge agrees with the asylum officer's decision, no further appeal is allowed, and the asylum seeker is deported immediately.

Congress has mandated that asylum applicants be detained throughout the "credible fear" process. These applicants are held at INS-operated detention facilities, if they are available, but many are detained at state and local jails, where they are housed with criminals. If they pass their "credible fear" interview, asylum applicants may be paroled out of prison. The parole decision is made by INS detention and deportation officials, and asylum seekers cannot appeal a negative parole decision to an immigration judge.

Even if the "credible fear" process is implemented exactly as it was designed, some of the refugees who are stopped at the border will not succeed in gaining an asylum hearing. The "credible fear" system forces asylum applicants to ask for asylum right at the airport, from a uniformed INS official, just after they get off of the plane. Most refugees come from countries where uniformed officials are not to be trusted, and many of them have been tortured and imprisoned by government officials in their home countries. Refugees who have suffered rape or sexual assault would not normally be willing to talk about these events with a stranger at an airport. Not realizing that this is their only chance to tell their story, some refugees say nothing about the persecution they experienced and are deported before they even have a chance to apply for asylum.

The expedited removal system, moreover, has not been implemented exactly as it was designed. Some applicants who do manage to articulate a claim for asylum at secondary inspection are deported without receiving "credible fear" interviews, due to the misconduct of individual INS inspectors. There are no outside observers at the secondary inspection interviews, and the INS has turned down requests from nonprofit organizations to monitor secondary inspections. There are no tape recordings or transcripts made of secondary inspections interviews, and the only record made of these proceedings are the notes taken by the INS inspectors themselves. If an inspections official decides to abuse his authority and deport an alien, even after the alien has asked for asylum, no one will ever know about it. The alien will be removed from the country, the official can fill out the paperwork falsely, and no other record of the event will exist.

While it is difficult to know how often this happens, refugee advocates have documented a number of individual cases where asylum applicants were deported without a "credible fear" interview.[2] One of them, an ethnic Albanian refugee from the Kosovo region of Serbia, arrived in the United States on a flight from Mexico City on January 20, 1999. The INS official in secondary inspections did not give him a chance to apply for asylum, even though he indicated he was afraid and said he was a Kosovar of Albanian ethnicity. The INS officer handcuffed him and put him on a plane back to Mexico City. He later managed to enter the United States successfully and applied for asylum with the assistance of the Lawyers Committee for Human Rights. Had he not succeeded in reentering the United States, no one would have ever known about the INS official's misconduct.[3]

Another Kosovar, named Rame Vataj, was forced out of the United States through expedited removal proceedings at Newark airport on February 15, 1998, despite expressing a fear of being returned to Yugoslavia. He returned to the United States a few months later and succeeded in entering this time. Three other asylum seekers were removed but did not succeed in reentering. Two men from Ecuador asked for asylum at New York's JFK International Airport on July 15, 1997, but were returned to Ecuador. They went into hiding and managed to escape again, this time to Europe. Another asylum seeker, Arumugam Thevakumar from Sri Lanka, was forced out of the United States after asking for asylum on January 16, 1999. He was sent back to Turkey, the country where his flight originated, and was detained and beaten by Turkish authorities upon arrival. He later managed to contact the U.N.

2. For more examples, see the case studies in "The Expedited Removal Study: Report on the First Three Years of Implementation of Expedited Removal," Karen Musalo, May 2000, pp. 71–120, and "Is This America? The Denial of Due Process to Asylum Seekers in the United States," Lawyers Committee for Human Rights, October 2000, Appendix 2.

3. "Kosovo Highlights Injustice of Expedited Removal," Jerry Fowler, Lawyers Committee *Advisor,* Summer 1999.

High Commissioner for Refugees in Ankara, Turkey, but it is unclear what happened to him after that.[4]

The INS officials in secondary inspections have failed to use interpreters and have treated asylum applicants rudely and cruelly. In several cases documented by the Lawyers Committee for Human Rights, INS inspectors did not use a professional interpreter but spoke to the applicant through another INS officer or an airline official who did not translate effectively. In several other cases, INS officials used an interpreter who did not speak the applicant's native language but who used a second language that the applicant did not speak well. One INS official told an English-speaking applicant from Nigeria, "Go back to your own country—America doesn't grant asylum." Another official told an applicant that the INS would contact his country's government.

INS officials have also denied applicants food or medical care while in their custody. Immigration officers tried to make Arumugam Thevakumar sign papers that they did not explain to him, and told him he would not be given food unless he signed. Another applicant was kept at the airport for two days and given only two meals during that time. One woman who fled China because of its laws against having more than one child was detained at the airport and began having cramps, chills, and muscle spasms while in INS custody. Even when she fell to the floor from illness, INS officials did not call a doctor; they laughed at her instead.

Some asylum applicants have even suffered physical abuse while in secondary inspections. One asylum applicant, a sixteen-year old from Liberia named Mekabou Fofana, was taken for fingerprinting but did not understand what was going on because the INS had not told him through a translator what they were doing. When he resisted, four officers seized him and tried to fingerprint him by force. He fell and hit his head against the desk and had to be taken to the hospital for stitches. A Guinean asylum seeker was also injured while being forcibly fingerprinted, cutting his head on

4. This example, and those in the following four paragraphs, are taken from "Is This America?" Lawyers Committee for Human Rights, October 2000, and the "Report on Expedited Removal," Karen Musalo, May 2000.

a doorknob, but was not taken to the hospital for treatment. He was also not given the opportunity to apply for asylum, and no official explained the asylum process to him in his own language. Instead, four INS officers carried him to the airplane to be sent back. He struggled and fell three times, hurting his shoulder, and they finally gave up and took him back to the airport and shackled him to a bench. After all these struggles, he managed to speak to another INS official, to whom he explained, in halting English, that he was afraid to go back to Guinea. This official finally referred him to a "credible fear" interview.

Those asylum seekers who do make it through secondary inspections face further hardships before being granted a "credible fear" interview. The 1996 law states that all aliens must be imprisoned until their "credible fear" interviews and may be kept in prison, at the discretion of the INS, until their court hearing. After an arriving alien asks for asylum at secondary inspections, he or she is put in leg irons and handcuffs and forced to wait in a holding area at the airport until the INS can find staff to handle the transfer to a detention facility. Some aliens have been forced to wait for hours, shackled to a bench at the airport. One applicant, a young man from Afghanistan, was held at the airport for twenty-seven hours; another man, from China, was detained for eighteen hours. Both were kept shackled to a bench for most of that time.

Asylum applicants are taken either to INS-run prisons or to state or local criminal jails that agree to take INS detainees on a contract basis. At these detention facilities, asylum seekers are strip-searched, forced to shower within view of the guards, dressed in prison uniforms, and locked into cells. No translator is assigned to explain to them what is happening, why they are being detained, or the rules of the jail or detention center. At INS-run prisons they are detained with other immigration prisoners, but those asylum applicants who are taken to state or local jails are mixed with American criminals.

After being taken to jail, asylum applicants usually wait several days until they hear from the INS again. An asylum officer puts a telephone call through to them at the jail and explains to them, through an interpreter, that they are being detained while they wait for a "credible fear" interview. The asylum officer explains what the interview is, and tells them the date when it will be conducted. One of the few good aspects of the implementation of expedited removal has been the asylum office's conduct of "credible fear" interviews. The asylum office has been careful in its assessment of asylum seekers' credibility, and has referred 88 percent of all "credible fear" applicants to court for a full hearing.[5]

In the Washington, D.C., area, there are no INS prisons, so asylum applicants are first held in county jails near the district office. From there, INS detention officers place applicants in handcuffs and leg irons and transfer them to the office for their "credible fear" interview. After the interview, asylum applicants are moved to a more distant county jail while they await their full hearing before a judge. To avoid the trouble of transporting applicants from these distant jails to the immigration court, the INS and the courts have begun using a video conference system for hearings. The INS has installed video cameras, microphones, and video screens in two county jails, and the Arlington immigration court has put similar equipment in one of its courtrooms.

The video conferencing system has made it possible for the INS to detain asylum seekers in jails hundreds of miles from Washington, D.C., making it difficult for their families and their attorneys to communicate with them. In the last three years the INS has detained most asylum seekers either at the Virginia Beach jail, about four hours away from Washington by car, or at the Piedmont Regional Jail in Farmville, Virginia, which is about three and a half hours distant. Attorneys representing detained asylum seekers normally communicate with their clients by accepting collect calls, which cost eighty-nine cents per minute, or by visiting their clients in person at the jail, a seven-hour roundtrip.

I have assisted a number of imprisoned asylum seekers, but the story of one particularly illustrates the inherent problems of the current "expedited removal" system. Julie Rukongeza, a twenty-eight-year-old woman, came to the United States from the Democratic Republic of Congo. She was born in Rwanda but had

5. "Report on the First Three Years of Expedited Removal," Karen Musalo, May 2000.

lived in Congo since she was a teenager and had a Congolese passport. She managed to get to the United States by plane, but she
had no visa to enter the United States, and the INS official at the
airport told her she would have to go back to Africa. At this point
she began to cry and said she would be killed if she returned there.
The INS officer referred her to "credible fear" proceedings.

Julie was handcuffed and taken away to the Arlington County
Jail. She was searched and her clothing was taken away from her;
in its place she was given an orange prison uniform. Julie did not
understand why this was happening, and no one explained it to
her. Julie speaks no English, and no one at the jail spoke French.
Neither the INS nor the jail authorities provided any translators to
explain to her the rules and procedures of the jail.

Julie spent several days in jail before anything else happened.
She had no friends or family in the United States, but she did have
the phone number of a man who had been her neighbor in Congo
and had moved to the United States years earlier. Unfortunately,
she could not figure out how to use the phones at the jail to call
him.

After three days an INS asylum officer called Julie to explain,
through a translator, that she was being detained until her first
asylum interview, and that this interview would take place in a few
days. The asylum officer asked Julie if she wished to contact
the local office of the United Nations High Commissioner for
Refugees (UNHCR) or if she needed help finding a lawyer. She answered yes to both questions. The asylum officer called the U.N.
on her behalf, and a UNHCR staff person then called me and
asked if I could help her.

By the time I was notified of the case, it was the day before
Julie's interview. I had appointments all day, so I did not talk to
Julie until the morning of her "credible fear" hearing. This hearing
took place at the INS Washington district office in Arlington, Virginia. The INS has two small prison cells there for immigration detainees who are being transported or deported, and they conduct
"credible fear" interviews in a small office near the cells.

I introduced myself to Julie, gave her my business card, and
explained why I was there. She was eager to talk. She explained
that she was a Tutsi, born in Rwanda, who had lived for many

years in Kinshasa, the capital of Congo. In 1998, a year after Laurent Kabila's rebel movement had overthrown the former dictator, Mobutu Sese Seko, a second civil war broke out between rebellious former soldiers, mostly Tutsis, who controlled the eastern part of Congo, and troops loyal to Kabila, who controlled Kinshasa and western Congo. Kabila, who had capitalized on Tutsi antagonism against Hutus in the civil war that brought him to power, now stirred up antagonism against his Tutsi former supporters, calling them "foreigners" and "invaders."

Julie became a victim of this hatred. Soldiers came to her house many times and beat and raped her. She was afraid they would one day kill her. Her friends and neighbors collected money to help her and used it to bribe officials to issue her a Congolese passport. They also bought her a plane ticket. She managed to get on a flight for the United States, despite having no visa to enter the country, and she asked for asylum at the airport.

She had only one question for me: would she be able to leave the jail that day? In their phone conversation two days earlier, the asylum officer had told her she would be eligible for parole after her "credible fear" interview. She had misunderstood this to mean that she would be released immediately after the interview was over. I explained to her that while she would be eligible for release that day, she would not be released immediately—the INS district office would have to approve her release, and she would have to show them that she had a place to go to. As soon as she heard that she would not be leaving the jail that day, she began to weep, and soon she was sobbing, doubled over with her face in her hands. She wept for ten minutes before I could get her to speak again. Then she did not wish to talk about her life in Africa or her reasons for seeking asylum in the United States. She just begged me to get her out of jail. "I'm going to die in jail—please, please, get me out of prison," she said, over and over again.

She was still sobbing when the asylum officers came in. There were two asylum officers present that day—one to do the interview, and an officer-in-training who was there to observe. Julie was still crying, but she was no longer sobbing and could talk. The asylum officers began the interview. Julie and I had been speaking directly to each other in French, but the asylum officers had to use

an interpreter. They set up a speakerphone connection to the
AT&T translation service and began the interview. Julie continued
to cry, but she calmed down when the asylum officers explained to
her that she needed to answer their questions if she wanted to
leave prison. I advised her that she should concentrate on their
questions and answer them as best she could. She agreed to try.

Despite her efforts, Julie said she could not remember many
things about her life. She had never known her place of birth, she
said, beyond the fact that it was in Rwanda, and she could not remember the name of the town where she had grown up. She could
not say exactly how old she was when her parents were killed.
After their death, she went with her younger sister to live at her
grandmother's house. When her grandmother died of natural
causes, Julie was orphaned, and she began living on the street. She
took her little sister and moved west, eventually ending up in Kinshasa, in what was then Zaire. She lived in Kinshasa for many
years until the civil war forced her to leave and come to the United
States.

While Julie claimed she had been born in Rwanda, her passport had been issued by the Congolese government and described
her as a Congolese citizen. She could remember almost nothing
about her childhood in Rwanda, but she could describe the life of
fear, beatings, and rape that she had experienced during the pre-
ceding six months. When the asylum officer pressed her for more
details about her life before these events, she just began to cry and
said, "I don't know, I don't know. . . . I can't remember."

I asked the asylum officers to give me some time to talk with
her alone, and they allowed me to do so. I suspected that Julie was
not being honest in some aspect of her story because she thought if
she told her true story she wouldn't be granted asylum. I suspected
that she was actually a Congolese citizen but was claiming to be a
Rwandan because she thought this would help her win asylum.

I explained to Julie that it didn't really matter what her story
was as long as she told the truth. Regardless of her country of origin, it was clear that she had suffered greatly, and her asylum case
was obviously a strong one. There was no reason to lie or to hide
the truth from the asylum officers. She insisted that she wasn't
lying but that she just couldn't think. "My thoughts just spin

around and around," she said. "All I can think of is getting out of jail. When I think of my life before, all I can think of is the soldiers, and what they did to me and my little sister. . . . I'm so worried about my sister." She began to cry again.

The asylum officers returned. I told them about our conversation, and I explained that memory loss was common with people who had survived severe emotional traumas. There is a name for this condition—post-traumatic stress disorder—and asylum officers are trained to recognize it and to take it into account when making case decisions. "She's obviously afraid of something," one of them said, "we're just not sure what." But they still had to continue with the interview until they had enough information to make a preliminary assessment of her case, and determining her actual country of citizenship was an important part of her case which they could not just skip over.

The interview went on for about two more hours. The asylum officers took a break for lunch, and then questioned Julie for another hour. While she still could not remember many details about her life, they eventually got enough information to make at least some sense of her story. In the end they found that she had a "credible fear" of persecution in either Rwanda, her country of origin, or Congo, her country of "last habitual residence." They found that it was likely she was a citizen of Rwanda, but that she would have to offer more testimony about her actual country of citizenship when she applied for asylum before the immigration judge.

Julie's court hearing would not take place for another four to eight weeks, and in the meantime she was eligible for release from jail. To be paroled, however, she would have to find a sponsor who was willing to take her in and be responsible for her care. She had not been able to contact her former neighbor, and she did not know anyone else in the United States. I told her that I would help her contact this neighbor, or find a church or shelter that was willing to take her in, but that she would have to stay in jail until we worked something out. I expected to have her out of jail within one week, if everything went well.

Her former neighbor had somehow heard that she was in jail, and he called the INS on his own. I made a written request for parole, and he went to the INS to sign a statement saying he was able and willing to take care of her—but it turned out that he did not have permanent status in the United States. He had temporary status and a work permit, but the INS's rules allow only for someone with permanent status to act as a sponsor. I had to start over, this time with a shelter for refugees called the International Friendship House in York, Pennsylvania.

Meanwhile, Julie had been transferred from the Arlington jail to the Piedmont Regional Detention Center in Farmville, Virginia, about 150 miles from Washington. This new jail had different rules from the Arlington jail, including a rule that prisoners could not have long hair. Julie's hair had been braided, and she had long artificial braids coming down to her shoulders. She did not understand why they were cutting her hair, and she thought she was being punished. She began to protest, in French, that she had not done anything wrong, and she began to struggle, resisting being put into the barber's chair. The guards handcuffed her and forced her into the chair, and held her down as they cut off her braids. She screamed and cried, but they continued cutting her hair until it was very short. She spent the rest of the week in jail, frightened and unsure if she would ever get out.

The INS detention office had not told me that Julie was being moved to Farmville. Her "credible fear" interview had taken place on a Tuesday, and I visited her on Friday of the same week to reassure her that I was still working on her parole. I went back to see her the next week to tell her about the progress of her parole request. When I got to the Arlington jail, I found that she was no longer there. The jail personnel tried to help, but they could not find any record of where the INS had taken her—they knew only that she had been moved the day before.

I called Julie's detention officer the next day and learned that she had been moved to Farmville. I also found that she had had her first court hearing that morning, a hearing I had not been notified about. By this time Julie was terrified. She had been transferred from one jail to another, her hair had been cut off—apparently in punishment for something—and at her hearing before the judge, her lawyer had not even shown up. The hearing process itself was strange and frightening to her—she could see the judge on a little television, and hear him and the translator through a speaker, and apparently the judge could hear and see her as well. She told the judge that she had a lawyer, but she didn't know where he was and she wanted to get out of jail. He told her that he had to wait until her lawyer appeared, and that he would reschedule the hearing for the next week.

Next week! Julie felt like she would die if she waited that long. In any case, she thought her lawyer had abandoned her, and she had no way of finding a new lawyer. If she had no lawyer next week, would the judge order her out of the country? What could she do? Unfortunately, there was no way for me to reassure Julie that I was still working on her case. At that time the jail did not accept incoming calls for inmates,[6] and Julie could not call me because the phone system at my office does not accept collect calls. I did not have time to travel all the way to Farmville just to reassure her. Instead I spent my time working on her request for parole. The only shelter near Washington, D.C., that is willing to accept refugees is one in York, Pennsylvania, called the International Friendship House. This shelter houses asylum seekers who have been released from the York County jail, a local prison which has contracted with the INS to house hundreds of immigration detainees. The volunteers and staff at the International Friendship House agreed to help Julie and sent a letter to the INS stating that their shelter would house and provide for her if the INS would release her from jail. I spoke to Julie's detention officer that day, and he said he had passed the letter along to his supervisor.

After a few days passed, I called the detention officer's supervisor to ask about the progress of Julie's parole request. She told me that she had forwarded the request to the district director and that he would look at it as soon as he had time. When I asked her how long this would take, she said it would take perhaps one week, maybe two or three—it was hard to say. I asked her if she could intervene with the district director to have him make this more of a priority, and she said it was out of her hands. If I wanted

6. The jail has since changed this policy and is quite accommodating in setting up phone calls between detained asylum seekers and their representatives.

him to move quickly on the request, I would have to talk to the director myself.

Instead of transferring my call to his office, she put me on hold. I waited about ten minutes while I did some other work, but no one ever picked up the phone. I called her back, but she did not listen to what I had to say—as soon as she heard my voice, she said, "Hold on, I'll transfer you," and put me on hold again. I hung up and called her several more times, but she had stopped answering her phone.

I left an angry voice mail message for her, and then called another number at the district office and managed to get transferred to the director's office. I left a message with his secretary, as he was not in the office when I called. In both my message to him and my message to the deportation supervisor, I threatened to contact the *Washington Post* about Julie's situation. I referred to the negative media attention they had received earlier with another of my clients, Aster Cheru.

I left work at five o'clock that day feeling defeated and foolish for having lost my temper and having made empty threats. The next morning, however, I checked my voice mail and found a message that had been left at 6:30 that evening. The district director had reviewed Julie's parole request and approved it. She would be released as soon as someone was able to pick her up at the jail.

I could not go to the jail that day because I had a court appearance scheduled for the afternoon, but I was able to pick her up the following day. Julie was sad and looked at me uncertainly when I met her at the jail. She was thinner than when I had seen her the week before, and her eyes were red and swollen from crying. One of the guards gave her back her own clothing, and she went to change, but she still didn't seem to believe she was really leaving. When she came out dressed in her own clothes, the guard, trying to joke with her, said, "You're leaving—are you going to smile now?" I told him that she didn't speak English and couldn't understand what he was saying. "All she's done is cry since she came in here," he said.

Julie didn't smile when we walked out of the jail, and she remained silent until we had driven out of sight of the prison. Then she began to talk, all in a rush. "That jail was a terrible place . . . a terrible place!" It was old and dirty, she said, the food was strange to her and tasted bad, and it was noisy all the time, making it impossible for her to sleep. The Arlington jail, she said, was a nice place by comparison.

I drove Julie from Farmville, Virginia, to York, Pennsylvania, a journey of about three hundred miles. The drive is a beautiful one, through the foothills of the Appalachian Mountains, passing forest, pastureland, and the occasional farm. Julie did not talk much but seemed to enjoy looking out the window. From time to time she would sigh happily and say, "I have left the prison."

When we arrived at the shelter we met the other residents, all of them former INS detainees. About ten of them were living there at the time, and they were quite a mix: a young man from Russia, two women from China, a man from Pakistan, and several Africans. One of the Africans, a young man from Nigeria, spoke some French; another, a young woman who was also a Rwandan Tutsi, spoke French fluently. She greeted Julie warmly.

The other residents had been detained in large jails with many other immigration detainees. They were all surprised that Julie had been released so quickly. "Two weeks!" they kept repeating. One had been in jail for two months, another for five. Most of them had had to stay in jail until their cases were decided by the judge.

As difficult as Julie's experience had been, the other asylum applicants were right when they told her that she was comparatively lucky. Each INS district director sets his own policy about the parole of asylum applicants. INS headquarters issues guidelines, but in practice district directors have nearly unlimited power to detain any applicant until he or she gains status. In the Washington District, which has jurisdiction over Virginia and the District of Columbia, the district director usually grants parole to asylum seekers, provided they have a person willing to sponsor them. In most cases the Washington District Office also requires the asylum applicant or the sponsor to post a $5,000 bond. The Maryland district director paroles most asylum seekers but not all, and, as we saw with Philippe's case, the Baltimore district office can take a very hard line. At the extreme end of the spectrum, the INS district directors in New York and New Jersey almost never parole asylum applicants until their cases are decided. Some asylum seekers, denied asylum at their court hearings, have spent years in INS jails in New York and New Jersey, waiting for their appeals to be heard by the BIA.[7]

Some detained asylum seekers receive even worse treatment than Julie did. Yudaya Nanyonga, an asylum seeker from Uganda, was transferred from the Wackenhut INS detention center in Queens, New York, to the York County Prison in York, Pennsylvania, where she was assigned to the maximum-security section. She became frightened and began crying uncontrollably. Prison officials responded by stripping her naked, injecting her with sedatives, and placing her in a four-point restraint. Prison officials claim that she was put in maximum security due to an administrative error, and that she was stripped, sedated, and restrained because they were afraid she would commit suicide. Yudaya thought she was treated this way as a punishment for complaining about conditions at Wackenhut; one York prison official told a representative of a nonprofit agency that she was in fact being "made an example of."[8]

At the Virginia Beach jail, in Virginia, immigration detainees complained that prison guards taunted them with racist statements and woke them up late at night by dragging their keys against the cell bars. The prison was so crowded that some detainees had to sleep on mattresses on the floor for lack of beds. Inmates were allowed outside to the exercise yard only twenty minutes per week. When an Amnesty International delegation complained, the officer in charge replied that "there was no constitutional right to recreation," and that "this facility passed inspection and was found to be in compliance." If the inmates wanted recreation, he said, "they could do push-ups and other exercises in the area outside their cells."[9]

The situation of children in INS detention is particularly difficult. Each year thousands of minors are picked up by the INS and placed in detention facilities. INS regulations state that children

---

7. "Lost in the Labyrinth: Detention of Asylum-seekers," *Amnesty International,* September 1999, pp. 24–39, and "Refugees Behind Bars: The Imprisonment of Asylum Seekers in the Wake of the 1996 Immigration Act," pp. 25–32.

8. "Lost in the Labyrinth," pp. 45–46.

9. "Lost in the Labyrinth," p. 56.

should be detained in noncriminal settings, such as foster homes, group homes, or shelters, but there are so many minors in detention that the INS cannot provide these settings for all child detainees. In fact, 34 percent of juvenile detention stays take place in criminal facilities, where children detained by INS are housed with U.S. citizen children who have been convicted of crimes.[1]

Some children are even placed in adult detention facilities. If INS disputes a noncitizen's claim to be under eighteen, it uses dental exams and an x-ray exam of the bone structure of the applicant's wrist to verify the applicant's claim. The INS continues this practice despite protests from professors of dentistry and the American Dental Association that dental testing is not accurate. At the New York airport, a dentist, not a doctor, examines the x-rays as well as the dental records to determine age. This dentist, whose fee is paid by the INS, determines that a person claiming to be a minor is actually over eighteen in approximately 90 percent of his examinations.[2]

In 1998 a delegation from Human Rights Watch visited an INS contract facility for children, the Berks County Youth Center in Leesport, Pennsylvania. They found many violations of the INS's own regulations on treatment of juvenile detainees, established after INS agreed to a settlement in a 1997 class-action lawsuit, *Flores v. Reno*.[3] These violations included not giving lists of legal services providers to the detainees, not providing Chinese translators despite the presence of many Chinese juveniles at the facility, and inadequate educational and recreational programs. Children were also handcuffed on the way to and from court, and some eligible for release to family members had their release delayed unnecessarily, sometimes for months.[4]

Many of these problems have existed for years, but Congress

1. Jo Becker, "Children in Detention Suffer Denial of Basic Human Rights," *Detention Watch Network News*, Lutheran Immigration and Refugee Services, April/May 2000.

2. Chris Hodges, "Airport Dentist Crucial to INS Gatekeeping," *New York Times*, July 24, 2000.

3. *Flores v. Reno*, 113 S. Ct. 1439 (1993). The regulations were published as "Processing, Detention, and Release of Juveniles," in the *Federal Register*, vol. 63, p. 39,759 (July 24, 1998), and amended 8 C.F.R. section 236.3.

4. "Detained and Deprived of Rights: Children in the Custody of the U.S. Immigration and Naturalization Service," by Jo Becker and Michael Bochenek, *Human Rights Watch*, December 1998.

and the INS have recently made them worse. In 1996 the immigration law changes passed by Congress made it mandatory for the INS to detain asylum seekers and immigrants who have been convicted of certain crimes, but Congress did not give the INS enough money to build enough new detention facilities to accommodate these prisoners. When the law took effect, the average number of immigrants in INS detention at any given time doubled from 8,279 in 1996 to 16,400 in 1999;[5] the INS estimates that this number will reach 23,000 by 2001.[6] Since most INS detainees do not stay in jail long, the number of individuals detained by the INS in the course of a year is actually much higher: in 1998 the INS detained 153,517 individuals.[7] With so many new detainees, the INS had to find space for them and greatly increased its reliance on criminal jails. INS headquarters issued new standards for INS detention centers in 1998, but these standards applied only to INS-managed jails and few jails run by private contractors.[8] Later, after being pressured by immigrants' rights groups, the INS issued standards that state and local jails would be required to adhere to. The jails, however, will not be required to meet these standards until 2003; until that time the INS holds them to no standards at all.

Under the current system, when advocates for asylum seekers complain to local INS officials, we are told that the jails set policies for the treatment of inmates and that we must talk to the jail officials if we have a concern. The jail officials treat all inmates the same and refuse to make special allowances for immigration detainees. Many officials do not even understand that some INS detainees are asylum seekers who have committed no crime. One official, an INS deportation officer assigned to the Wicomico County jail in Maryland, did not even acknowledge a difference between asylum seekers and other detainees. In an interview with the Women's Commission for Refugee Women and Children, he complained, "You keep using the term asylum seekers, like there

5. "INS Reinterprets Mandatory Detention Provisions, Proposes Other Detention Changes," *Interpreter Releases*, July 19, 1999, pp. 1082–1086, 1099–1102.

6. "Locked Away: Immigration Detainees in Jails in the United States," *Human Rights Watch*, September 1998.

7. "INS Reinterprets Mandatory Detention Provisions," p. 1084.

8. "Detention Operations Policy Manual," INS Detention Management Branch, reprinted in the *Detention Resource Manual*, Lutheran Immigration and Refugee Services, March 1998.

are good people and bad people. They're all the same. You can't educate them or rehabilitate them. They're in detention."[9]

How can this situation be improved? The INS and Congress need to remember that there are fundamental differences in the reasons for the detention of asylum seekers and the detention of criminals. In theory, asylum seekers are detained only so that the government can be sure they will not abscond before their hearings. Since asylum seekers have committed no crimes, it is not necessary to detain them in high-security settings. Many asylum seekers have suffered imprisonment, torture, rape, and other trauma in their home country, and one goal of a detention policy should be not to traumatize these people further. Most of all, the detention of asylum seekers should be used only where necessary to ensure attendance at a hearing, and should never be used as a deterrent or a punishment for applying for asylum.

The INS could adopt a humane and fair detention policy if it had the funds and the political will to do so. When Congress mandated a detention policy but did not provide enough funds to implement it, it virtually forced the INS to keep INS detainees in criminal jails. But even if the INS did have enough money to build its own detention facilities, it is unlikely that INS officials would build low-security, shelterlike facilities. INS officials do not consider the nontraumatization of asylum seekers to be a priority. INS detention officials are trained to put enforcement first: to ensure that large numbers of unauthorized aliens are caught, detained, and deported as quickly as possible. While more compassionate officials at the asylum office make decisions about "credible fear" hearings, the INS leaves decisions about parole to the district directors and their subordinates in the Deportation and Detention division. As long as decisions on detention and parole rest with these officials, the INS will continue to detain large numbers of asylum seekers with little regard for the conditions of their detention.

INS headquarters has issued guidelines about the parole of asylum seekers but leaves district directors wide authority to determine their own parole policy and does nothing to discipline or

---

9. "Liberty Denied: Women Seeking Asylum Imprisoned in the United States," Women's Commission for Refugee Women and Children, April 1997, p. 11.

overrule directors who do not follow the guidelines. To me, this is one of the most puzzling and frustrating aspects of the whole issue of detention. For some reason the New York district director can openly ignore the directives of his supervisors and almost never grant parole to detained asylum-seekers without getting into any trouble. The representatives of nonprofit agencies meet regularly with INS headquarters officials, and this issue is brought up at almost every meeting. To date the headquarters officials have done little about the problem and have refused to allow detainees to appeal district directors' parole decisions.[1]

While the INS has done little to protect asylum seekers in detention, the Board of Immigration Appeals has taken action to help detained asylum seekers find legal representation. On October 4, 2000, the Catholic Legal Immigration Network, Inc. (CLINIC), one of the nation's largest immigration legal services agencies, and the Capital Area Immigrant's Rights Coalition (CAIR) announced that they would begin operating a pilot project to help detained aliens find representation for appeals at the BIA. Because most BIA appeals are done entirely in writing and do not involve new testimony or oral argument, a lawyer can represent an alien's case on appeal even if he or she does not live near where the alien is detained. The appeals project matches volunteer lawyers with aliens in need of representation. The BIA itself provides funding and administrative support for the CLINIC/CAIR project, and the American Bar Association has encouraged its members to participate and has provided funding for other organizations that assist asylum seekers in detention.[2]

1. On December 28, 2000, the INS released interim regulations "clarifying" the Immigration and Nationality Act, stating that other officials at INS headquarters had the authority to grant parole to detained aliens. *Interpreter Releases,* January 8, 2001, pp. 49, 224–226; citing 65 Federal Register 82254–56. In a meeting with nonprofit legal services agencies shortly before the regulations' publication, INS headquarters officials explained that under the new regulations they still would not consider appeals from aliens. They stated that INS headquarters officials would overturn the parole decisions of district directors only in rare cases, such as those in which there was adverse publicity. Meeting with the INS Office of International Affairs, November 8, 2000.

2. "Pro Bono Update: BIA Approves Pilot Project; ABA President Urges Greater Awareness, Volunteerism," *Interpreter Releases,* October 30, 2000, pp. 1552–1553, and personal interview with Andrea Siemens, CAIR.

What would a humane detention system be like? First, most asylum seekers would not be detained at all. In cases where they must be detained, they should be allowed to live in low-security, shelterlike settings, where they would be housed with other asylum seekers, not with criminals. Social workers and volunteers fluent in their languages should be on hand to help them adjust to their arrival in the United States and to help them overcome any trauma that they experienced in their home countries. The INS should especially make sure that juvenile detainees, both asylum seekers and others, are detained in appropriate settings and have access to legal counsel.

The INS could administer these detention shelters themselves or could contract their administration out to private companies or nonprofits. Most European countries use such a system with success. But the INS will not open similar shelters until Congress instructs them to do so and gives them adequate funding. Advocates for asylum seekers have discussed the possibility of legislation on this point, but so far no member of Congress has proposed a bill to fundamentally reform the INS detention system.

Senator Dianne Feinstein of California introduced a bill that would make the detention system treat children more fairly. The "Unaccompanied Alien Child Protection Act of 2000," introduced on September 27, 2000, as Senate Bill 3117, would establish an Office of Children's Services within the Department of Justice to oversee government actions involving unaccompanied alien children and would make the best interest of the child the guiding principle of all government actions. The bill would require the prompt parole of unaccompanied alien children in INS detention to U.S. relatives and would require that children without relatives be kept in appropriate, nonsecure facilities. The government would appoint legal counsel and a guardian *ad litem* for any child without relatives in the United States. The bill would also change technical aspects of current immigration law to make it easier for children to obtain legal immigration status, and would require special training for INS officials who work with unaccompanied minors. If passed, the bill would largely fix the problems of INS abuse of unaccompanied alien minors. It was introduced without any co-sponsors, and only a few other senators have declared support for the bill. Without additional support from other senators, particularly Republicans, it is not likely that the bill will succeed.

While no members of Congress have proposed doing away with the entire expedited removal system, a bill has been proposed that would limit the use of expedited removal and discourage the detention of asylum seekers. This bill, the Refugee Protection Act, proposed in 1999 by a bipartisan coalition of senators, would end the practice of expedited removal and reinstate the pre-1996 system of allowing every asylum seeker the chance to be heard by a judge. Expedited removal procedures would be used only in rare cases when the attorney general declared an "immigration emergency," and even in such emergencies the use of expedited removal would be limited. The bill also contains language that discourages the detention of asylum seekers while they await their hearings.

The Refugee Protection Act has not yet been considered by the Senate Judiciary Committee, let alone the full Senate. And, despite lobbying efforts by refugee advocates, no one has introduced a corresponding bill in the House of Representatives. Until Congress makes this issue a higher priority, the INS will continue to arrest, detain, and deport asylum seekers under the current expedited removal procedure.

A week after Julie's arrival in York, Pennsylvania, she managed to contact her friend in North Carolina, and her friend's church, whose congregation were mostly immigrants from Congo, agreed to assist her. She moved from Pennsylvania to North Carolina, and living with people from Congo helped her begin to recover from her trauma.

Julie's hearing was held about five months after her arrival. I anticipated two problems with her case, both of them serious. First, the INS would be able to use the notes from her "credible fear" hearing against her. Her account of her life during the "credible fear" hearing was incoherent, and in many places the notes of that interview disagreed with her actual story. Also, the INS would argue that even if her story were true, she would be safe in returning to Rwanda, her country of citizenship. The rapes and other persecution she had suffered in Congo would not be relevant to her case, as her suffering in Congo did not indicate that she would be in danger in Rwanda. In fact, the government of Rwanda was now controlled by Tutsis, so the INS would have a strong argument that she could return there safely.

To overcome the problem of credibility, I arranged for her to see a psychologist expert in post-traumatic stress disorder, who could work with her and then testify that Julie's story was true. For the second problem—that she would not be in danger of persecution in Rwanda—I could make two arguments. I researched current conditions in Rwanda and found that, although the government was controlled by ethnic Tutsis, Hutu rebel groups were still operating in the country, and they sometimes killed Tutsi civilians. This was a weak argument, however, and I thought it unlikely that the judge would find that these isolated attacks supported a well-founded fear of persecution in Rwanda.

I could also argue that, even if Julie did not have a well-founded fear of future persecution in Rwanda, she should not be forced to go there for humanitarian reasons related to the severity of her past persecution. She had not lived there since she was a small child, had no friends or family there, and had suffered extreme persecution there at an early age. There was support in the case law for granting asylum to a refugee based on past persecution alone, even where there was not a well-founded fear of future persecution. The example usually cited in the case law is that of Jewish citizens of Germany after World War II. Even though country conditions had changed after the defeat of the Nazis, so that it might have been safe for Jews to return, it would have been inhumane to force them to return to countries where they had suffered so greatly. This general idea was implied by the wording of the U.N. Protocol on the Status of Refugees and the U.S. law implementing that protocol, the Refugee Act of 1980. The idea was given specific form in U.S. case law in a decision called *Matter of Chen*, and was also written into the asylum regulations.[3]

---

3. 20 I&N Dec. 16 (BIA 1989). Mr. Chen was a Chinese citizen who had suffered severe persecution as a child because his father was a Christian minister. The BIA found that conditions had changed in China so that he no longer had a well-founded fear of future persecution, but granted him asylum for humanitarian reasons and because of the severity of the past persecution he had suffered. This ruling was codified in the regulations at 8 CFR 208.13 (b)(ii), but the regulations were changed in 2000 to make it more difficult for victims of past persecution to be granted asylum. This change is discussed in more detail in the next chapter.

I worked with Julie to write down the specifics of her story, and to go over them with her so that she could testify with confidence. I also wrote a brief analyzing the legal issues in her case. I contacted Dr. Judy Okawa, who works as the director of the Program for Victims of Torture and Trauma at the Center of Multicultural Human Services, a social service agency located near Washington, D.C. Dr. Okawa agreed to see Julie, but her schedule was too full for her to see Julie before her hearing, which was scheduled for October 2000. I asked the judge to postpone the hearing to a later date so that Dr. Okawa could talk to Julie and give testimony as an expert witness.

The judge assigned to Julie's case was Wayne Iskra. Judge Iskra is a strict judge but a fair one, who believes strongly in giving asylum applicants the right to present evidence and call witnesses, and to be given due process in their hearings. Judge Iskra would not postpone the hearing, but he agreed to hold a second hearing, at a later date, at which Dr. Okawa could testify. We proceeded with Julie's testimony. I had Julie tell her entire story, again, to the judge, and I followed along with the written statement that Julie and I had prepared, to see if her oral testimony contradicted her written statement. She did fairly well, and her testimony in court followed her written statement nearly exactly. Her memory of her childhood years was still vague, however. She could not tell how far apart her parents' house and her grandmother's house were, and she still could not remember the name of the village in Rwanda where she had lived. She could not remember her age at the time of each significant event in her life, or estimate how much time had passed between significant events.

Where she could remember things, Julie's testimony and her written statement were fairly consistent. During cross-examination the INS attorney addressed some of the contradictions that Julie had made in minor factual matters, but the attorney was unable to make her contradict herself further during cross-examination. She did, however, seem confused by the INS attorney's questions and often replied to questions about her past by stating that she didn't know or couldn't remember. The attorney also read parts of the "credible fear" interview notes to Julie, pointing out the contradictions and asking Julie for an explanation. Julie answered that she did not remember saying these things during the "credible fear" interview and could not explain why the answers she had given at that time were different.

The inconsistencies between the "credible fear" notes and Julie's testimony were considerable. The notes indicated that Julie said her parents were killed when she was fifteen years old, that she had lived with her grandmother until she was seventeen, and that she had attended high school in Rwanda. The notes indicated that Julie had said she left Rwanda in 1997 or 1998 and had lived in Congo for only eight months before coming to the United States. Julie had also stated that her parents had died two years ago, which contradicted her statements in the same interview that her parents had died when she was fifteen.

While Julie was unable to explain these inconsistencies at the hearing, I knew why they were there, having attended the "credible fear" hearing myself. The INS interviewer, frustrated with Julie's inability to answer even simple questions, began asking leading questions, such as "So this happened when you were seventeen, right?" to which Julie often answered "yes" without really listening to or understanding the question. Unfortunately, as her legal representative, I could not also act as a witness to what had occurred in the "credible fear" interview. I had considered asking the asylum officer who had conducted that interview to appear as a witness, but I had decided against it. I thought it might be difficult to get the asylum officer to agree to testify, and I also thought the psychologist's report and testimony would be enough to establish Julie's credibility.

After the INS attorney finished, I had the opportunity to ask Julie questions again, but I asked only a few. I asked her about her mental state during the "credible fear" interview, and she answered that she was confused, scared, and depressed. She said she had had a hard time answering questions, and she couldn't remember much at that time because her head was spinning with thoughts and worries. She still had a problem with her memory, she said, but she was much better now than when she was in jail. The judge asked a few questions, as well, trying to get her to clarify her answers on certain points, but she was unable to answer many of his questions because of her poor memory and her confusion. He then adjourned the hearing, telling us to return in January 2001, when he would hear testimony from Julie's psychologist.

Dr. Okawa asked for Julie to come in for two days of psychological interviewing and testing. Dr. Okawa spent about four hours with Julie each day, talking to her about her life history and her current emotional state. The sessions may have had some therapeutic value, but they were primarily meant to be testing sessions. Dr. Okawa was evaluating Julie's mental health for the court and was forming her own expert opinion as to whether Julie's memory lapses and confusion were caused by trauma or were evidence of dishonesty.

In addition to the clinical interviews, Dr. Okawa administered several tests, including the "Traumatic Experiences Inventory" and the "Trauma Symptom Inventory." The "Traumatic Experiences Inventory" is a simple list of traumatic experiences, but the "Trauma Symptom Inventory" is more sophisticated. It asks about emotional and psychological states, such as "dissociation," in which a person withdraws from the world around her into her own memory, and "intrusive experiences," in which a person suffers sudden, strong, and painful memories of the trauma while engaged in unrelated thoughts and activities. This test is particularly reliable because it measures symptoms that most laypersons do not know to be associated with traumatic stress. To falsify a positive result on this test, a person would have to be both a good actor and well informed about the nature and clinical symptoms of post-traumatic stress disorder.

Julie scored high on these tests, establishing that she had symptoms indicative of post-traumatic stress disorder. Dr. Okawa also tested her short-term memory and found it to be significantly impaired. For example, on the "Digit Span Forwards" and "Digit Span Backwards" subtests of the "Wechsler Adult Intelligence Test—III," Julie could remember and repeat back only two or three numbers in a series, where most people can remember and repeat back at least seven digits, as in a telephone number, or more. This indicated to Dr. Okawa that Julie suffered from cognitive confusion, meaning that she was distracted by thoughts, feelings, and memories that result from her experience of trauma. This cognitive confusion would explain some of the difficulties

Julie had in testifying accurately at her "credible fear" interview and in court.

Dr. Okawa wrote a nine-page report on her findings, and I submitted it to the court. At Julie's final hearing in January, Dr. Okawa testified for an hour and a half. On direct examination, I asked her to explain her methods and her findings. I then asked her to give her expert opinion on whether the statements on Julie's asylum claim were true and whether the harm that Julie had suffered as a child was, in her opinion, particularly severe. Dr. Okawa answered that, despite Julie's problems with her memory and her confusion on details, she was sure that Julie had truly experienced the persecution she had described, and that the harm she suffered from this persecution, especially in view of how young she was when it happened, could be classified as extremely severe.

I knew that Judge Iskra might not take Dr. Okawa's testimony seriously if he thought she was overly sympathetic and uncritical, so I asked her how she tested for the possibility that Julie was faking her symptoms or lying. Dr. Okawa explained how the tests contain safeguards against this possibility, and she also described how she checked for dishonesty, or what she called "malingering," in her clinical interviews. She observed that, of the approximately thirty times she had been asked to testify in court for an asylum case, she had found that the applicant was "malingering" in about one-quarter of those cases.

Dr. Okawa stated that Julie's case was unusual in the amount of confusion she evidenced and her lack of memory of so many childhood events. Because of this, Dr. Okawa had considered seriously the possibility that Julie was malingering and had tested extensively for it, but she was convinced in the end that Julie's confusion did not indicate dishonesty. Instead she felt that the confusion was a result of the severity of Julie's experience of trauma, which she suffered at such a young age, as well as the psychological damage she suffered by growing up as a street child and the physical harm that had come from a childhood of malnutrition and poverty. Dr. Okawa noted that Julie often spoke as if she were still a small child, and her memory of events, even recent ones, was like a child's memory. She said that Julie seemed to suffer from a kind of developmental delay, almost a form of retardation.

The INS attorney asked some good questions during cross-examination, having Dr. Okawa define her terms more exactly and asking her whether Julie's symptoms might be evidence of some other psychological condition, not post-traumatic stress disorder. The INS attorney also asked if Dr. Okawa could state, with certainty, which exact account of Julie's life was correct—the account she gave in her "credible fear" interview, the account she gave in her written statement for court, or the slightly different account she gave in her oral testimony. Dr. Okawa admitted that some of Julie's symptoms could be evidence of other disorders, but the kind and combination of symptoms clearly indicated post-traumatic stress. She could not say, with certainty, that any of Julie's accounts were accurate in every detail, but she reaffirmed that Julie's basic story of trauma was true.

On "re-direct," or my turn to ask questions again, I corrected possible problems and misunderstandings that had arisen during cross-examination. The judge then asked a few direct questions. "Dr. Okawa, do you think that Julie's parents were murdered when she was a child?" "Yes." "Why?" Dr. Okawa gave a summary of the reasons why she believed this part of Julie's story. "Do you think that Julie was raped in Congo?" "Yes." "Why?" Dr. Okawa explained her reasons for this. "Do you think that Julie is telling the truth?" "Yes." "Why?" Dr. Okawa explained her reasons for believing Julie's story, despite the gaps in Julie's memory and her contradictory statements. The judge thanked Dr. Okawa, and she left the witness stand.

When a judge asks direct questions like this, it is a good sign. It means he is listening and seriously considering what is being said. In my closing statement I emphasized that Julie's story should be believed despite the gaps and contradictions in her testimony. Dr. Okawa's expert testimony explained the reasons for these gaps and contradictions and affirmed the truth of Julie's claim. I then argued that Julie still had a well-founded fear of persecution in Rwanda, and that even if she did not, she deserved a grant of asylum on past persecution alone. The judge asked, "What's the past persecution?" I answered that Julie's persecution consisted of the emotional and psychological harm that resulted from the death of her parents, and also the loss of food, shelter, an education, and her later status as a child beggar. The severity of this persecution, along with other humanitarian factors, justified a grant of asylum regardless of whether the court found that Julie had a well-founded fear of future persecution.

The INS attorney argued that, despite the testimony of Dr. Okawa, the contradictions in Julie's testimony were so substantial that her story simply could not be found credible. He pointed to problems in Dr. Okawa's testimony and emphasized that she herself admitted that she could not say with certainty which version of Julie's story was true. Even if Julie were telling the truth about her parents' death, one could not be certain that her parents died due to ethnic violence; they could have been murdered as part of a personal dispute or during a robbery. Even if they were killed for reasons of ethnic hatred, conditions had changed in Rwanda, so that now, with a Tutsi-led government in place, it would be safe for Julie to return.

Judge Iskra began to read his decision. Just as Judge Grant had done in Aster Cheru's case, Judge Iskra did not immediately tell us whether he would approve the case. He read into the record the basic tenets of the law of asylum, including the law relating to the grant of asylum where the applicant demonstrates past persecution but no well-founded fear of future persecution. He stated that he found Dr. Okawa's testimony and evaluation to be credible, but he also found many inconsistencies in Julie's testimony. He began to list them, one by one, and they sounded particularly severe. In some cases an inconsistency existed between the "credible fear" interview notes and the asylum application, but in others there were three versions of the same story—one in the "credible fear" interview, one in Julie's written statement, and one in Julie's oral testimony. The judge listed about ten inconsistencies that he had found and added that many aspects of Julie's testimony were vague and lacking in detail—another indicator of noncredibility.

By this point I was somewhat worried, as it looked like the judge might deny Julie's case. Fortunately he went on to say that while "in most cases, this court would find the respondent to be noncredible," in this case he placed "great weight" on Dr. Okawa's testimony. He felt that Julie's demeanor while she was testifying was childlike, so his own observation corresponded to

Dr. Okawa's diagnosis of Julie's impaired psychological development. The judge also noted that he was willing to accept Dr.
Okawa's diagnosis of cognitive confusion as an adequate explanation for the vagueness and inconsistencies in Julie's testimony.

Judge Iskra went on to say that he could not be sure of every
fact in Julie's case, but that he could make certain basic factual
findings. He found that it was true that she was a Rwandan citizen, of Tutsi ethnicity; that her parents were killed as a result of
ethnic violence; that she lived with her grandmother for some
time, then with an abusive caretaker, then as a street child, finally
ending up in Kinshasa; and that she was raped by Congolese soldiers in Kinshasa because of her Tutsi ethnicity. All of this supported his finding that Julie was a victim of past persecution and
that she did not have firm resettlement or a "safe haven" in
Rwanda.

The judge declined to comment on the issue of future persecution and based his decision on the severity of past persecution. He
noted that the law, as stated in *Matter of Chen,* gave him the ability to grant asylum based on past persecution alone, when discretionary and humanitarian considerations argued in favor of doing
so. He stated that this case clearly fell within those provisions.
Julie had been "severely traumatized" and "psychiatrically
harmed" as a result of her persecution, and "to send her, a woman
with no family, back to Rwanda, is something that I am not going
to do. Accordingly, it is ordered that her application for asylum be
granted."

I felt a tremendous feeling not of happiness but of relief. Julie
did not seem especially moved by the result, but I think she was
too exhausted to feel much of anything. After we left the courtroom, Julie asked me when she would get a work permit. She was
worried about her little sister, whom she had talked with a few
weeks earlier on the phone. Her sister was not doing well in Kinshasa—without Julie there to provide for her, she did not have
enough to eat, and she had been ill with fever. We applied for employment authorization that day, but it would be two months before the INS sent her a work permit. Meanwhile Julie would have
to continue to wait, as she had been doing for the last eight
months. I gave her some money to send to her little sister in Kin-

shasa. I almost never give clients money for relatives overseas, but in this case, as Julie had no other surviving family and had suffered so much in her life, I thought that giving her the money would be justified.

Julie also asked me how she could bring her little sister to the United States to live with her. I had to answer that I did not know. The law allows for asylees to bring their spouses and children to the United States, but not their siblings. Even if we could somehow argue that Julie's little sister should be considered as an adopted daughter, her sister was over twenty-one years old and not eligible for a visa as Julie's dependent. The only way to bring her to the United States would be through the U.S. refugee resettlement program, possibly with assistance from the U.N. High Commissioner for Refugees. As a single woman, in danger in her country of first asylum, Julie's sister would be eligible for consideration for resettlement in the United States. Getting her sister into the program would be difficult, however, as there were millions of refugees in Africa eligible for the resettlement program and only fifteen thousand visas available for them each year. I can advocate for Julie with the United Nations and the U.S. State Department, but there is no certainty that this advocacy will be successful.

Julie's own future in the United States will be difficult, but fortunately there are many people willing to help her. Her church has already done much to provide for her material needs and to give her emotional support, and she can continue to rely on them in the future. She has been studying English by listening to instructional cassette tapes, and there are English as a Second Language classes offered in the area of North Carolina where she lives. She should be able to find employment, though she will probably never have the education or skills to find a high-paying job.

While Julie has been able to find safety in the United States, I wonder sometimes if she will ever be able to find happiness. She told Dr. Okawa that she still has nightmares about the persecution she has experienced, and often feels frightened and alone. Sometimes she still acts and talks like a child, and it seems as if she has never fully recovered from the trauma she suffered when she was eight years old. Psychological counseling may help, but there are no organizations that counsel torture and trauma survivors in

North Carolina, and Dr. Okawa can do little to help Julie from so far away.

Julie takes much comfort in her religious faith and reads the Bible often. When she feels frightened at night and cannot sleep, she reads the Bible as a way of comforting herself. As Jesus said, "Blessed are you who are in need; the kingdom of God is yours. Blessed are you who now go hungry; you will be satisfied. Blessed are you who weep now; you will laugh."[4] For Julie's sake, and the sake of so many of my clients, I hope his words come true.

4. Luke 6:20–21 (Revised English Bible translation).

10

⊓⊔⊓⊔⊓⊔

The Future of Asylum

IN ITS CURRENT FORM, the asylum system can be considered a qualified success. The future of the system, however, is in doubt. Asylum seekers are increasingly being regarded by lawmakers and the general public as just another kind of illegal immigrant. Congress has passed legislation that makes it more difficult for applicants to be granted asylum, and the INS and the BIA have adopted policies that limit asylum seekers' access to protection. In doing so, our government has failed to uphold America's historic role as the protector of the persecuted and a refuge for those seeking freedom. If this trend is not reversed, we may cease to be a leader in promoting freedom in the world, and we risk losing an element of the American character that is central to our identity as a nation.

Recent developments in European countries show what could happen in the United States if we are not vigilant in maintaining a fair asylum system. All Western European countries have signed and ratified one or both of the international treaties on refugee protection, the 1951 U.N. Convention and the 1967 Protocol Relating to the Status of Refugees. They are thus bound by law to protect refugees and to allow foreigners to apply for asylum. At the same time these countries do not have a history of welcoming immigrants; they seek to preserve their ethnically and culturally homogenous character. Many European countries are willing to allow a small number of refugees to receive protection, but they consider large numbers of asylum applicants, who may change the ethnic makeup of the population, to be a threat.

In past decades, relatively small numbers of aliens applied for asylum in Western Europe, and the governments of these countries adjudicated asylum applications fairly. During the late 1980s and the 1990s, however, hundreds of thousands of refugees came to Western European countries to apply for asylum. At first they came from the former Warsaw Pact states during and after the fall of communism in Eastern Europe, then from the former Yugoslavia. There were also ethnic Kurds from Turkey and refugees from political violence in former European colonies seeking asylum.

The end of the Cold War and the economic and political integration of Western Europe opened borders. Refugees from Eastern Europe and Turkey found they could enter Western Europe easily for the first time in decades. Open borders within Western Europe allowed refugees to travel from one country to another, and to choose the country in which they would apply for asylum status. If a refugee was denied asylum status in one country, he could move to another and try again.

European governments reacted to this influx of asylum seekers by placing restrictions on the grant of asylum. Germany, the country with the largest number of asylum seekers, was the first to adopt "safe third country" legislation in 1993. Under this rule, an asylum seeker may be deported without consideration of the asylum claim if the applicant could have applied for asylum in one of the countries that he or she passed through on the way to Germany. Under the new law, Germany sent applicants back to the country of transit so they could apply for asylum there.

After Germany passed a "safe third country" law, other European countries followed suit.[1] In 1997 the Dublin Convention took effect, putting into place a "safe third country" procedure for all member countries of the European Union. After the passage of these laws, refugee advocates have found that "chain deporta-

---

1. Judith Kumin, "Asylum in Europe: Sharing or Shifting the Burden?" *World Refugee Survey 1995*, U.S. Committee for Refugees.

tions" often occur, in which asylum seekers are deported repeatedly from one country to another. Sometimes they continue being deported until they leave Europe and reach a country without effective asylum application procedures, or are even returned to the country where they fear persecution.[2]

European countries also grant a much smaller proportion of asylum cases than the United States does. Many of them have adopted "expedited removal" procedures and other barriers for asylum seekers. Germany, for example, has declared that all the countries on its borders are "safe third countries" in which asylum applicants could receive protection, so that all asylum seekers arriving by land are turned back at the border. Germany has created an accelerated procedure for applicants who come from a country of origin deemed not to be a violator of human rights, and an expedited procedure for applicants who arrive at an airport with documents deemed to be false. Germany denies asylum to applicants who fear persecution by agents other than the government and has limited asylum grants to applicants who may have a safe haven available to them within their own country. In 1999 Germany granted asylum to only 4.3 percent of all applicants. And this percentage, small as it is, does not take into account the thousands of asylum seekers turned back at land borders.

Most other European countries have adopted similar restrictive application procedures and grant only a small percentage of asylum cases.[3] In the United Kingdom, for example, stricter procedures have caused approval rates to decline from a high of 32 per-

2. A new European Union treaty on asylum applicants, the Treaty of Amsterdam, took effect on May 1, 2000. It reaffirmed member governments' commitment to the Dublin Convention and provided for the standardization of asylum processing procedures and their partial administration under the government of the European Union. As of this writing, it is unclear whether this change in administration will help or hurt asylum seekers. See Steven Edminster, "The High Road or the Low Road: The Way Forward to Asylum Harmonization in the European Union," U.S. Committee for Refugees, 2000.

3. Some countries deny most asylum applications but grant many applicants temporary legal status on "humanitarian" or other grounds. Norway, for example, granted refugee status to only 3 percent of applicants in 1999 but gave temporary residence permits to 43 percent of applicants on "humanitarian grounds." These temporary permits are renewable each year, and temporary residents can receive permanent residence after three years.

cent in 1989 to only 6 percent in 1996. The approval rate in 1999 for cases "given full consideration" was 42 percent but this number does not include those applicants who were denied asylum on "safe third country" or "noncompliance" grounds. France has also adopted restrictive procedures. The French authorities detain applicants who arrive with documents deemed to be false and use expedited removal procedures to deport applicants with "manifestly unfounded" claims; in 1999, France approved only 17 percent of all claims. Other European countries also have approval rates much lower than the United States: 13 percent in Belgium, 17 percent in Denmark, 3 percent in Holland, 3 percent in Norway, 6 percent in Portugal, 12 percent in Spain, 6 percent in Sweden, and 6 percent in Switzerland. A notable exception in 1999 was Austria, which approved 50 percent of all cases; this was due to a large influx of refugees from Kosovo, most of whom were granted asylum.[4]

Since the passage of the Refugee Act in 1980, the American asylum system has faced three large influxes of asylum seekers, similar to the crises in Europe. The first of these, the influx of Cuban boat people in 1980, caught U.S. officials by surprise. Nearly all of the Cuban entrants were eventually granted legal status, either asylum, legal permanent residency, or a special "parole" status created for Cubans only. The crisis consisted mainly of the inability of the federal government to handle the large number of asylum seekers, the inadequate social services offered to the Cubans, and the prolonged and inhumane detention of many applicants.

The second crisis, the influx of Central Americans during the 1980s, was handled differently. In the Cuban crisis, asylum seekers were allowed to stay, both for humanitarian reasons and for reasons of foreign policy. Most Central American asylum seekers were not granted asylum status. Since the American government supported right-wing governments in Guatemala and El Salvador, and the anti-Communist guerrilla movement in Nicaragua, granting asylum to the victims of these allies' human rights abuses

4. Information taken from the *World Refugee Survey 2000*, U.S. Committee for Refugees.

would have undermined our foreign policy goals. The government also opposed granting asylum for reasons of domestic policy. It viewed the new applicants as "economic migrants," undocumented aliens who were seeking better jobs in the United States.

The third asylum crisis was the attempt of large numbers of Haitians to seek asylum in the United States during the late 1980s and early 1990s. The Bush administration, and later the Clinton administration, met this crisis by preventing Haitians from applying for asylum at all. The government sent boats to intercept the Haitian refugee boats and send them back to Haiti. Refugee advocates challenged this policy in court, but the U.S. Supreme Court allowed the practice to continue.[5] The Court ruled that because the Haitian boat people were neither U.S. citizens nor on U.S. territory, they had no constitutional rights, and the president and Congress could do what they wished with them under their authority to regulate immigration and conduct foreign policy. Finally, the Clinton administration persuaded Haiti's dictator to step down by threatening to invade the country, and the number of boat people diminished, but the interdiction policy continued.

Since the formation of the Asylum Corps in 1991 and the passage of asylum reform legislation in 1994, the U.S. asylum system has operated at a relatively high level of fairness and efficiency. There have been no new political crises in neighboring countries that threatened to bring a large number of asylum seekers to the United States. The 1994 reform of asylum procedures reduced the number of fraudulent applicants and allowed genuine applications to be processed quickly. The creation of the Asylum Corps also made the hearings process more fair and efficient. The end of the Cold War made the asylum process less political, so that asylum seekers from all countries could receive a fair hearing.

As the process became more fair, more applicants won asylum status. From its lowest point in fiscal year 1993, when only 15 percent of applicants were granted asylum, the approval rate rose to 38 percent in 1999, when twenty thousand cases were approved. While this is only a fraction of the hundreds of thousands of immigrant visas granted each year, it was enough to attract the

---

5. *Sale v. Haitian Centers Council, Inc.*, 509 U.S. 155 (1993).

attention of policymakers and lobbyists who oppose high levels of immigration. Some members of Congress view asylum seekers as little better than illegal immigrants, and the 1996 laws passed to restrict illegal immigration included provisions that make obtaining asylum more difficult. The Clinton administration followed Congress's lead and introduced regulations that strictly implemented the law. The Board of Immigration Appeals issued precedent decisions that limit asylum even further.

These restrictions on the right of aliens to apply for asylum are harmful to asylum seekers and harmful to our nation's values of freedom, justice, and compassion. They are particularly inexcusable because they come from people who should know better. While the general public may confuse the issue of illegal immigration and the legal process of applying for asylum, policymakers in Congress, INS officials, and the Board of Immigration Appeals are informed on the issues and capable of making better choices.

The new methods of restricting access to asylum are more subtle than those used in the past. The government no longer denies asylum applications based on purely political factors, as it did in the 1980s. Instead the government limits the grant of asylum by putting procedural and legal obstacles in the way of applicants. Filing deadlines, evidentiary requirements, denials of employment authorization, and mandatory detention are used to discourage refugees and prevent them from gaining asylum status. These legal restrictions are less visible and dramatic than sending Coast Guard cutters to intercept boats, but they have the same effect: they deny protection to refugees, forcing them back to countries where they face torture, rape, and death.

The nature of the changes is sometimes technical and may be difficult to understand, but the effects of these changes are important. Philippe Fontem was incarcerated for two months and nearly deported because of a change in the regulations regarding motions to reopen, and because an immigration judge declared that he was absent from his hearing when he was in fact only late. Aster Cheru spent seven months in jail and lost custody of her children because of the INS's interpretation of one sentence in the law regarding the imprisonment of aliens convicted of aggravated felonies.

The restrictions adopted by Congress include the one-year filing deadline, the broadened definition of "aggravated felony," the long wait before asylum applicants receive work permits, the use of expedited removal, and changes in the procedures followed by immigration courts. The INS has made these changes even more detrimental by adopting an overly harsh interpretation of the law pertaining to the detention of asylees and aliens convicted of crimes, by failing to process asylees' work permits in a timely fashion, and by delaying the processing of asylees' petitions for their spouses and children. Finally, the immigration court system has failed to protect asylum seekers from judges who consistently make bad decisions on asylum cases.

Current Problems with the Asylum System

The one-year filing deadline. In 1996, Congress passed into law a rule that aliens must apply for asylum within one year of their arrival in the United States. At first, when Lamar Smith, chairman of the House Immigration Subcommittee, proposed a time limit on asylum applications, he suggested thirty days. Refugee and immigrant advocates protested, but supporters of a time limit on applications for asylum said that they were simply trying to limit the number of fraudulent applications for asylum. If a person came to the United States seeking protection from persecution, why would he or she not ask for protection soon after arrival? When an alien waited many years before applying for asylum, they reasoned, the request for asylum was probably fraudulent—a true refugee would ask for protection right away.

Refugee advocates, and sympathetic senators and representatives, argued that there were legitimate reasons why an asylum seeker might wait before applying. An asylum seeker might not know about the procedure or might be afraid to approach a government official to ask for help. A survivor of torture or other trauma might need months to recuperate before even being able to think about applying for asylum. It would also take most asylum seekers time to find an attorney and get together the evidence they needed to prove their claim.

These arguments succeeded in convincing most senators and representatives not to support a thirty- or sixty-day deadline, and to allow exceptions to the deadline. After a number of proposals and counterproposals, the House and Senate agreed to lengthen the filing deadline to one year. They reasoned that a year would be enough time for most asylees to figure out the system and apply, but they also allowed the INS to permit late filings where an applicant could show that he or she qualified for an exception to the one-year rule.[6]

Congress did not specify what these exceptions might be and let the INS formulate the regulations about the exceptions. These are quite liberal in the granting of exceptions, and asylum officers are sympathetic in their adjudications. As a result, the damage caused by the one-year filing rule has been limited.[7]

While these efforts by the INS to mitigate the effect of the deadline have been helpful, it has raised an unexpected problem for applicants who enter the United States without documents, or by using false documents. Refugees who enter the country on false documents are almost always told to destroy or return their passports after they enter the country. Adele and Philippe Fontem both returned their passports to their original owners after entering the United States, and Therese Kabongelo threw hers away. They do this because the people who helped them enter do not want to get into trouble for doing so, and destroying or returning the passport removes any evidence that might indict them. Other asylum seekers must rely on criminal alien smugglers to escape their countries and find safety. These smugglers insist on knowing the names and addresses of the asylum seekers' family members, so that they can make reprisals if the asylum seekers fail to destroy or return their travel documents or say anything to the authorities that would get the smugglers in trouble with the law.

Asylum seekers who entered the country using false documents or no documents usually have no evidence they can use to

6. For an extensive discussion of the efforts of advocates to preserve the asylum system during the debates on the changes in immigration law in 1996, see Philip Schrag, *A Well-Founded Fear: The Congressional Battle to Save Asylum in America* (New York, 1999).

7. The INS published interim regulations on the one-year deadline on March 6, 1997. Final regulations on the one-year deadline were published with the final regulations interpreting the Illegal Immigration Reform and Immigrant Responsibility Act of 1996, and were published in 65 Federal Register 76121–38, December 6, 2000. The regulations are reprinted in *Interpreter Releases,* December 11, 2000, pp. 1695–1704, 1714–1731.

prove their date of entry, and thus cannot prove that they applied for asylum within one year of their arrival. The INS's regulations state that asylum applicants must prove the date of their arrival in the United States through "clear and convincing evidence," so asylum seekers without documents to prove their entry date must provide this evidence through credible and detailed testimony. Many do not remember their trip to the United States clearly, particularly those who traveled while ill or still in a state of emotional shock from the trauma they suffered before leaving their home countries. These asylum seekers cannot always give detailed testimony about their trip and their experience at the port of entry.

Asylum officers and judges are also inconsistent in their evaluation of testimony about date of entry. Some are sympathetic and understanding, and give the asylum seeker the benefit of the doubt, while others are skeptical. As asylum seeker's chance of being denied asylum for reasons related to the one-year deadline have more to do with the individual asylum officer or judge who hears the case than with the asylum seeker's own story or testimony.

Since the one-year deadline went into effect in 1998, thousands of asylum applicants' cases have been denied for their failure to meet the requirements of the rule. No statistics exist for one-year denials in immigration court, but the statistics for rulings by the asylum office are telling. In fiscal year 1998, when the deadline was in effect for only one part of the year, only 968 cases were referred to court for reasons related to the one-year rule. In fiscal year 1999, 3,960 cases out of the 57,933 adjudicated, or 6.8 percent, were referred to court, and in fiscal year 2000, 6,052 out of a total of 61,869 cases, or 9.8 percent, were referred to court because of the one-year rule.[8]

Overall the effect of the one-year deadline has been less harmful than some advocates feared, thanks to the INS's fairly lenient interpretation of the exceptions to the deadline. Even so, thousands of deserving refugees have been denied asylum simply because they waited too long to apply or because they lacked

8. These statistics were provided by INS headquarters in a meeting with nonprofit organizations on November 6, 2000.

documentation of the date they entered the United States. Congress should repeal the one-year deadline and return to the system that existed before 1996.

Increased penalties for aliens convicted of crimes. The 1996 immigration bill also changed the laws regarding aliens convicted of crimes, expanding the definition of an "aggravated felony" to include twenty-one different kinds of crimes—including alien smuggling, document fraud, crimes of embezzlement or fraud where the amount of money stolen is more than $10,000, and crimes of theft and crimes of violence where the sentence imposed is at least one year.[9] Congress forbade federal court review of most decisions made by the INS and immigration judges[1] and did not allow these judges to grant waivers of removal to aliens convicted of aggravated felonies.[2] Congress also ordered the law to be applied retroactively, so that even decades-old convictions could lead to an alien's deportation.[3] The BIA also ruled that crimes later expunged from an alien's criminal record would still be considered convictions for immigration law purposes.[4] The INS prosecuted the new law harshly, seeking to imprison and deport aliens with minor criminal convictions and refusing to grant parole to most aliens who requested it.

Only a small number of asylum seekers have been convicted of crimes in the United States, but they are seriously affected by the changes in the law. The new laws on "aggravated felons" caused Aster Cheru to be imprisoned for seven months and nearly deported. She was not able to pursue her asylum claim and had to apply for restriction on removal status, which is more difficult to obtain and offers fewer benefits. Even though she was ultimately granted restriction on removal, her imprisonment caused her much emotional trauma and the loss of custody of her children.

Congress has gone too far with this attempt to fight crime by deporting aliens with criminal convictions. Noncitizens who have committed only minor crimes and who present no danger to the

---

9. Immigration and Nationality Act (INA), Section 101(a)(43).
1. INA, Section 242(g).
2. INA, Section 212(c).
3. INA, Section 101(a)(43).
4. *Matter of Roldan,* Int. Dec. 3377 (BIA 1999).

community are being deported. Aliens with genuine claims for asylum protection, but who have criminal records, are denied the opportunity even to apply for asylum. The old law already contained provisions preventing serious criminals from obtaining asylum status. Congress should change the definition of "aggravated felony" back to what it was before 1996 and should return to immigration judges the authority to grant waivers of deportation to aliens who have U.S. citizen spouses and children.

Delays in receiving work authorization. Most developed countries provide for asylum seekers' basic survival needs while they wait for the government to adjudicate their claims. The United States has never done this, but the government used to grant asylum applicants temporary work permits so they could support themselves while they were waiting for their cases to be adjudicated. In 1994 this policy changed, and asylum applicants were neither allowed to work nor given any public assistance for at least six months while they waited for the government to make a decision on their applications. The INS often takes months to process work permits, even after applicants have become eligible for them, and these processing delays cause further hardship for asylum seekers.

Asylum applicants who do not have friends or family to support them face frightening and difficult choices. Many of my clients came to the United States because they had heard it was a place to seek freedom, but they had no friends or family here to help them after they arrived. Some, like Therese Kabongelo, sought help by talking to taxi drivers at the airport; others looked for a church or mosque where they could ask for assistance. Others simply wandered around, confused, until a stranger saw them and offered to help.

One of my clients, an Ethiopian woman, was forced to flee her home country after being arrested and tortured several times for her political activities. She was desperate to leave the country, so she accepted a job as housekeeper for a wealthy family in Bahrain, a small country in the Persian Gulf. When she arrived in Bahrain, she found herself in an even worse situation. Her employer took her passport away and locked her in the house. He beat her and abused her sexually. She wanted to leave, but

Bahrain's legal system provides no protection to refugees, foreign employees, or women, and she could not escape. Finally the family went on vacation to the United States and took her with them. She ran away from them at a shopping mall but did not know where to go or what to do next. Another Ethiopian woman found her there, crying, and offered to help her. The woman took her home with her and allowed her to stay in her house for the next seven months until she won her asylum case, received a work permit, and found a job.

Another client, a young woman from Vietnam, fled her country as a stowaway on a boat, after having been arrested, raped, and tortured for being found in possession of a banned anti-government newspaper. She went to the United States because she had heard one could be free there, but she did not know anyone in the United States and did not know where to go for help. Another stowaway helped her travel from their arrival point on the West Coast to Washington, D.C., but abandoned her at the bus station once they got there. She did not know whom to ask for help and was afraid she would be sent back to Vietnam; she stayed at the bus station, crying and not knowing what to do. An American man saw her there and realized she was lost and in trouble; he called a Cambodian co-worker who spoke some Vietnamese, and the two of them convinced her to trust them and let them help her. She stayed with the American man for eight months while she waited for her asylum application to be approved, and finally moved out when she had a work permit and a job.

Not all asylum seekers are as lucky as these two women in finding people willing to help them. Some of my clients spent months in homeless shelters before being granted asylum and a work permit. Other asylum seekers meet worse fates—forced into prostitution or slave labor, either by the smugglers who brought them to the United States or by others after they arrive.

Congress bears considerable responsibility for these refugees' suffering. When Congress "reformed" the asylum system in 1994, it denied work permits to asylum seekers for the first six months after applying for asylum, in an effort to discourage fraudulent claims for asylum. The policy was successful in discouraging fraudulent claims but has caused considerable harm to genuine refugees. Congress should reduce the time that asylum seekers must wait before they receive work authorization, or should provide for asylum seekers' basic needs while their cases are being adjudicated.

Procedural changes in the law. The 1996 immigration law placed limits on appeals, motions to reopen, and motions to reconsider adverse decisions made by immigration judges. Under current law, negative decisions made after an applicant is late to or absent from an immigration hearing cannot be appealed at all. The applicant's only means of preventing deportation is to file a motion to reopen the case, arguing that extraordinary circumstances made it impossible for him or her to attend the hearing on time. An applicant may usually file only one motion to reopen or reconsider, and, depending on the reasons for filing the motion, must file the motion within 90 or 180 days of the judge's decision.

These restrictions on motions and appeals have had devastating consequences for asylum seekers. For example, Philippe Fontem never received a hearing on the merits of his asylum claims because he arrived at the immigration court late, and the judge had already ordered him removed *in absentia*. Philippe did not qualify for a motion to reopen, because his reason for being late would not be considered an "exceptional circumstance" under the law. Had it not been for Adele, he probably would have been sent back to Cameroon.

Why are the consequences so severe for asylum applicants who are late to or absent from their hearings? As with the rules on work permits, the rules on motions and appeals were adopted in reaction to past abuses. Aliens in deportation proceedings sometimes use delaying tactics to prevent judges from making a final ruling in their case. Each delay represents a victory, since the goal of most people in deportation proceedings is to stay in the United States as long as possible. The severe penalties for not attending a hearing are an attempt to prevent aliens from using nonattendance as a way of delaying the legal process. Likewise, the restrictions on motions to reopen and motions to reconsider were imposed to prevent aliens from delaying their deportation by filing numerous motions.

While there must be rules to prevent these kinds of abuses,

Congress and the BIA have gone too far in enforcing them. The BIA should take into consideration the difficult situation of indigent asylum seekers such as Philippe, who must rely on others for transportation to court. The BIA should also take into account the terrible consequences that deported asylum seekers face. Under current law, asylum seekers are deported to countries where they face torture and death for the simple fact of being late to or absent from their asylum hearings. This may make the immigration court system more efficient, but it does not make it more just.

Regulations that limit the grant of asylum. On June 11, 1998, the INS and the Executive Office of Immigration Review (EOIR), the branch of the Department of Justice that manages the immigration courts and the Board of Immigration Appeals, proposed a rule that would limit the grant of asylum in certain types of cases. Many asylum advocates and agencies commented on the proposed rule, disagreeing with its provisions and asking for changes, but it was enacted on December 6, 2000, in almost its original form. Under the old regulations, if an applicant had proved past persecution, it was presumed that the applicant had a well-founded fear of future persecution, unless the INS could rebut this presumption with evidence of changed country conditions. The new regulation states that the INS may also rebut the presumption by proving that there has been a "fundamental change in circumstances such that the applicant no longer has a well-founded fear." This "fundamental change in circumstances" is a broader standard than the old standard of changed country conditions.

The new rule also limits the factors that adjudicators may consider in deciding cases on past persecution alone. Under the old system, established by regulation and the case precedent in *Matter of Chen,*[5] adjudicators considered many factors in deciding cases based on past persecution, including the existence of human rights abuses in the applicants' home country, the continued possibility of persecution, the severity of past persecution, the lack of close family ties in the home country, and the length of time spent outside the applicant's home country. The new regulation limits consideration to only one major factor: if the applicant "has

5. 20 I&N Dec. 16, 18 (BIA 1989).

demonstrated compelling reasons for being unwilling or unable to return to the country arising out of the severity of the past persecution."[6] By limiting the factors that an adjudicator may consider, this regulation makes it more difficult for victims of past persecution to win asylum in the United States.

Finally, the new rule states that adjudicators should deny an asylum claim where the INS has shown that the applicant "could avoid future persecution by relocating to another part of the applicant's country of nationality." The rule does provide that where an applicant has proven past persecution, or where the persecutor is the government, adjudicators should presume that relocation would not be reasonable unless the INS can rebut this presumption with a "preponderance of the evidence." This limits the effect of the new rule by requiring the INS to prove that relocation would be reasonable. Still, the rule adds a new obstacle that asylum applicants must overcome in order to gain protection.

One of the strange aspects of the new regulation is that it was not prompted by any change in the law. The 1996 reform of the immigration law did not change the law of asylum, and no recent BIA precedent decisions have addressed these issues. Many commenters argued that, by changing substantive aspects of asylum procedure through regulation alone, the INS and EOIR were exceeding their authority as agencies of the executive branch and were, in effect, writing new laws without the authorization of Congress. Asylum advocates also criticized the new law for the limitations it placed on grants of asylum. While it is not clear to me why the Department of Justice has instituted these new regulations, it appears that, with the approval rate for asylum cases going up each year, the regulations were meant to reduce the total number of asylum grants.

Delays in processing asylee relative petitions. Approved asylees may bring their spouses and children to join them in the United States. While the INS is supposed to process these applica-

---

6. 8 CFR 208.13 (b)(1)(iii)(A). The new regulation also states that an applicant may be granted asylum if the applicant has established "a reasonable possibility of other serious harm upon removal to that country." This provision would cover very rare cases in which an applicant fears harm that is as serious as persecution but is not connected to one of the five grounds.

tions in thirty days, it actually takes the INS six months to approve them. After the INS approves an asylee relative petition, the file goes to the State Department's National Visa Center, then to the U.S. embassy in the country where the asylee's relatives live. These final steps take an additional two to three months, meaning that asylees must usually wait eight to nine months after their approval to bring their families to join them.

The delay in processing these petitions causes many hardships for asylees and their families. We have already seen how the delay in processing Adele's petition for Philippe caused him to spend more time in jail, and how the delay in processing Therese's fingerprints, coupled with the expected delay in processing the relative petition, influenced her decision to return to Africa to visit her children. Many of my clients have experienced similar problems. An asylum applicant has often come to the United States after the death of a spouse, leaving their children behind with relatives. The children live under the constant threat of reprisals and may be in hiding. A wife or husband who is left behind after the asylum seeker flees the country is in especially great danger of being targeted by government forces, who aim to punish the asylum seeker.

The danger to family members could be reduced if the INS would process asylee relative petitions quickly. The INS allocates staff resources to case processing according to the direction given it by the president and Congress, and policymakers have made border enforcement and the processing of citizenship applications the INS's priority. Asylum seekers have no political voice, and their needs are overlooked. The INS should reallocate resources to the processing of asylee relative petitions, so that asylees may bring their families quickly out of danger.

The use of detention as a deterrent. The INS detains all asylum seekers who are apprehended entering the United States with documents suspected of being false. They do this because the 1996 law made detention mandatory for these asylum seekers. Once applicants pass their "credible fear" interviews, however, they are eligible for parole. Some INS district offices grant parole liberally, but others, particularly the New York district office, almost never grant parole. Some district offices even keep asylees in jail after they have won their cases in court, because the judge's decision is under appeal. In theory, asylum seekers are only detained so that they do not abscond before their hearings, but in practice, detention is used as a deterrent, both to encourage asylum seekers to abandon their applications and accept deportation and to discourage other persecuted people from seeking asylum in the United States.

Both the law and the INS's implementation of it must change. The incarceration of asylum seekers—people who have committed no crime other than seeking safety and freedom in the United States—is a terrible violation of refugees' human rights. Congress should put an end to the mandatory detention of asylum seekers and order the INS to use shelterlike detention facilities, with available medical and social services, for the small number of asylum seekers who must be detained. Congress should allocate sufficient funds for the INS to effect these policies. The INS should also reform its own institutional culture so that it no longer treats asylum seekers like criminals. INS headquarters should oversee the administration of detention of asylum seekers and should take action to change the practices of district offices when, as in New York, individual district directors violate national INS policy.

Asylum advocacy organizations, such as Lutheran Immigration and Refugee Services, the Catholic Legal Immigration Network, Amnesty International, Human Rights Watch, Lawyer's Committee for Human Rights, and many others have been advocating in favor of these changes for years. Their pleas have been ignored by both the president and Congress. It is time for the government to stop imprisoning asylum seekers and to return to our traditional values of welcoming and helping victims of persecution.

Unfair practices of individual judges and asylum officers. Asylum officers are Justice Department employees who can be hired and fired just as civil service employees can. Immigration judges are administrative judges, employed by the Department of Justice in the executive branch of government. Unlike federal judges who serve in the judicial branch of government, they are not appointed for life, and it does not require impeachment proceedings to remove them from the bench. They can be fired like any other federal employee.

In practice, however, asylum officers and immigration judges are almost never disciplined or forced to resign, no matter how badly they abuse their power. As a result, some individual asylum officers and judges make consistently unfair decisions, discriminating against certain nationalities or types of applicants, without being questioned. Their decisions may be overturned on appeal, but the appeals process takes three years and asylum applicants suffer greatly while waiting for their appeals to be processed.

There is a similar problem in the Asylum Office. Asylum officers control the entire interview, with the applicants' representatives limited to making a few remarks at the end of the interview. An attorney can do little to offset an asylum officer who interviews poorly or adopts a confrontational attitude during the interview. Asylum officers are almost never fired, even very bad ones, and some officers have biases against applicants from certain countries or with certain kinds of claims. At times I have feared—before the interview even began—that my client's case was going to be denied, simply because I knew the biases of the officer to whom the case was assigned.

Several factors nonetheless mitigate the harm that these individual officers can do. First, asylum officers are selected and trained to be sympathetic to applicants and to give nonconfrontational interviews. As time passes, the asylum corps has been more successful in selecting good officers; most of the "bad" officers in the Arlington office have been there for many years. Also, asylum officers' decisions are reviewed by supervisors, who can overturn bad decisions. If it is clear that the first interviewer has done a poor job, supervisors can call an applicant back for an interview with another officer.

The situation is different with immigration judges. Judges hear a wide range of immigration cases, many of which involve aliens accused of criminal offenses and fraud. Inevitably judges become more skeptical of the truth of immigrants' statements when so many of the people they see in their courtrooms are in fact guilty of making false statements or other crimes. Many judges retain an enforcement mentality, learned while working for the INS. They are not trained to be sensitive to asylum seekers' psychological states and trauma.

Unlike asylum officers, immigration judges are not supervised directly, and no supervisor reviews their decisions. A judge's decision can be overturned by the Board of Immigration Appeals, but the judge's decision will stand for at least three years while the case is on appeal. Asylum seekers whose cases are denied within 180 days of the application date are not eligible for a work permit during the entire three years their case is on appeal. Detained asylum seekers usually remain in prison throughout the appeals process.

Immigration judges know that asylum applicants will have to wait three years, with no means of supporting themselves, if their applications are denied, and some of them abuse this power. They make decisions that are sure to be overturned on appeal, hoping that imprisonment or lack of work authorization will discourage asylum seekers, causing them to withdraw their appeals and accept removal from the United States.

The rate at which individual judges approve asylum cases varies widely. While some variation in approval rates is normal, the variation in approval rates among judges is so extreme as to show that some judges are abusing their authority and denying good cases. While the average grant rate for court cases is 31.4 percent, some judges almost never grant asylum to aliens. Judge William Cassidy of Atlanta, Georgia, has heard 3,722 asylum cases but has granted asylum to only 66 applicants—a rate of only 1.7 percent. Other strict judges include William F. Jankun of New York City, who has approved only 18 cases of the 1,511 (0.1 percent) he has adjudicated; Daniel A. Meisner and Eugene Pugliese of Newark, New Jersey, who have approved respectively only 80 of 927 (0.9 percent) and 78 of 1,108 cases (0.7 percent); Roy J. Daniel of Los Angeles, who has approved only 21 out of 1,333 cases (1.5 percent); and G. Mackenzie Rast of Atlanta, who has approved only 29 of 1,351 (2.1 percent) cases he has heard.[7]

The very low approval rates of these judges may in part re-

---

7. The information in this paragraph and the three following paragraphs is taken from a study done by the journalist Rick Tulsky, who obtained a 1,134-page printout of asylum adjudication records by filing a Freedom of Information Act request with the Justice Department. He analyzed this printout and published the results in a series of articles in the October 17, 2000, edition of the *San Jose Mercury News*.

flect the makeup of their caseload, not just their own strict standards. Judges who hear many asylum cases from countries with low approval rates, such as Mexico and China, or who hear asylum cases from aliens who are applying for asylum only as a last-ditch attempt to prevent deportation, will naturally have a lower approval rate than judges who hear stronger cases. Significantly, most judges in Los Angeles approve only a small fraction of the cases they hear, which indicates that the low approval rates of the judges listed above are to a certain extent normal for the caseload they hear. The most lenient judge in Los Angeles, for example, Judge Lawrence O. Burman, has approved only 70 of the 701 cases he has heard (10 percent).

Still, even within one geographical jurisdiction there are wide variations in the approval rates of judges. Since cases are assigned to judges randomly, any difference in the cases themselves would average out over time, so the judges' own opinions and disposition would be the most important variable in explaining the difference in approval rates among judges in the same jurisdiction. In New York, for example, the most liberal judge, Victoria Ghartey, has approved 460 of the 1,210 cases she has heard (38 percent), making her 380 times more likely to approve a case than Judge William F. Jankun (0.1 percent). In Newark the most liberal judge, William Strasser, has approved 118 of 425 cases (28 percent), making him roughly 30 times more likely to approve a case than his colleagues Daniel A. Meisner (0.9 percent) and Eugene Pugliese (0.7 percent).

In the Arlington and Baltimore immigration courts, where I usually practice, the variation is not as extreme. In Arlington, Judge Joan V. Churchill approves only 14 percent of the cases she hears, while Judge Wayne R. Iskra, the judge in Julie Rukongeza's case, approves 20 percent. Judge John M. Bryant approves 27 percent of the cases he hears, and Christopher M. Grant, the judge in Aster Cheru's case, grants 28 percent. In the Baltimore court, the approval rates range from 26 percent for Judge Bruce M. Barrett and John F. Gossart to 40 percent for William P. Greene, Jr. and 51 percent for Lisa Dornell. Still, in both jurisdictions, the most liberal judge grants twice as many cases as the strictest one.

In my opinion, the variation in approval rates among judges

does not reflect excessive leniency by the more liberal judges, who I believe to be interpreting the law correctly, but excessive strictness on the part of the judges with low approval rates. Some judges grant asylum so rarely that their decisions can only be called biased and unjust. In my own practice, and the practices of my colleagues, I have seen judges make decisions that are clearly unfair and even unethical.

One judge in the Washington area used to manipulate his calendar in such a way as to deny the opportunity for work authorization to almost all asylum applicants. The law states that asylum applicants should have their cases adjudicated within 180 days of applying and can receive a work permit if the court has not reached a decision by that date. This "180-day clock" stops, however, if an applicant does not accept the first available hearing date. At master calendar hearings the judge in question would ask the applicant if he or she wanted an individual hearing date the next day, or a few days in the future. No attorney would accept an individual hearing date so soon, because there would not be sufficient time to prepare the case, so the applicant and the attorney would ask for a later date. The judge would then assign them a date months in the future and stop the 180-day clock for work authorization.[8] Other judges must have done the same thing, because in April 2000, Chief Immigration Judge Michael J. Creppy issued a memorandum that forced judges to discontinue this practice.[9] The memo instructed judges to give attorneys at least two weeks between the master calendar date and the individual hearing date, so they would have time to prepare.

The same judge has engaged in unethical practices by trying to pressure applicants into withdrawing their asylum applications. At the individual hearing of a Somali applicant, who was represented by a colleague of mine at another agency, this judge turned off the tape recorder and went "off the record." He offered to

8. I have had this experience twice in cases that I represented before this judge, and many other legal practitioners in the Washington area have had the same experience.

9. "Operating Policy and Procedures Memorandum No. 00–01, Asylum Request Processing." Michael J. Creppy, Chief Immigration Judge, March 22, 2000. Reprinted in *Interpreter Releases*, April 17, 2000, pp. 526–535.

grant the applicant withholding of deportation, without even having a hearing, if the applicant would agree to waive his right of appeal. If the applicant would not agree to this bargain, the judge said, he would deny both asylum and withholding, regardless of what transpired during the hearing. The applicant decided not to accept this deal and insisted on having a full hearing. The judge heard his case and denied it. As of this writing, the client still has years to wait for the BIA to hear his appeal, and he has no work permit and no legal status in the meantime.[1]

Another area judge has a reputation for almost never granting asylum claims, regardless of the strength of the evidence presented or the severity of the persecution suffered by the applicant. I have represented only a few cases before this judge, but I had the opportunity to observe a particularly unjust decision that she made in a case that I assisted with. The applicant, a sixteen-year-old girl, had been sexually assaulted and tortured by soldiers when she was only fourteen. The soldiers had sought information about the whereabouts of her older siblings, who were wanted for arrest because they were members of an outlawed political party.

The girl had been severely traumatized by these events and was in psychotherapy. The INS attorney subjected the girl to a tough cross-examination, asking for detailed information about the sexual abuse. The judge overruled the girl's attorney's objections to the line of questioning and then followed up with her own questions. The girl's therapist was present at the hearing and wanted to testify on the girl's behalf, but the judge ruled that her therapist, a licensed clinical social worker, could not testify because she did not have a Ph.D. or an M.D. and was therefore not an expert witness. The girl's older sister was present, but the judge also did not allow her to testify on the grounds that the sister's own application for asylum had been denied (it was on appeal at the BIA), and therefore the sister's testimony would, by definition, be noncredible.

The judge also discovered that the girl had been born in an-

---

1. Personal interview, July 2000. The attorney for this case has asked not to be named in the book, so as not to jeopardize future cases with this judge.

other African country because her father and mother were living there briefly while her father worked there. The girl passed through that country on her way to the United States. The judge asked for evidence proving that the girl was not a citizen of that country, but she denied the girl's attorney's request for more time in which to find that evidence. In the end, the judge denied the girl's case, stating that the girl's testimony contained inconsistencies and therefore lacked credibility, and that she had not proven that she was not a citizen, or could not find firm resettlement, in the country where she was born. Her case is still on appeal at the BIA.

In my opinion, these rulings do not represent mere differences of opinion about the interpretation of asylum law; they represent a violation of basic fairness and legal ethics and an abuse of judicial power. These judges should be disciplined or even fired by their supervisor, Chief Immigration Judge Michael J. Creppy. Judge Creppy has done little to monitor judges' decisions, however, or to discipline those judges who consistently make unfair or incorrect rulings.

I attempted to interview Judge Creppy for this book, to allow him the opportunity to explain his point of view on this issue. He would not agree to be interviewed, but he has commented about this issue previously. In an interview with the *Los Angeles Times*, he said he was "pleased" with the wide disparity in judges' decision-making. "Every judge is exercising his own discretion in deciding what they believe," he said. "Every case is different."[2]

Rick Kenney, a spokesman for the Executive Office of Immigration Review, said that Judge Creppy does not think it is appropriate to second-guess judges' decisions and does not challenge their interpretations of the law. Since individuals can appeal decisions to the BIA, he does not think it is appropriate to exercise his own influence over judges' decision-making. Kenney did say, however, that Judge Creppy takes complaints seriously. Yet a recent *Los Angeles Times* article profiled a case in which no action was

2. "Few Applicants Succeed in Immigration Courts," *Los Angeles Times,* April 15, 2001.

taken to discipline a judge who was accused of a profound breach of ethics and procedure.[3] During Judge Creppy's tenure, some judges had been "disciplined," Kenney said, and one had been removed from his position for inappropriate behavior in the courtroom. But no judges had lost their jobs due to incompetence, bias, or poor decision-making.

For my own part, I find Judge Creppy's hands-off approach to managing immigration judges difficult to understand. I agree with him that a statistical analysis of approval rates is, by itself, a limited tool by which to analyze discrepancies in the decision-making of judges. Some judges in certain jurisdictions may have valid reason for approving fewer cases, because the caseload in those jurisdictions includes a great many weak or fraudulent applications. Within one geographical area, however, the distribution of cases among judges is random, and there is no reason why judges' approval rates within the same jurisdiction should vary as widely as they do.

While a simple analysis of approval rates may be inappropriate, it is legitimate to track the number of decisions made by each judge which are overturned on appeal. If a judge's decisions are often overturned, it may indicate that the judge is incompetent or biased and in need of further training or even replacement.

I agree with Judge Creppy that immigration judges should have extensive freedom to decide cases without micromanagement from their supervisors. But asylum seekers also have the right to a fair hearing. Those who fall victim to biased or incompetent judges face a wait of three years before being granted protection and risk being returned to countries where they will be tortured or killed. By taking no action to discipline or replace biased and incompetent judges, Judge Creppy is not meeting his responsibilities as chief immigration judge and is allowing many vulnerable asylum seekers to come to harm.

Board of Immigration Appeals decisions that limit the grant of asylum. The Board of Immigration Appeals interprets immigration law by publishing "precedent decisions" whose interpreta-

3. "Judges Behavior Sparks Outrage But Little Relief," *Los Angeles Times*, April 15, 2001.

tions are binding on immigration judges and asylum officers. In theory the BIA should act as an impartial body, concerned only with implementing the law in a just manner. Between 1990 and 1996, the Board of Immigration Appeals decided asylum cases in a balanced fashion, publishing some precedent decisions in which asylum was granted and others in which asylum was denied. After the political climate changed with the passage of the 1996 immigration law, the BIA changed its pattern of decision-making. From 1997, the majority of the BIA's published precedent decisions involve cases where asylum was denied. Some of these precedent decisions have severely limited the ability of asylum seekers to be granted asylum.[4]

Even as late as 1996, the BIA ruled in favor of asylum applicants in three important cases. In *Matter of Kasinga*,[5] it granted asylum to a young woman from Togo who feared she would be subjected to female genital mutilation, a traditional practice that involves cutting off some or all of a woman's external genitalia, if she were forced to return to Togo. In doing so, the BIA found that she was a member of a protected "social group" and that female genital mutilation constituted persecution. The decision cleared the way for many other women and girls to seek asylum on the same grounds and forced immigration judges to take such claims seriously.

In *Matter of H-*,[6] the BIA granted asylum to a Somali applicant based on his membership in a Somali clan that had suffered persecution at the hands of the warlords and militias who rule Somalia. In doing so, the BIA made a precedent ruling that a Somali clan constituted a valid "social group" and that applicants could be granted asylum from a country even if it had no functioning government. The decision made it possible for hundreds of other Somalis to win asylum in the United States.

4. The analysis presented here examines BIA precedent decisions made between 1997 and 2000. Karen Yarnold has studied unpublished BIA decisions for the years 1980–1987 and found that the BIA was more likely to rule in favor of asylum applicants from enemy countries. Karen Yarnold, *Refugees Without Refuge: Formation and Failed Implementation of U.S. Political Asylum Policy in the 1980s* (University Press of America, 1990).

5. Int. Dec. 3278 (BIA 1996).

6. Int. Dec. 3276 (BIA 1996).

In *Matter of S-P-*,[7] the BIA ruled that an asylum applicant may be granted asylum because of a political opinion that his persecutors imputed to him, even if he did not actually have that opinion. Again, this set a precedent that went beyond a narrow, literal reading of the asylum statute and allowed more applicants to gain asylum protection.

After 1996 the BIA changed course. It issued twelve precedent decisions holding against asylum seekers, but it issued only four precedent decisions in which it granted asylum. Three of the four positive decisions involved cases where the applicants came from countries that were traditional enemies of the United States. Two of the three positive decisions, *Matter of X-P-T-*[8] and *Matter of C-Y-Z-*,[9] involved Chinese applicants who had applied for asylum because of their fear of forced sterilization in China. Congress had just passed a law making the fear of forced sterilization a valid ground for asylum, and the BIA decisions interpreted this new law. The third positive decision, *Matter of O-Z- & I-Z-*,[1] ruled in favor of two Jewish asylum seekers from Russia. The fourth decision, *Matter of S-A-*,[2] is discussed below.

The negative decisions involved asylum seekers from poor countries, such as Mauritania, Peru, Guatemala, and Afghanistan. These countries are not traditional enemies of the United States, and immigrants from these countries do not have much political influence here. All the negative decisions set a binding precedent on immigration judges and asylum officers, and have limited the circumstances in which adjudicators may grant asylum.

The BIA issued precedent decisions in several cases where asylum applicants had been targeted by persecutors who were acting from both political and nonpolitical motives. For example, in *Matter of T-M-B-*[3] and *Matter of V-T-S*,[4] the BIA ruled against applicants from the Philippines who had been targeted by guerrilla groups both because of their political opinions and because

7. Int. Dec. 3287 (BIA 1996).
8. Int. Dec. 3299 (BIA 1996).
9. Int. Dec. 3299 (BIA 1996).
1. Int. Dec. 3346 (BIA 1998).
2. Int. Dec. 3433 (BIA 2000).
3. Int. Dec. 3307 (BIA 1997).
4. Int. Dec. 3308 (BIA 1997).

the guerrillas wanted to extort money from them. In *Matter of C-A-L-*,[5] the BIA ruled against a Guatemalan ex-soldier who was targeted by guerrillas both because of his political support of the government and because they wanted to recruit him to use his skill as an artillery specialist. In all three cases the BIA denied asylum, declaring that the harm suffered by the applicants was not persecution because it did not occur on account of one of the five protected grounds.

Many of these precedent decisions limited grants of asylum by raising the standards for the kind of testimony aliens must provide to meet their "burden of proof." In *Matter of A-S-*,[6] which concerned the application of an alien from Bangladesh, the BIA reaffirmed its practice of deferring to a judge's ruling the credibility of an alien's testimony in most cases. Since many cases are denied because of a judge's adverse credibility finding, the *Matter of A-S-* decision limited the possibility for appeal. In *Matter of E-P-*,[7] the BIA ruled against a Haitian applicant for asylum because his testimony lacked detail and because country conditions had changed since the applicant had fled Haiti.

The decisions that have most seriously affected the ability of aliens to receive asylum are *Matter of S-M-J-*,[8] *Matter of Y-B-*,[9] *Matter of O-D-*,[1] and *Matter of M-D-*.[2] These four decisions set new standards for the amount of corroborative evidence that aliens must provide to meet the burden of proof and be granted asylum.[3] In the past, immigration courts took into account the difficulties that asylum applicants faced in providing documentary

5. Int. Dec. 3305 (BIA 1996).
6. Int. Dec. 3336 (BIA 1998).
7. Int. Dec. 3311 (BIA 1997).
8. Int. Dec. 3303 (BIA 1996).
9. Int. Dec. 3337 (BIA 1998).
1. Int. Dec. 3334 (BIA 1998).
2. Int. Dec. 3339 (BIA 1998).
3. The BIA denied asylum in two other cases not listed above; the reasons for the BIA's denial are difficult to summarize briefly. In *Matter of N-M-A-*, Int. Dec. 3368 (BIA 1998), the BIA denied asylum to an applicant from Afghanistan, despite his experience of past persecution there, in part because country conditions had changed and a new group of rulers had replaced the government that had persecuted him. In *Matter of A-E-M-*, Int. Dec. 3338 (BIA 1998), the BIA denied asylum to a Peruvian applicant for a number of different reasons, including changed country conditions, the availability of safe relocation within Peru, and the contention that the harm the applicant had suffered was merely harassment, not persecution.

evidence to support their claims and allowed applicants to prove their cases through their own testimony alone, provided their testimony was detailed and credible. The four decisions set a precedent that asylum applicants must now provide extensive corroborating evidence to support their claims or must explain why that evidence is not available.

In *Matter of S-M-J-*,[4] the BIA stated that an applicant must provide corroborative evidence proving specific facts of his case "where such evidence is available," but also stated that an applicant was not required to provide such documentation where the applicant had a "reasonable explanation" of the documentation's lack of availability. The BIA cited the U.N. High Commissioner for Refugees' *Handbook on Procedures and Criteria for Determining Refugee Status* in emphasizing that applicants often had difficulties obtaining evidence and that they should be given "the benefit of the doubt" when evaluating their claims.

The BIA soon went beyond *Matter of S-M-J-* and increased its requirements for supporting documentation. In *Matter of Y-B-,* a Mauritanian man had fled persecution in his home country, had stayed in a refugee camp in Senegal for two years, and had then come to the United States to apply for asylum. The immigration judge denied the man's asylum claim, and the BIA upheld the judge's denial. The BIA agreed with the judge's finding that the applicant's testimony was not credible. It also found that the applicant had failed to prove his case because he had not provided documentation of his stay in the refugee camp in Senegal.

The BIA went a step further in another 1998 decision, *Matter of M-D-*. This case also involved a Mauritanian refugee who had been beaten and imprisoned, who fled Mauritania to a United Nations camp in Senegal, and who then came to the United States to apply for asylum. The BIA did not say whether it found his testimony credible or not. It upheld the judge's denial of the case based

4. The analysis that follows is indebted to Margaret Kuehne Taylor's article, "The Mogharrabi Rule in 1998: A Review of Recent BIA Asylum Decisions," published in *Interpreter Releases*, vol. 75, no. 25, July 6, 1998, pp. 901–910, and to Robert Jobe, Mark Silverman, and Larry Katzman, *Winning Asylum Cases,* published by the Immigrant Legal Resource Center, April 2000.

only on the fact that the applicant had not produced documents to prove he had resided in the refugee camp. In fact the applicant's attorney had written the United Nations to ask for corroboration from their records, but the U.N. could not provide this corroboration as it lacked the resources to maintain complete records of the residents of its camps in Senegal. The BIA ignored the applicant's reasonable explanation for his lack of corroborating evidence and denied his case.

As it turned out, *Matter of M-D-* was such a bad decision that it was overturned on appeal. The U.S. Court of Appeals for the Second Circuit, in a decision issued on November 13, 2000, declared the BIA's ruling invalid and sent it back to the BIA for reconsideration. In its decision, the appeals court stated that the BIA had violated its own precedent, as well as federal asylum law, in making its decision. The court ruled that the BIA had erred by failing to rule explicitly on the credibility of the applicant's testimony, since, by BIA and federal court precedent, an application for asylum may be granted on the basis of credible testimony alone. The court found that the applicant had "plainly provided substantial corroboration of the specifics of his story." The court found that the BIA had not explained in its decision why further corroborative evidence was necessary, nor why it found the applicant's explanations for the failure to provide other corroborating documents not reasonable and sufficient.[5] The appeals court's decision was an important victory for asylum seekers in that it rendered invalid one of the BIA's most harmful decisions.

Finally, in *Matter of O-D-,* the BIA addressed the issue of false documents submitted to prove an asylum claim. In this case an applicant, again from Mauritania, submitted an identity card that the INS forensics laboratory discovered to be false and a birth certificate that INS found to be "probably counterfeit." The BIA found that the presentation of these false documents, which they considered to be central evidence in his claim to be a refugee, "compromised the integrity of his entire claim." A dissenting opinion, filed by Lory Rosenberg and joined by BIA chairman

---

5. *Diallo v. INS,* No. 98-4131, 2000 WL 1592934 (2nd Cir. Nov. 13, 2000).

Paul Schmidt and John Guendelsberger, argued that the BIA should consider the totality of the evidence, giving special weight to the applicant's testimony, in adjudicating an asylum claim, and should not allow one or two pieces of evidence to outweigh all other evidence presented with the claim.

The BIA made one other major decision in 1999 limiting the grant of asylum. In *Matter of R-A-*,[6] it denied asylum to a Guatemalan woman, Rodi Alvarez Pena, who had been beaten severely, raped, and threatened with death by her husband.[7] The BIA agreed that the abuse was severe enough to constitute persecution and that the Guatemalan government was either unwilling or unable to protect her from her husband if she were returned to Guatemala. The BIA denied her asylum application, however, because it found that the persecution she suffered did not occur on account of one of the five protected grounds—political opinion, race, religion, nationality, or social group.

The BIA was divided in its decision, with ten members voting to deny her application and five members to approve it. The dissent stated that Ms. Pena feared persecution on account of both her membership in a particular social group and her political opinion. Unlike the majority, the dissent found that Ms. Pena was a member of a valid social group, defined as "Guatemalan women who have been involved with Guatemalan male companions who believe that women are to live under male domination." The dissent found that this definition of social group met the standards for the definition of social group set by the BIA in its decision in *Matter of Kasinga* and an earlier case, *Matter of Acosta*.[8] The dissent also found that "opposition to male domination and violence against women, and support for gender equity, constitutes a political opinion."

In 2000 the BIA ruled on another case of domestic violence, *Matter of S-A-*,[9] and this time approved the woman's application

6. Int. Dec. 3403 (BIA 1999).
7. I am indebted here to Karen Musalo's analysis in her article, "*Matter of R-A-*: An Analysis of the Decision and Its Implications," published in *Interpreter Releases,* vol. 76, no. 30, August 9, 1999.
8. 19 I&N Dec. 211 (BIA 1985).
9. Int. Dec. 3433 (BIA 2000).

for asylum. In this case a woman had fled Morocco because she was abused by her father, a conservative Muslim. The BIA ruled that her case was different from *Matter of R-A-* because she was persecuted on account of religion. Her attorney, Millicent Y. Clarke, welcomed the victory but stated that "the gender aspects were primary" in the case and that the BIA "copped out by choosing to decide the case on religion."[1]

Why has the BIA issued so many negative precedent decisions on asylum cases in the last four years? I put this question to Paul Schmidt, chairman of the BIA, who denied that there was any plan to issue anti-asylum decisions or any anti-asylum bias on the part of the BIA. He explained that its members make decisions independently, on a case-by-case basis, and that the BIA as a whole does not meet to decide which issues to resolve through the issuance of precedent decisions.

Schmidt thought the rise in precedent decisions denying asylum in the last four years had more to do with the accidental composition of BIA panels than anything else. Each BIA member is assigned to a panel of three judges, and most appeals are decided by the panels. If a panel is split two-to-one on a case, the dissenting member can refer the case to the board as a whole, and the whole board votes on whether to hear the case. After deciding the case, the board also votes whether to make it a precedent decision.

During the last four years, Schmidt, who usually votes in favor of asylum seekers, was assigned to a panel with another pro-asylum board member, Lory Rosenberg, and a board member who often opposes granting asylum, Gerald Hurwitz. Their panel often voted in favor of asylum seekers' appeals, with Hurwitz dissenting and referring the decision to the full board. The board then usually agreed with the dissent and issued a precedent decision denying asylum, with Schmidt, Rosenberg, and one or more other members dissenting.

While Schmidt's explanation is accurate, I believe there are other factors that influence the decisions of BIA members. Contin-

---

1. "Unpublished BIA Decision Grants Asylum in Domestic Violence Case," *Interpreter Releases*, March 20, 2000. *Matter of S-A-* was first decided as an unpublished case and was then made a precedent case in April 2000.

gent factors, such as the assignment of members to panels, may influence the decision of which cases are referred to the full board, but the fact remains that the BIA has chosen mostly anti-asylum decisions to publish as precedent decisions. The members are responding to what each of them sees as the need of the asylum office and the immigration courts for guidance, and they are choosing to instruct these adjudicators to grant fewer cases.

One possible explanation for the BIA's practice is the fact that the approval rate for asylum cases has gone up in recent years. The judges may feel that the number of asylum grants is too high and may be issuing anti-asylum precedent decisions in an effort to keep the number of approvals low. Also, the BIA may be following what it sees as the intent of Congress, which changed immigration law in 1996 to make it more restrictive.

A third explanation lies on the background and mind-set of the BIA judges themselves. They are administrative law judges, employees of the Department of Justice within the executive branch of government. Like immigration judges, most come from prior careers in the INS, and few have experience working as advocates for refugees. Of the twenty-one board members, four have prior work experience as INS trial attorneys, ten have worked in other departments of the INS or the immigration court system, and nine have other government work experience. Seven board members have held positions as professors in law schools. Only four BIA members have experience working in a private law firm, and only three have worked in nonprofit organizations. Two of those three, Cecelia Espinoza and Juan Osuna, were hired only recently, in July 2000. Only two BIA members, Gustavo Viallageliu and Lorne Mathon, have worked in the field as immigration judges.

Most board members do not have experience working directly with asylum applicants. They do not appreciate the obstacles that asylum seekers face in finding legal representation, obtaining evidence to support their claims, understanding the American legal system, and articulating their testimony to U.S. officials. Since they lack an understanding of these difficulties, they are quick to assume that inconsistencies in testimony and lack of supporting evidence are signs of fraud, not signs of confusion, trauma, or the inability to pay for effective legal counsel. In making precedent decisions, they may place more weight on the importance of preventing fraud and abuse of the system than on the importance of protecting refugees.

One other aspect of the BIA appeals process should be mentioned here, as it has a significant negative effect on asylum seekers. The BIA is overworked and has a large backlog of appeals to adjudicate; as of this writing, most asylum seekers must wait three years for the BIA to hear their appeal. If they were not granted work authorization at the time of the judge's decision, asylum applicants cannot get work authorization during the time their appeal is pending. As the government provides no assistance to asylum seekers, they must either work illegally or depend on friends and relatives to survive while waiting to have their appeal heard.

The BIA has recognized this problem and has taken steps to correct it. The size of the board has been increased, allowing more decisions to be adjudicated. Appeals of detained asylum seekers have been placed on an expedited docket, reducing the waiting time from three years to six months for these applicants. The BIA has also adopted a process by which an immigration judge's decisions on certain matters can be "affirmed" by one judge, rather than the usual panel of three judges, without a written opinion.

When this policy was announced in the *Federal Register* on October 19, 1999,[2] advocates were concerned that it would hurt asylum seekers by allowing one BIA member to affirm an immigration judge's decision to deny asylum without giving proper consideration to the appeal. But the BIA has made it clear that it does not intend to use this process on asylum cases. In two memoranda issued on August 28 and November 1, 2000, the BIA listed sixty-three categories of cases that would be subject to the new streamlined procedures; none of these categories concerned asylum cases, except for those cases where an alien is precluded from even applying for asylum due to a criminal conviction.[3] In my interview

2. 64 *Federal Register* 56135–42.
3. These memoranda are discussed and reproduced in *Interpreter Releases*, November 6, 2000, pp. 1573–1575, and pp. 1584–1595.

with Chairman Schmidt, he emphasized that asylum cases would probably not be subject to the streamlining process, because asylum cases involve too many factual and legal issues that require a full panel review. He also affirmed the BIA's commitment to giving asylum cases serious consideration, emphasizing that asylum cases involve matters of "life and death" and that the BIA is "the last chance at justice" for many of the asylum seekers who make their appeals to the board.[4]

Positive developments since 1996. There have been only a few positive changes in the law or in INS procedure since 1996. The approval rate and the total number of asylum approvals increases each year, but this is a result of changes instituted before 1996. There are more asylum officers and immigration judges than ever before, so the total number of asylum claims adjudicated has increased. The approval rate has also increased as a result of a decline in fraudulent claims, not a change in the thinking of adjudicators.

The INS has adopted some interpretations of the law that benefit asylum seekers. It released guidelines on the adjudication of gender-related asylum claims in 1995 and guidelines on the adjudication of children's claims for asylum in 1998. These guidelines encourage asylum officers to listen sympathetically to these kinds of cases and to take into account the difficulties that women and children may have in articulating their claims. The guidelines encourage asylum officers to use a broad definition of the law of asylum when considering whether the harm suffered by an applicant constitutes "persecution" and whether it falls into one of the five protected grounds. Unfortunately the INS issued these instructions in the form of guidelines, not regulations; guidelines are not legally binding on asylum officers or on immigration judges.

On December 7, 2000, the INS and the Executive Office of Immigration Review issued proposed regulations which would overturn the interpretation of gender-based claims and domestic violence claims that the BIA had established in its decision in *Mat-*

4. Personal interview, January 16, 2001.

ter of R-A-[5] Later the attorney general vacated *Matter of R-A-* itself and ordered the BIA to reconsider the case under the new regulations.[6] The regulations will become legally binding only if the Department of Justice approves a final version. Since Justice is now under a different administration than the one that proposed the rule initially, it is not certain if the proposed regulations will indeed be made final. Political considerations, including lobbying by immigrants' rights and women's groups, may determine the fate of the proposed regulations.

If they are made final, the proposed regulations will correct the decision in *Matter of R-A-* and make the law of asylum claims based on gender or domestic violence consistent with earlier decisions in *Matter of Acosta* and *Matter of Kasinga.* The proposed rule states that victims of domestic violence can be considered "members of a particular social group," one of the five grounds for granting asylum, and that domestic abuse, if severe enough, can be considered "persecution." The preamble to the rule emphasizes that not all victims of domestic violence can gain asylum in the United States, and the body of the rule sets restrictions on the grant of asylum to victims of domestic violence, particularly where the victim could receive effective protection from the government of her home country. Still, the proposed regulation represents a major victory for asylum seekers. If made final, the regulation will make it possible for hundreds of abused women who cannot find safety in their home countries to obtain asylum in the United States.

Congress provided some relief to asylum applicants with criminal convictions when the Senate ratified the U.N. Convention Against Torture in 1998 and Congress passed legislation implementing it in 1999. There are no exceptions to the convention's provision that a government cannot return aliens to a country where they will be tortured, so aliens with criminal convictions

5. The proposed regulation was published in 65 *Federal Register* 76855–98, December 7, 2000, and has been reproduced, with commentary, in *Interpreter Releases,* December 18, 2000, pp. 1737–1746 and 1760–1770.

6. *Interpreter Releases,* January 22, 2001, p. 256.

may receive protection under the convention. It thus provides the only possible protection for those refugees who have committed crimes in the United States that disqualify them from receiving asylum or restriction on removal status.

Congress also passed legislation in 1999 allocating $10 million in funding for fifteen torture treatment centers, to be located in areas where there are large numbers of refugees and asylees. These centers already existed, supported by private funding and small amounts of government money, but the increase in funding allowed them to greatly expand their operations. The centers provide medical assistance, psychological treatment, and legal assistance to torture victims. The Center for Multicultural Human Services, where Dr. Judy Okawa has her practice, received money from this source of funds, and this money helped pay for her evaluation of and testimony on behalf of Julie Rukongeza.

Finally, the Office of Refugee Resettlement, a bureau within the Department of Health and Human Services, issued a policy ruling on June 15, 2000, that for the first time made asylees eligible for cash and medical assistance. Under prior policy, aliens with "refugee" status, who had been brought to the United States from refugee camps by the State Department, received cash assistance and Medicaid for their first eight months in the United States. The new policy expands this assistance to include asylees, and states that the eight months of eligibility does not start with their date of entry into the United States but with the date that they are granted asylum. The amount of cash assistance is small, only $220 per month for a single adult, but the medical insurance is particularly helpful for those asylees with medical problems resulting from having suffered rape, torture, and imprisonment in their home country. On April 5, 2001, the Office of Refugee Resettlement and the Social Security Administration changed the regulations on Social Security cards, making it easier for asylees to get them and enabling them to work legally without having to apply for an INS work permit.

Future Developments

What can our government do to improve the treatment of asylum seekers? Change must come from two sources. Congress must revise the immigration laws to allow for more humane treatment of asylum seekers and must allocate sufficient funds so that the INS can implement the policies. The INS, the immigration courts, and the BIA must change their policies and institutional culture so that asylum seekers are treated with compassion and fairness.

Congress should repeal the provisions of the 1996 immigration law that instituted the one-year filing deadline and expedited removal. Lawmakers should allow asylum seekers to receive work permits earlier or should provide for asylum seekers' basic needs while they wait for their cases to be adjudicated. Congress should end the practice of detaining asylum seekers in state and local jails or in INS detention facilities that are similar in character to prisons. If Congress decides that some asylum applicants must be detained, it should allocate money for the INS to operate minimum-security shelters, where asylum seekers have access to medical care and social services.

The membership of the Board of Immigration Appeals must also change. Too many of its members have too strict a viewpoint on the adjudication of asylum claims. New appointees to the BIA should come from all backgrounds, not just from backgrounds as INS attorneys. Since asylum issues make up a large part of the BIA's caseload, more of its members should have work experience that enables them to understand the real difficulties that asylum seekers face in making their claim.

Finally, the immigration court system must change so that immigration judges have a better understanding of asylum seekers' special needs, and the system must prevent individual immigration judges from abusing their authority. The Department of Justice should hire more judges from backgrounds in private practice and nonprofit organizations, and fewer judges who have worked as INS trial attorneys. All immigration judges should receive more training on the special needs of asylum seekers, similar to the training given to asylum officers. Individual immigration judges who abuse their authority should be disciplined or dismissed.

Current Legislative Proposals to
Reform the Asylum System

Several refugee and immigrant advocacy organizations lobby Congress and the INS to improve the asylum system. They have identified several issues as priorities. The Florence Project, a nonprofit agency that works with INS detainees in a large INS prison in Florence, Arizona, has been selected to operate a pilot project to assist minors in INS detention. If that effort is successful, the INS may replicate the project nationwide. The INS has also agreed to hold state and local jails to minimum standards for the treatment of immigration detainees, and it expects to have this program in place by the year 2003.

Senator Diane Feinstein of California has introduced a bill called the "Unaccompanied Child Protection Act of 2000," which would reform the INS detention system to protect unaccompanied minors in INS proceedings. While the bill would represent an excellent reform, as mentioned before it has attracted no co-sponsors and its passage seems unlikely. A more successful effort has been the Refugee Protection Act, S. 1940, introduced in the Senate in November 1999 with bipartisan sponsorship. The act would end the use of expedited removal except in "immigration emergencies" declared by the attorney general. The term "immigration emergency" is not defined in the bill, but it is clear that the bill's sponsors have the 1980 influx of Cuban asylum seekers and the Haitian boat people of the 1990s in mind. Even during an "immigration emergency," the expedited removal process would have to incorporate safeguards that would reduce the likelihood of true refugees being returned to their home countries. The bill would discourage the detention of asylum applicants who are in expedited removal. A final provision of the bill, not related to expedited removal, would encourage the INS to be more liberal in granting exceptions to the one-year deadline.

The Refugee Protection Act was introduced by Patrick Leahy, a Democrat from Vermont, and has been co-sponsored by two Republican senators, James Jeffords from Vermont and Sam Brownback from Kansas, and seven Democratic senators, Richard Durbin of Illinois, Russell Feingold of Wisconsin, Bob Graham of

Florida, Frank Lautenberg of New Jersey, Edward Kennedy and John Kerry of Massachusetts, and Paul Wellstone of Minnesota. Progress on the bill was slow because 2000 was an election year, and senators had other concerns, more pressing to their home constituents, to consider. As of this writing, no member of the House of Representatives has proposed a counterpart to the Senate bill, which has not moved out of the immigration subcommittee.

How can the asylum system be changed? Refugee advocates are already doing all they can to bring changes in the system, but their voices are few. Only when American citizens stand up for the rights of asylum seekers will Congress devote serious attention to the issue.

Organizations That Assist Asylum Seekers

ASYLUM APPLICANTS, looking for assistance with a case, should contact the local INS office for a list of nonprofit agencies that help immigrants. The INS is required by law to keep and distribute such a list. For the address of the nearest INS office, call the INS customer service line, 1-800-375-5283, or look on the INS website, www.ins.usdoj.gov.

Readers who wish to donate volunteer time or money to an agency that assists asylum seekers should contact the INS for a list of agencies in their area, or one of the national offices of the agencies that assist asylum seekers. These agencies include:

Catholic Legal Immigration Network, Inc. (CLINIC). CLINIC and Catholic Charities together are the largest network of refugee assistance organizations in the United States and one of the most effective. 415 Michigan Ave., N.E., Washington, DC 20017; (202) 635-2556; www.cliniclegal.org.

Immigration and Refugee Services of America (IRSA). IRSA operates a number of affiliates that offer direct assistance to asylees. The U.S. Committee for Refugees (USCR), which publishes the *World Refugee Survey, Refugee Reports,* and many reports on refugee issues, is a part of IRSA. 1717 Massachusetts Ave., N.W., Suite 701, Washington, DC, 20036; (202) 797-2105; www.refugees.org.

Lawyer's Committee for Human Rights (LCHR). LCHR offers direct representation to asylum seekers, researches human rights conditions in other countries, and is one of the main supporters of lobbying efforts to reform the law of asylum. 333 Seventh Ave., 13th Floor, New York, NY 10001; (212) 845-5200; www.lchr.org.

Lutheran Immigration and Refugee Services (LIRS). LIRS, in conjunction with the Presbyterian church, manages a fund which grants money to nonprofit agencies that assist asylum applicants. 700 Light St., Baltimore, MD 21230; (410) 230-2700; www.lirs.org.

The Women's Commission for Refugee Women and Children. This group, a project operated by the International Rescue Committee, is one of the main supporters of legislation to reform asylum law. 122 East 42nd St., 12th Floor, New York, NY 10168-1289; (212) 551-3088; www.intrescom.org/wcrwc.

Asylum Cases Filed with Immigration and Naturalization Services Asylum Officers Approved, Denied, or Referred After Interview, by Selected Country of Origin April 1991–September 2000

	Cumulative April 1991–Sept. 2000		
Country	Approval Rate for Cases Decided	Cases Granted	Cases Denied or Referred After Interview
TOTAL*	26.0%	93,245	264,962
Iraq	84.5%	3,357	616
Bosnia	75.2%	562	185
Sudan	73.1%	2,154	792
Somalia	68.8%	6,635	3,052
Burma	67.9%	1,403	663
Syria	67.0%	1,168	575
Iran	62.1%	3,629	2,216
Cuba	61.4%	2,388	1,504
Ethiopia	61.4%	5,954	3,738
Afghanistan	53.6%	1,259	1,090
Yugoslavia***	51.0%	4,592	3,456
Liberia	49.8%	3,398	3,432
Egypt	42.0%	1,048	1,447
Colombia	41.5%	1,540	2,173
Russia	38.7%	2,342	3,718
Sri Lanka	34.0%	278	539
India	30.3%	5,434	12,499
Ukraine	29.2%	785	1,906
Peru	24.3%	1,603	4,999
Mauritania	24.0%	1,126	3,562
Lebanon	23.5%	364	1,188
Haiti	22.9%	5,115	17,228
Pakistan	22.4%	1,740	6,030
Laos	20.1%	276	1,097
Nigeria	19.1%	487	2,067
China	18.9%	5,927	25,499
Nicaragua	13.4%	1,431	9,224
Bangladesh	13.2%	760	4,999
Ghana	9.4%	190	1,842
Guatemala	8.4%	3,289	35,809
Honduras	6.9%	516	6,976
El Salvador	5.4%	1,424	24,826
Philippines	3.7%	218	5,714
Mexico	0.8%	209	26,245

| | | Approval Rate for | | Cases Denied or Referred | Cases Pending |
| | Cases | Cases | Cases | After | as of |
Country	Received	Decided	Granted	Interview	9/30/00
TOTAL*	48,054**	51.8%	16,693	15,549	329,115
Iraq	338	82.0%	233	51	167
Bosnia	49	65.8%	24	17	30
Sudan	580	77.7%	429	123	209
Somalia	2,415	74.1%	1,689	589	981
Burma	630	74.0%	307	108	342
Syria	46	60.5%	26	17	59
Iran	934	70.5%	596	250	605
Cuba	490	71.1%	96	39	2,390
Ethiopia	1,507	79.0%	1,259	335	783
Afghanistan	230	30.9%	253	565	150
Yugoslavia***	749	62.1%	415	253	621
Liberia	1,082	58.5%	584	415	859
Egypt	575	55.2%	294	239	208
Colombia	2,747	67.8%	1,165	553	1,238
Russia	946	50.7%	389	378	887
Sri Lanka	119	44.4%	36	45	74
India	1,615	49.6%	539	547	1,918
Ukraine	239	39.7%	71	108	280
Peru	205	45.6%	77	92	306
Mauritania	847	25.8%	92	264	586
Lebanon	77	41.2%	21	30	188
Haiti	4,683	22.2%	613	2,156	15,365
Pakistan	540	54.6%	215	179	468
Laos	8	35.0%	14	26	774
Nigeria	109	34.1%	31	60	189
China	6,476	54.8%	2,522	2,078	4,021
Nicaragua	268	50.0%	12	12	12,956
Bangladesh	312	32.5%	54	112	256
Ghana	62	36.4%	12	21	121
Guatemala	2,084	20.1%	223	889	98,601
Honduras	196	7.7%	13	155	560
El Salvador	2,686	12.4%	131	922	172,765
Philippines	156	24.5%	13	40	778
Mexico	3,936	7.9%	36	421	1,056

Note: In April 1991, a new corps of asylum officers assumed responsibility for adjudicating asylum claims. This chart is based on decisions made by asylum officers only. Since January 4, 1995, asylum officers generally have not been authorized to deny asylum to deportable aliens. Since that date, such cases not granted have been referred to immigration judges. Many other applications for asylum are filed directly with immigration judges, particularly in the context of deportation proceedings.

* The total includes all nationalities, not just those listed here.
** Includes 40,697 newly filed and 7,357 reopened cases.
*** Includes applicants who identify their country of origin as Yugoslavia, Croatia, or the former Yugoslavia (excluding Bosnia).

Source: U.S. Department of Justice, Immigration and Naturalization Service; Compiled by the U.S. Committee for Refugees.

Asylum Cases Decided by Immigration Judges Approved or Denied by Selected Country of Origin, FY 1989–2000

Country	Cumulative FY 1989–2000 Approval Rate for Cases Decided	Cases Granted	Cases Denied
TOTAL*	23.3%	46,984	154,863
Bosnia	73.6%	89	32
Afghanistan	66.0%	2,330	1,200
Burma	64.6%	288	158
Sudan	61.9%	397	244
Sri Lanka	58.0%	863	626
Russia	56.6%	1,723	1,333
Egypt	53.1%	651	576
Somalia	53.0%	1,825	1,621
Iraq	52.8%	423	378
Iran	52.1%	1,469	1,348
Yugoslavia**	51.2%	1,868	1,777
Ethiopia	50.9%	1,630	1,570
Liberia	48.0%	903	978
Ukraine	46.3%	755	877
Mauritania	34.6%	919	1,739
Peru	31.4%	1,376	3,009
Cuba	31.1%	1,645	3,644
Nigeria	30.1%	727	1,691
Lebanon	29.3%	280	675
Syria	29.2%	121	294
Colombia	27.9%	484	1,250
India	26.7%	2,523	6,943
Pakistan	23.9%	1,121	3,571
Nicaragua	21.4%	3,139	11,516
Laos	20.8%	151	575
Bangladesh	20.2%	733	2,890
China	20.0%	5,134	20,487
Ghana	16.3%	307	1,574
Haiti	10.9%	1,487	12,107
Honduras	9.5%	429	4,111
El Salvador	9.4%	2,350	22,752
Philippines	7.9%	202	2,347
Guatemala	7.8%	1,570	18,579
Mexico	2.7%	232	8,419

		FY 2000			
Country	Cases Received	Approval Rate for Cases Decided	Cases Granted	Cases Denied	Cases Pending as of 10/01/00
TOTAL*	50,838	31.4%	7,336	16,013	55,720
Bosnia	18	77.8%	7	2	22
Afghanistan	227	83.0%	151	31	148
Burma	191	68.6%	81	37	151
Sudan	231	57.0%	65	49	194
Sri Lanka	402	68.4%	171	79	235
Russia	1,091	63.9%	417	236	1,435
Egypt	459	74.4%	218	75	483
Somalia	1,772	42.8%	410	548	935
Iraq	231	59.9%	82	55	190
Iran	807	47.9%	171	186	861
Yugoslavia**	871	55.1%	249	203	764
Ethiopia	655	53.9%	233	199	530
Liberia	525	45.9%	94	111	572
Ukraine	239	43.4%	96	125	321
Mauritania	532	23.0%	98	328	533
Peru	379	36.4%	250	437	237
Cuba	1,532	28.9%	99	243	503
Nigeria	408	28.7%	79	196	340
Lebanon	193	35.6%	48	87	176
Syria	92	50.0%	18	18	104
Colombia	1,439	40.6%	186	272	1,871
India	1,540	43.0%	515	684	2,424
Pakistan	634	42.4%	178	242	743
Nicaragua	184	6.8%	4	55	24
Laos	279	7.7%	6	72	175
Bangladesh	399	34.7%	174	328	479
China	8,669	***44.7%	***2,463	3,051	8,539
Ghana	154	20.8%	22	84	121
Haiti	5,031	9.9%	204	1,855	5,613
Honduras	575	9.8%	15	138	239
El Salvador	2,927	9.5%	145	1,375	2,300
Philippines	345	21.7%	34	123	598
Guatemala	2,562	12.7%	187	1,289	1,823
Mexico	5,471	10.5%	48	410	11,264

Note: This chart shows asylum decisions in proceedings before immigration judges. INS asylum officers refer cases not granted to immigration judges, who examine the claim in deportation proceedings. Other asylum claims may arise in deportation or exclusion proceedings for cases coming directly before immigration courts without an INS asylum officer referral. FY 89 is the first year for which complete data are available under the Executive Office for Immigration Review's automated data system.

* Includes all nationalities, not just those listed here.
** Includes applicants who identify their country of origin as Yugoslavia or Serbia/Montenegro.
*** Includes 1,850 Chinese granted "conditional" asylum in FY 2000.

Source: U.S. Department of Justice, Immigration and Naturalization Service; Compiled by the U.S. Committee for Refugees.

Bibliography

THE LITERATURE on asylum law and policy in the United States is not extensive, and I have read most of it in preparing this book. Since I have already cited specific sources in the footnotes in the text, I have here provided a selective, annotated bibliography, with recommendations for those readers interested in finding further information on specific subjects.

Books

Do They Hear When You Cry? by Fauzia Kassindja and Layli Miller Bashir (New York, 1998), is a memoir of an asylum seeker written with the help of one of her attorneys. Ms. Kassindja, the applicant in *Matter of Kassinga,* BIA Int. Dec. 3278 (BIA 1996), was the first refugee to win asylum status based on a fear of female genital mutilation. She was detained for two years under brutal conditions before winning her case and being released.

Also recommended is *A Well-Founded Fear: The Congressional Battle to Save Asylum in America* by Philip Schrag (New York, 1999). Mr. Schrag, a professor of law at Georgetown University, was one of the leaders of the effort of refugee advocacy groups to oppose the most harmful provisions of the proposed 1996 immigration law, such as the thirty-day deadline for applying for asylum. The book describes in detail the congressional politics of the time and the lobbying effort.

*Calculated Kindness: Refugees and America's Half-Open Door,
1945 to the Present* by Gil Loescher and John Scanlan (New York,
1986), is an informative and well-written study of the development of
U.S. refugee and asylum policy.

Finally, *The Congressional Politics of Immigration Reform* by
James Gimpel and James Edwards (New York, 1999), is a good study
of the political battles over the immigration law and the debates that
led to the 1996 changes in the law. Gimpel and Edwards discuss all
aspects of immigration policy; asylum issues are only a small part of
the book.

There are also a number of books on asylum that were written
for practitioners of immigration law rather than for general readers.
The most useful are:

A Guide for Immigration Advocates, written and published by
the Immigration Legal Resource Center (San Francisco, 1999). An in-
troductory guide to immigration law for lawyers and paralegals, written in plain English with a minimum of legal jargon.

Detention Resource Manual, Lutheran Immigration and Refugee
Services, 1998.

Law of Asylum in the United States by Deborah Anker. Refugee
Law Center, 1999. The most complete survey of asylum law and
court decisions available.

AILA's Asylum Primer by Regina Germain. American Immigration Lawyers Association, 2000. Useful both as an introduction to
asylum law and a reference work for experienced practitioners.

Immigration Law and Crimes by Dan Kasselbrenner and Lory
D. Rosenberg. West Group, 1999.

Asylum Case Law Sourcebook by David A. Martin. Federal Publications, 1998. A useful summary of federal appeals court decisions,
indexed by subject matter.

Refugee Law and Policy: Cases and Materials by Karen Musalo.
Carolina Academic Press, 1997. A good textbook and reference work
on the law of asylum, with an emphasis on analysis and the history of
the development of asylum law.

Winning Asylum Cases by Mark Silverman, Robert Jobe, and
Larry Katzman. Immigrant Legal Resource Center (San Francisco,
2000). A well-written, easy-to-use guide for attorneys wishing to spe-
cialize in asylum law.

Reports

"Detained and Deprived of Rights: Children in the Custody of the U.S. Immigration and Naturalization Service" by Jo Becker and Michael Bochenek. Human Rights Watch, 1998.

"The Expedited Removal Study: Report on the First Three Years of Implementation of Expedited Removal" by Karen Musalo. Center for Human Rights and International Justice, University of California, Hastings College of the Law, May 2000.

"Is This America? The Denial of Due Process to Asylum Seekers in the United States." Lawyers Committee for Human Rights, October 2000.

"Liberty Denied: Women Seeking Asylum Imprisoned in the United States." Women's Commission on Refugee Women and Children, April 1997.

"Locked Away: Immigration Detainees in Jails in the United States." Human Rights Watch, September 1998.

"Lost in the Labyrinth: Detention of Asylum-seekers." Amnesty International, September 1999.

"Refugees Behind Bars: The Imprisonment of Asylum Seekers in the Wake of the 1996 Immigration Act." Lawyers Committee for Human Rights, August 1999.

Journals

Interpreter Releases, published by Federal Publications, is the single best source for news and analysis on immigration law; most practitioners of immigration law subscribe to it. I have used information from *Interpreter Releases* throughout my career and throughout the writing of this book. The following articles were particularly useful:

"*Matter of R-A-:* An Analysis of the Decision and its Implications" by Karen Musalo (August 9, 1999).

"The *Mogharrabi* Rule in 1998: A Review of Recent BIA Asylum Decisions" by Margaret Kuehne Taylor (July 6, 1998).

"Update on Precedent Decisions of the Board of Immigration Appeals" by Paul Wickham Schmidt and Carolyn Anne Elliot (April 17, 2000).

"Precedent Decisions of the Board of Immigration Appeals: An Update" by Paul Wickham Schmidt and Carolyn Anne Elliot (September 28, 1998).

"Update on Precedent Decisions of the Board of Immigration Appeals" by Paul Wickham Schmidt and Carolyn Anne Elliot (November 3, 1997).

"Precedent Decisions of the Board of Immigration Appeals: An Update" by Paul Wickham Schmidt and Carolyn Anne Elliot (August 19, 1996).

The *Detention Watch* newsletter, published by Lutheran Immigration and Refugee Services, is a quarterly and provides information about the detention of asylees and other immigrants in the United States. Subscriptions are free, though a donation is suggested for those who can afford to do so, to help cover costs. To subscribe, contact LIRS at 700 Light St., Baltimore, MD 21230; (410) 230-2700; www.lirs.org.

Refugee Reports, published monthly by the U.S. Committee for Refugees (USCR), provides good updates and analysis on the status of refugees and asylees in the United States. The U.S. Committee for Refugees also publishes a yearly publication, the *World Refugee Survey*, which is the best source of statistics and country-by-country information on the status of refugees worldwide. The *World Refugee Survey* is also available on the USCR website, www.refugees.org. Unfortunately, *Refugee Reports* is not available on this site.

"Making Asylum Policy: The 1994 Reforms" by David Martin. *Washington Law Review*, July 1995. This is an excellent article on the politics behind asylum reform, written by one of the main architects of the reforms.

Documentary Films

With Liberty and Justice for All. In 1997 the First Mondays project sponsored a thirty-minute documentary film about the harmful effects of the 1996 immigration law. The film focuses on two immigrants— an asylum applicant from Liberia and a longtime legal permanent resident facing deportation because of a criminal offense he committed more than ten years earlier. The film provides an excellent introduction to these issues and shows the perspective of both the immigrants and their attorneys. It can be ordered from the Alliance for Justice, 2000 P St., N.W., Suite 712, Washington, DC 20036 (202) 822-6070; www.afj.org.

A Well-Founded Fear. Two documentary filmmakers, Shari Robertson and Michael Camerini, spent two years interviewing asylum officers, asylum applicants, and their attorneys, and filmed actual asylum interviews with the applicants' permission. This two-hour film puts the viewer in the place of an asylum officer, and shows how these officers make their decisions. It can be ordered from their web site, www.wellfoundedfear.org. The film is not related to Philip Schrag's book *A Well-Founded Fear.*

Internet Sites

The Internet is the first place to look for information on asylum law, refugees, and human rights. This information changes regularly, making any listing of sites out of date almost upon publication. The following websites are up to date, accurate, useful, and free.

The INS website (www.usins.doj.gov) is excellent. It contains copies of all the INS forms, which can be downloaded and printed out, as well as the text of the Immigration and Nationality Act, the regulations that interpret the act, and the complete text of all BIA decisions from 1976 to the present.

The United Nations operates two good websites with information on refugees: the website for the U.N. High Commissioner for Refugees (www.unhcr.ch) and "RefWorld," a database of U.N. reports and other information (www.unhcr.ch/refworld).

Several websites offer information about human rights law and asylum law. Two of the best of these are the website for the University of Minnesota Human Rights Library (wwwl.umn.edu/humanrts) and a new website designed to provide free assistance to asylum legal practitioners (www.asylumlaw.org).

Readers, asylum applicants, and legal practitioners seeking human rights information about a specific country should consult the websites of Amnesty International (www.amnesty.org), Human Rights Watch (www.hrw.org), and the Lawyers Committee for Human Rights (www.lchr.org). Also useful are the State Department's *Country Reports on Human Rights* and *Report on Religious Freedom,* published annually and available at www.state.gov.

Other useful websites include the USCR website, at www.refugees.org, and the website for the documentary film *A Well-Founded Fear* (www.wellfoundedfear.org).

Index

A NOTE ON THE AUTHOR

Christopher Einolf, an accredited legal representative for asylum applicants, has acted on behalf of more than three hundred refugees from over thirty-five different countries. He was educated at Davidson College and Columbia University, where he received a master's degree in international affairs. He now works for the Pennsylvania Immigrant Resource Center as director of advocacy for children in INS detention, and lives in Arlington, Virginia.